CAUSAL EXPLANATION AND MODEL BUILDING IN HISTORY, ECONOMICS, AND THE NEW ECONOMIC HISTORY

Causal Explanation and Model Building in History, Economics, and the New Economic History

by PETER D. McCLELLAND

CORNELL UNIVERSITY PRESS

ITHACA AND LONDON

First published 1975 by Cornell University Press.
Published in the United Kingdom by Cornell University Press Ltd., 2-4 Brook Street, London W1Y 1AA.

International Standard Book Number 0-8014-0929-2
Library of Congress Catalog Card Number 74-25372
Printed in the United States of America

FOR MRS. STANDFAST

Acknowledgments

Compiling a list of acknowledgments is not unlike establishing the causal antecedents for a book. Neither task can be accomplished to the complete satisfaction of the author. The initial impetus for this study came from Allan Bogue. His request for an article instigated an inquiry that quickly developed into a work larger than either one of us had anticipated. Beyond this obvious impulse, however, the scope of the subject matter confounds the ready identification of intellectual forces and contributing personalities. Although in no way to blame for defects in the final product, those legions who have, in great and small ways, contributed to my education are all responsible—all causal factors not without influence, as the historians like to say.

Within that list, two men have played a crucial role. I went to Harvard as a graduate student with one ambition: to study economic history under the tutelage of Alexander Gerschenkron. For over a decade he was, initially, instructor; later, colleague; and ultimately, wise counselor and friend. Without his influence, this book could not have been. Through the good fortune of being a resident tutor in Eliot House, I came to know W. V. Quine, or Van as he is known to members of the Senior Common Room privileged to share his erudition. My debt to him is also enormous. I am not sure whether it was said of Plato or Dr. Johnson or both that whatever path one traveled, one always met him coming back. That is where I invariably met Van and always emerged the wiser from our encounters.

To the members of Gerschenkron's Economic History Workshop, especially Peter Temin, I am grateful for influence exerted during the formative years of my training as an economic historian. From members of Harvard's department of economics I gained much that was directly applicable to the problems of Chapters III and V, particularly from James Duesenberry, Dale Jorgenson, Stephen Marglin, Gail

Pierson, Marc Roberts, and Janet Yellen. Among the Cornell faculty, Edwin Burton and Henry Wan, Jr., must be singled out for giving so generously of their talents to strengthen, amend, and correct defective passages throughout the manuscript. Also helpful were discussions with, and suggestions from, Erwin Blackstone, William Brock, Walter Galenson, Michael Haines, T. C. Liu, Dennis Mueller, and William Taylor. A number of graduate students read all or part of the manuscript and made helpful recommendations, including Robert Andrew, W. Davis Dechert, Alan Dillingham, Roy Gardner, John Hagens, John Hiller, and William Hogan. Historians, economists, and economic historians who kindly gave of their expertise to make constructive criticisms include Allan Bogue, Alfred Eichner, John Hughes, Fritz Machlup, Albro Martin, Donald McCloskey, William Parker, Nathan Rosenberg, Morton Rothstein, Cushing Strout, and the members of the economic history seminars at Columbia and Chicago universities.

For faithful assistance and helpful suggestions I am indebted to several research assistants, but especially to Michael Brown-Beasley. Few could match his many talents and resourcefulness. Between initial scrawl and finished manuscript there have been many drafts, almost all of which have been typed and retyped by Deborah Archie with patience, accuracy, and above all cheerfulness.

Looking back upon the terrain traversed to write this book, I realize that for all the diverse intellectual forays required, my greatest debt remains to that companion whose comfort and encouragement never faltered; who never once, for all my doubts, gave way to doubts herself. And so the miles were shortened.

PETER D. MCCLELLAND

Ithaca, New York

Contents

CAUSAL EXPLANATION AND MODEL
BUILDING IN HISTORY, ECONOMICS,
AND THE NEW ECONOMIC HISTORY

Introduction

This book is concerned, if somewhat obliquely, with the enigmatic problems of human knowledge: with what we mean when we claim to "know" something or to have "proven" something, and within the context of those meanings, with what determines the limits of our knowledge and our ability to prove. It is concerned specifically with how generalizations are used to explain phenomena in three different but related fields: history, economics, and economic history. In recent decades that usage has been radically changed in at least one of these fields. The new economic history, often called cliometrics, constitutes a revolution both in the kinds of generalizations employed and in the manner in which generalizations are formulated and applied in historical analysis. The result has been a barrage of charges and countercharges between cliometricians and more conventional historians concerning the nature of historical explanation and the uses and abuses of scientific techniques in attempting such explanations.

In that debate can be found the formative impulses for this book. The specific impulse was a request to write a survey article on the techniques of the new economic history for a special edition of the *American Behavioral Scientist* devoted to new methods in historical analysis. The article developed into a book in response to difficulties which, in retrospect, should have been anticipated from the outset. Assessment of the techniques in question can proceed only after three questions have been resolved: (1) What is the nature of causal explanation in general? (2) What is the nature of causal explanation in history? (3) What is the nature of causal explanation and model building in economics? Once these questions have been carefully explored, the nature of causal explanation and model building in the new economic history becomes readily apparent. If they are never explored, the latter topic cannot even be intelligently discussed. The literature analyzing the merits and demerits of the new economic history has not only failed to resolve the questions noted, but has seldom evidenced any awareness of the need to broach its subject matter from the broader vantage point suggested.

As the work progressed, two other objectives materialized. To answer the second question—What is the nature of causal explanation in history?—the original plan was simply to borrow some of the thoughts of major writers on this topic. From the framework developed to deal with the first question—What is the nature of causal explanation in general?—came two surprising results. The defects in the views of such authors as Carl Hempel, Michael Scriven, and William Dray concerning causal explanation in history became readily apparent, and an alternative to those views suggested itself that seemed to be relatively consistent with the practices of most historians. To present these defects and that alternative view of causal explanation in history therefore became the second objective of this book.

The third objective emerged in attempting to resolve the third question—What is the nature of causal explanation and model building in economics? That discipline suffers from a curious malaise. For as long as I have been a member of the profession—and no doubt long before that—my senior colleagues have complained about the limited ability of their students, graduate and undergraduate, "to think like economists." This failure is somewhat remarkable in that it concerns not the ability to grasp advanced literature but rather the ability to apply the causal mechanisms and thought processes found in any introductory textbook. It is even more remarkable because, as those same professors are quick to point out, none of the material in question seems to be intrinsically complex. And yet students of economics are surely neither better nor worse on the average than students of any other subject. Why in this particular discipline should they have such difficulty grasping fundamentals which, one grasped, appear to be neither subtle nor labyrinthine? Perhaps part of the answer can be found in the defects of their educational program. Too often they are rushed toward mathematical sophistication. Almost never are the *fundamentals* of practice and theory pulled together within the broader context of a methodological discussion. To do so therefore became the third objective of this book.

The controlling premise in pursuing all three objectives is that the study of methodology is both an important and a treacherous undertaking. Its importance is implicit in the definition of methodology: "a branch of logic that analyzes the principles or procedures that should guide inquiry in a particular field."[1] If the principles and procedures are not understood, then practice will often be misguided in the extreme. The treacherousness results from the superficial simplicity of the subject. Many economists and historians assume that to study the methodology of their own discipline requires no special knowledge or training whatsoever. They are half right. Most, if not all, of the methodological issues of interest to them can be understood without any special training in philosophy. They cannot be understood, or at least fully understood, except against the backdrop of the larger philosophical problems that relate to each issue. To put the matter baldly, and perhaps too contentiously, economists and historians generally do not seem to understand the nature of causal explanation, the nature of counterfactual speculation, the problems associated with both, and the relationship between the two. The result, as will be documented throughout this book, is a confusion so pervasive that seldom can one detect what the substantive issues are.

A word on the road ahead. The structure of the book is dictated by the need to consider the questions noted at the beginning. The nature of causal explanation is explored in Chapter I. Arguments developed there provide the point of departure and the controlling reference for all subsequent discussion. Chapter II considers the nature of causal explanation in history. The main problem is to decide how the framework of Chapter I must be modified if the phenomena to be explained are human actions and the goals of the would-be explainer are those of the historian. The contrasts in objectives and techniques of the economist and the historian are examined in Chapter III. The framework in which they are examined is, predictably, a consideration of the nature of causal explanation and model building in microeconomics and macroeconomics. The first three chapters focus only upon causal explanation and do not consider the relationship between explanation of fact and counterfactual speculation. The latter has been the source of much heat and little enlightenment in the many interchanges between historians and

---

1. The word methodology may refer either to the study of methods (as noted in the above definition) or to the methods themselves ("a body of methods, procedures, working concepts, rules, and postulates employed by a science, art, or discipline"). Our main concern is with the first, although the word will occasionally be used in the second sense.

practitioners of the new economic history. The nature of counterfactual speculation in history and economics is therefore explored in
Chapter IV as a necessary prelude to Chapter V. The objectives of the
latter chapter are first to elaborate and then to assess the main analytical
techniques of the new economic history. The broader framework in
which both proceed is suggested by the title "Causal Explanation and
Model Building in the New Economic History."

Practitioners may well view such a proposed itinerary with a jaun-
diced eye. The attitude of many social scientists and historians toward
methodology is not unlike the attitude of most citizens toward the
sewage system: they know it is there, they assume that it works, and they
question the good sense of anyone who goes poking around in it. What
is too seldom realized is that most of the citizenry unconsciously poke
around in methodology most of the time. In private conversations with
economists, historians, and economic historians, I am always impressed
with how adamant the majority are concerning the prevalence of defective work in their own field. When pressed to account for this unsatisfactory state of affairs, they usually cite arguments that, at bottom,
concern the failure of their colleagues to understand the methodology
of their profession.

And yet doubts may linger. A dabbling in methodology may be enlightening for the student and helpful to the practitioner, the argument
might run, but surely a successful dabbling is possible without recourse
to a framework as broad as that attempted here. This particular challenge is easily met by noting both the pervasive confusion in the literature when a broad framework is not used and the ease with which those
confusions drop into place when that framework is used. A few examples
from later pages are perhaps required to drive the point home.

Chapter II.   As mentioned previously, the major contemporary
writers on the subject of causal explanation in history appear to be confused about the fundamental structure of causal explanation in general.
Once that structure has been explored, the defects in such writers as
Hempel, Scriven, and Dray become readily apparent.

Chapter III.   In recent years methodological debates by and for
economists have been dominated by the views of Milton Friedman
and, to a lesser extent, Paul Samuelson. The confusions and errors in
these debates can be easily seen and resolved, as they have not been

seen or resolved previously, using the general framework developed in Chapters I and II.

Chapter IV.   The role of counterfactual speculation as an appendage to causal analysis of fact cannot be understood until the nature of causal explanation is understood. That neither is fully grasped is suggested by the tendency of almost all new economic historians to argue—incorrectly—that every causal statement implies a counterfactual statement.

Chapter V.   One of the dominant characteristics of the new economic history is its attempt to combine causal explanations embedded in economic models with counterfactual speculation in order to partition the relative importance of various causal factors believed to have been operative in a given historical situation. The main argument here is a simple one: that the associated techniques cannot be fully understood unless they can be evaluated, and they cannot be adequately evaluated except within the context of a more general framework focusing upon the relevant philosophical problems. Which problems are relevant should be apparent from the three phrases that dominate the language just used: causal explanation, model building, and counterfactual speculation. Only when all three have been examined will the reader begin to get a sense of what the central dilemmas are for the new economic history as it is practiced today. To list those dilemmas here will not do. To explain what they are is the assignment of Chapter V, and in a very real sense, one of the main assignments of the entire book.

A final word on requisite expertise. *Nothing* in the following chapters requires for its understanding any formal training in philosophy. Wherever possible, jargon is relegated to footnotes, and such technical terms as cannot be avoided are explained as they arise. Those readers unfamiliar with philosophical literature may find parts of Chapter I slow going. They should be cautioned at the outset that however much their interest and patience are strained by the consideration given in that chapter to the meaning of terms, if philosophers have one agreed-upon message it is this: we cannot begin to understand what we are talking about if we do not take great pains to clarify the meaning of the words that will be central to our discussion. The proof of the pudding will be in the eating, and in this case the main dish is the remainder of the book. Therein will be found the type of confusions that arise when words are not carefully defined, such as those associated with Dray's use of "rational," Friedman's use of "validity," and Fritz Redlich's use of "figment."

With respect to economics, the book assumes that all readers will bring to Chapters III and V some training in that discipline, but not necessarily extensive training. More specifically, almost all of Chapter V should be easily understood by those whose formal training includes nothing more than an introductory course in economic theory. The same should be true of the main ideas developed in Chapter III. That chapter is admittedly written at a different pace, or pitched at a different level, than is Chapter V. The hope is that the more expert the reader, the more he or she will find in Chapter III. For all economists, novice and expert, its main objective is that outlined above: to pull together the fundamentals of practice and theory within the broader framework developed in Chapters I and II. It will also be found to be a logical stepping-stone to Chapters IV and V.

Many readers will be tempted to move directly from this introduction to that chapter concerned with their particular field of expertise. Do not do it. At a minimum, read carefully the six-page summary at the beginning of Chapter I. This is the foundation upon which all else is built. A failure to assimilate the arguments advanced there will ensure a failure to grasp all of the fundamental ideas of the book. This summary may well prove to be too condensed for most, in which case the rest of Chapter I develops the same ideas at a more leisurely pace.

I On Models, Theories, and Causal Explanations

> I always say the chief end of man is to form general propositions—adding that no general proposition is worth a damn.
>
> —Oliver Wendell Holmes[1]

> In science all is tentative, all admits to revision—right down . . . to the law of the excluded middle.
>
> —Willard V. Quine[2]

1. Introduction and Summary

Two themes dominate this book. The first is that Holmes has overstated his case, but Quine has not. Knowledge in all disciplines has its tentative aspects, but despite the associated uncertainties that knowledge has been an invaluable guide for human action. Generalizations may be imperfect, but (as Holmes well knew) to demonstrate that a tool is defective is not to prove that it is useless. The second theme concerns the unity of method in the causal explanations of all disciplines. In the twentieth century those explanations tend to be concerned only with efficient causation and are therefore governed by the central tenet of efficient causation: similar cause, similar effect. The implication is that causal explanations consist of subsuming specific facts under generalizations that link causes (C) to effects (E) in statements of the general form

$$\text{If } (C_1, \ldots, C_n), \text{ then } E.$$

(In the case of lighting a match, for example, the ignition would be the effect to be explained, and the causes would include such factors as the presence of oxygen, the chemical composition of the match, and the application of friction.) The basic requirement for understanding the nature of causal explanation is therefore an understanding of how these statements are constructed and what the various terms associated with these statements mean.

1. Howe 1961:II, 13.
2. Quine 1957:17.

Two questions come immediately to mind: (a) Should generalizations of this sort be prefaced with the word "Always," "Necessarily," or "Probably"? and (b) What is meant by similar in the statement "similar cause, similar effect"? In attempting to find answers, the reader will encounter two main stumbling blocks. One can be overcome only with an article of faith. The second cannot be overcome to all. To lay bare both the nature of these stumbling blocks and their implications for all causal explanations are the principal objectives of this chapter.

The nature of the first stumbling block becomes more apparent if all problems associated with the second are momentarily assumed away. Let us therefore assume that observable phenomena can be classified easily into homogeneous sets labeled "Causes of type C_1," "Causes of type C_2," "Effects of type E," etc. Assume further that all relevant causes for a given effect are known. In terms of the generalization

$$\text{If } (C_1, \ldots, C_n), \text{ then } E,$$

this implies that all the terms in $(C_1, \ldots, C_n)$ can be supplied, and—equally important—that whenever causes $(C_1, \ldots, C_n)$ occur, they are invariably followed by an effect of type E. The critical question is then to decide whether this generalization should be prefaced with the word "Always" or with the word "Necessarily."

Another way of raising the same puzzle is to ask whether causation consists of anything beyond observed correlations. The usual presumption is that causation consists of both correlation and mechanisms at work assuring that similar causes will indeed be followed by similar effects. In the natural sciences these mechanism ideas often relate to forces, or more generally, to the transmission of energy. The stumbling block was pointed out by David Hume. Our immediate experience, Hume noted, consists of observing correlations or constant conjunctions, but the idea of a necessary relationship between cause and effect is a product of the perceiving mind and is not founded upon immediate experience. In the case of litmus paper being immersed in acid, for example, we observe a constant conjunction between immersion and a change in color, but we cannot "see" the acid forcing or producing the change of color in the paper. Put another way, nothing in immediate experience (visual or otherwise) demonstrates the impossibility of litmus paper not turning pink when immersed in acid. The implication would seem to be that causation reduces to correlation and that causal generalizations should therefore be prefaced with the word "Always," and not with the word "Necessarily."

The issue, however, is not quite as simple as the litmus paper example suggests. Most human beings do believe that they can have direct or immediate experience of force. Participants in a football game, for example, generally argue that their experience of being struck head-on by another object of about the same size most definitely includes the immediate experience of force. The similarity between this experience and what is observed when billiard balls collide head-on is then used (in conjunction with other similar experiences) to infer that comparable forces are at work causing the observed motion of the billiard balls, even when the latter forces are not experienced directly.

The crux of the philosophical problem is whether any force can be experienced directly, and if it can, whether extrapolations of the sort just noted are ever justified. That extrapolation procedure would seem to be but one instance of a larger tendency that might be labeled "In search of similarities in the flux of observable phenomena." As will be outlined elsewhere, that search is central to the formulation of all causal generalizations, irrespective of whether one accepts or rejects Hume's ideas. Why, then, should this type of extrapolation of the idea of force be deemed unacceptable when other extrapolations in search of similarities are deemed acceptable? The answer can be found in only one source: the reader's own personal beliefs concerning the nature of direct experience and the extrapolations justified by that experience. The result will determine which of two very different perspectives will be brought to the main problems of this book. One viewpoint is to insist that causation implies only correlation and that causal analysis consists only in searching for the maximum consistent set of correlations. The other and more common view is to insist that force can be experienced directly and that this experience legitimates the extrapolation of the idea of force to other situations in which it is not experienced directly. Observed correlations in the latter case are then explained in terms of mechanisms at work assuring that similar causes must be followed by similar effects. Causal generalizations should be prefaced, according to the first view, with the word "Always," according to the second, with the word "Necessarily."   would it "should" be a better word...

The second stumbling block was buried in the assumptions noted at the outset. Once it is resurrected, the conclusion just noted must be discarded. The general problem concerns the meaning of similar in the statement "similar cause, similar effect." The starting point, apparent in the statement itself, is the unsurprising observation that effects to be explained by being subsumed under the same generalization must resemble one another, as must their antecedent conditions. Precise or universal causal generalizations—that is, generalizations that can be appropriately prefaced with always or necessarily—can be formulated if and only if (a) the flux of observable phenomena can be organized into homogeneous sets labeled "Causes of type C_1," "Causes of type C_2," "Effects of type E," etc.; and (b) the antecedent conditions $(C_1, \ldots, C_n)$ in the generalization

$$\text{If } (C_1, \ldots, C_n), \text{ then } E$$

can be viewed as being the complete list of causes, *known* to be complete.

All attempts to discover such generalizations invariably confront two kinds of problems. Reality can be organized into homogeneous sets only by abstraction—by ignoring as irrelevant some of the characteristics of a specific event. The would-be organizer frequently views the end product of this process as imperfect because he senses that too much has been abstracted and/or because he senses that, despite abstraction, what remains is not a collection of perfectly homogeneous entities. Consider, for example, the historian's problems of devising homogeneous categories for such diverse phenomena as political oppressions or revolutions. Even if all of the associated problems can be solved—even if reality can be organized into sets generally viewed as being homogeneous—the remaining difficulty would be to find, for a given type of effect, a complete list of causes known to be complete. Enter the second stumbling block. Causal explanation consists of subsuming specific facts under a generalization. In history and in the social sciences, the causal generalizations used for this purpose are usually viewed as being incomplete in the sense that the causes actually enumerated are not, by themselves, regarded as being the sum total of all relevant causes in the situation being analyzed. Even in the natural sciences, however, where generalizations can be found that appear to be extremely precise in the sense that E has always been observed to follow $(C_1, \ldots, C_n)$, the associated list of causes cannot be viewed as a complete list known to be complete. The reason is simple. All previous experimental situations may have included an unknown but relevant cause, and there is *no way* to prove that this was not the case. The point is far from trivial for both the practicing scientist and the philosopher. An example from physics will be explored in some detail in section 3 to suggest why.

To review: causal explanation consists of subsuming specific facts under generalizations of the form

$$\text{If } (C_1, \ldots, C_n), \text{ then } E.$$

Ideally these generalizations are constructed by (a) lumping diverse phenomena into homogeneous sets, and (b) relating one type of set—the effect—to another collection of sets—the causes—in such a manner that the first invariably follows the second. In practice, sets may or may not be viewed as achieving a high degree of homogeneity, but any given collection of causes can never be viewed as a complete collection known to be complete, however large that collection may be and however precise has been the observed relationship between the occurrence of those causes and the occurrence of the effect in question. Two inferences follow. The first is that all causal generalizations must be prefaced with the word "Probably," and not, as suggested earlier, with the word "Always" or "Necessarily." The second is that any exploration of the nature of causal explanation must include a consideration of the meaning of probability. The latter is therefore the final topic of Chapter I.

The word itself has two main reference points: what is outside the observer's head and what is inside that head. The first relates to frequency intrinsic to phenomena quite independent of our knowledge of it. The human perceiver attempts to discover such frequencies by observation, with observed frequencies then related to intrinsic or long-run frequencies by various articles of faith, some of which will be discussed in section 4. The second meaning of probability concerns what Rudolf Carnap calls "the degree of confirmation of the hypothesis h on the evidence e" (1945:72). More simply put, if one believes in a particular generalization of the form

$$\text{Probably, if } (C_1, \ldots, C_n), \text{ then } E,$$

the hypothesis is the generalization, the evidence concerns all the inputs leading to that generalization, and the associated degree of confirmation or degree of support given to that hypothesis by the evidence in question will determine the strength of the conviction with which that hypothesis is held.

By structuring all causal generalizations in this manner, one invites the question: how probable? A search for answers can proceed down two different paths. The question might be construed as calling for a numerical coefficient. The challenge is then to demonstrate that the probability associated with any given generalization of the form just noted can be translated into the betting odds that the individual advancing the generalization would be willing to accept that the next time events of type $(C_1, \ldots, C_n)$ occur, they will be followed by an event of type E. (The demonstration itself involves nothing more than the rudiments of decision making under uncertainty.) The second issue concerns the nature of the inputs leading to the formulation of those betting odds. From what sources come the evidence and assessment rules that will determine the degree of conviction with which a given causal generalization is advanced? To find the answer one might revert to the first meaning of probability: long-run frequency intrinsic to phenomena. This tack is a bit misleading on several counts. Intrinsic or long-run frequency connotes an aura of objectivity which in practice is seldom if ever realized. As will be illustrated in section 4, assertions about frequencies are profoundly influenced by the knowledge, experience, and beliefs of the asserter. More important, precise observations of past frequencies can seldom be brought to the problem of formulating most of the causal generalizations employed in history and the social sciences. What is brought has already been indicated above: the sum total of the knowledge, experience, and beliefs considered to be relevant to whatever generalization is being formulated. If it can be shown—and section 4 will argue that it can be shown easily—that no two people bring exactly the same evidence to the task of formulating most generalizations, then it follows that the probability coefficients associated with those generalizations will vary across individuals precisely because that evidence varies across individuals.

The final conclusion—hardly surprising, but crucial for the understanding of the principal arguments in this book—is that the criteria for adequacy in causal explanations are enormously conditioned by the perceptions and experience of the would-be judge. At every stage in the construction of causal explanations—the formation of quasi-homogeneous sets, the linking of different sets in a cause-and-effect relationship, and the assessing of how probable that linkage is—the knowledge, experience, and beliefs of the individual attempting such an exercise is crucial. In the remaining chapters of this book our task will therefore be as much psychological as methodological: to understand the mental rules and evidential inputs being employed when an historian or an economist or an economic historian scrutinizes the results of such labors and observes, "Now that's what I call a satisfactory causal explanation."

2. Problems of Definition

Preoccupation with meticulous definition of terms would seem to be an idiosyncrasy of the philosopher rather than a common trait. Most of humanity—at least by the standards of the philosopher—are usually not overburdened by the desire to reason rigorously, or by the desire to apply stringent criteria to the task of assessing what they do and do not know. Predictably, their use of language to describe any reasoning process is also less than rigorous. One therefore finds such words as axiom, postulate, premise, assumption, and hypothesis used interchangeably to designate the starting point of mental deliberation. Exact equality of meaning is not conceded by all of the reasoners all of the time. For some (but not others) "axiom" connotes a self-evident truth, while the other words merely designate what is to be taken for granted for the sake of getting on with the argument.[3] "Assumption" may or may not imply the prelude to reasoning, and "hypothesis" may be regarded as synonymous with "groundless assumption" or alternatively as "an assumption subject to verification or proof."[4]

Whatever terminology one prefers, the inescapable inputs for beginning a reasoned argument are statements accepted "as true without in any way establishing their validity."[5] This is merely a complicated phrasing for a simple point. Not all propositions can be derived from other propositions. If some are not derived but are merely asserted, the

3. For example, *Webster's Third New International Dictionary* (1961) includes in its many definitions of "axiom" the following: "Baconianism: an empirical rule or generalization based on experience. . . . Kantianism: an immediately certain synthetic a priori proposition." See also Feigl 1956:27.
   4. See, for example, the various definitions of these terms in either *Webster's Dictionary* or the *Oxford English Dictionary* (1933). The two definitions of hypothesis are from *The Concise Oxford Dictionary of Current English* (1958) and *The American Heritage Dictionary of the English Language* (1970). For an indication of how chaotic popular usage can be, see Machlup 1955:3 n. 2.
   5. Tarski 1965:118.

reasons for accepting them must be something other than their being reasoned inferences from other propositions. They are, as it were, the primitive propositions: the beginning.

At the other end of this mental process are conclusions or theorems. In the compact wording of the *Oxford English Dictionary*, a theorem is a "demonstrable theoretical judgement." In the less compact wording of the philosopher, a theorem is "simply a sentence which is the last member of a proof, where a proof is defined as a finite sequence of sentences each of which is either a postulate or is inferrable from earlier sentences in the sequence by means of the rules of inference."[6]

This brings us to the central semantic puzzle for purposes of this discussion. Man reasons in search of generalizations. That reasoning process, at least in economics, is often in pursuit of, and conditioned by, theories and models. What is the difference between the two? A precise answer is impossible because both words have a host of meanings, depending upon who uses them and in what context. The possible meanings of theory according to the dictionary range all the way from "an unproved assumption" to "the coherent set of hypothetical, conceptual, and pragmatic principles forming the general frame of reference for a field of inquiry."[7] The same word is frequently used by social scientists "to designate almost any general statement."[8] On those rare occasions when economists have attempted to be more precise, the proffered definition usually incorporates the empirical bias of their profession. Thus Samuelson defines a theory "as a set of axioms, postulates or hypotheses that stipulate something about observable reality" (1963:233). The philosopher may feel no compulsion to refer to observable reality at all, defining a theory in terms of "a set of laws which are so inter-related deductively that they can be arranged into an axiomatic system; i.e., so related that from a small set of them (the axioms) the rest (theorems) can all be logically deduced."[9]

Once the problem becomes one of explaining observable reality, the economist (unlike the logician) is forced to restructure his mental processes and his associated definitions of a theory to allow for uncertainty

6. Massey 1965:1156.
7. Both definitions are from *Webster's Third New International Dictionary*.
8. Nagel 1963a:211.
9. Wilson 1969:295–296. A theory is consistent if no sentence and its negation are both theorems of the system (Massey 1965:1158).

in his conclusions. His principal theorems, insofar as they relate to observable reality, are not necessarily implied by his premises; rather his theorems or conclusions are made more probable by the evidence marshaled in their support, but the absolute certainty associated with pure deductive reasoning *always* eludes him. Why this is so will become more apparent in subsequent analysis of the role of causal explanation in history and economics.

To return to our problem: perhaps the most popular usage of the words "theory" and "model" in economics reflects the viewpoint that the two words are synonyms.[10] Another viewpoint is to insist that the two words are only slightly different, models indicating "a simpler and more accurate determinable state of affairs, with the intention of facilitating deduction of further consequences which can then be tentatively reapplied to the more complex and elusive real system."[11] The latter part of this quotation concerns the purpose for having a model in the first place, a subject to which the discussion will return in Chapter III. At this juncture the appropriate focus is on the words "simpler" and "more accurate." One possible distinction between a model and a theory is the extent to which the former is a more precise specification of causal tendencies enunciated by the latter. *Webster's Dictionary*, for example, gives as one of its many definitions of model "a theoretical projection *in detail* of a possible system of human relationships (as in economics, politics or psychology)" (italics added). Willingness to embark upon detailed specifications of causal theories will be found to be a key distinction between the economist and the historian. If detail is abandoned, then models (in the sense noted above) can also be abandoned, and the nature of causal explanation is radically changed, as is the extent to which those causal explanations imply counterfactuals. (See below, Chapters II and IV.)

These considerations relate to the phrase "more accurate." What about the word "simpler"? For most (if not all) economists, "A model is a simplified and idealized abstraction whose purpose is to approximate

10. See, for example, Machlup 1960:569–570. For an indication of how this usage is *not* typical in the natural sciences, see Nagel 1961:90–115; also Achinstein 1965:102–108. The absence of consensus among social scientists concerning the appropriate usage of these two words is suggested by the fact that neither theory nor model is defined in general terms in the 1968 edition of the *International Encyclopedia of the Social Sciences.* For further evidence on prevailing confusion, see Harrod 1968:173–192.
11. Gellner 1964:434.

the behavior of a system. A model of necessity must always be a compromise between simplicity and reality."[12] Why of necessity? Why a
compromise? And how much simplicity is too much simplicity?

All three questions are merely a subset of those general problems that
arise when any causal explanation is attempted. To detail the various
usages of such words as "model" and "theory" is comparatively easy.
(To document how both are used with consummate laxness in the social
sciences is perhaps embarrassingly easy.) What is anything but easy is to
explain the various uses of the word "cause." For all its difficulty, that
task is the indispensable starting point for understanding the nature of
explanation and model building in history, economics, and the new economic history. It is therefore the main subject of this chapter.

3.   On Causal Laws

All philosophers, of every school, imagine that causation is one of the fundamental
axioms or postulates of science, yet, oddly enough, in advanced sciences . . . the
word "cause" never occurs. [Bertrand Russell][13]

It is beyond serious doubt that the term "cause" rarely if ever appears in the
research papers or treatises currently published in the natural sciences. . . . Nevertheless, though the *term* may be absent, the *idea* for which it stands continues to
have wide currency. It not only crops up in everyday speech, and in investigations
into human affairs by economists, social psychologists, and historians, it is also
pervasive in the accounts natural scientists give of their laboratory procedures, as
well as in the interpretations offered by many theoretical physicists of their
mathematical formalism. [Ernest Nagel][14]

Given that our subject is really causal explanation, let us begin with
the less demanding assignment of defining the second word in that
phrase. To explain is "to make plain or intelligible; to clear of obscurity
or difficulty"[15]—a formal definition that might be informally modified
to read "to make plain or intelligible to you." The appended words
merely underscore the subjective nature of the process. What is considered to be an adequate explanation will depend upon (a) the nature
of the initial puzzlement to be resolved and (b) the criteria accepted as
appropriate for resolving that puzzle. An adequate explanation is, after

12. E. A. Robinson 1967:125.
13. Russell 1918:180.
14. Nagel 1965:5.
15. *Oxford English Dictionary*.

all, nothing more—and nothing less—than an explanation which you happen to find adequate. It must therefore always relate "the object of inquiry to the realm of understanding in some comprehensible and appropriate way."[16] In many instances, that relating process will require no reference to causation. A child may ask, "What is a cat?"; the philosopher may inquire about the rules of logic; the linguist may seek to discover how the usage of a word has changed over time. A large percentage of our inquiries could nevertheless be reworded to read, "What is the cause of . . . ", although one might well resist the more sweeping suggestion of Aristotle, "Men do not think they know a thing till they have grasped the 'why' of it."[17]

What is required to give the individual who is puzzled a sense of having grasped the why of it varies across time, space, and personalities. Consider the problem of explaining an eclipse of the moon. A medieval theologian would find an explanation couched solely in terms of Newtonian equations singularly incomplete even if he understood the mathematics, while the African bushman would view all mathematical explanations as absolute gibberish. As self-evident as the point may seem to be, ignoring the subjective basis for criteria underlying adequacy in causal explanations has led to considerable dispute—and, in many cases, unnecessary dispute—among historians, economists, and philosophers. If we encountered a Canadian and a Russian arguing about the appropriate rules for the game of hockey, we would feel no compulsion to enter the debate in the interests of demonstrating one right and the other wrong. We would observe—correctly—that what is judged acceptable is strictly a matter of personal preference. The inquisitive social scientist might attempt to specify the rules actually used in each country, but one set of rules would have no intrinsic superiority over any other. Similarly, when we find—as we shall—Samuelson arguing with Friedman or Dray with Hempel about the rules for adequacy in causal explanation, we must beware of our natural tendency to label as intrinsically superior those rules that happen to appeal to us. Our central problem, as noted at the outset, is as much psychological as methodological: to understand the mental rules being employed when an historian or an economist says, sometimes with pride and

16. Scriven 1962:202.
17. Quoted in Kim 1967:159.

usually with assurance, "Now that's what I call a satisfactory causal explanation."

As might be expected, the philosophers provide the obvious starting point for pursuing such a topic. This is not to suggest that their own views on the subject have at all times been entirely devoid of ambiguity and confusion. W. K. Clifford, for example, maintains that the word represented by "cause" has sixty-four meanings in the writings of Plato and forty-eight in those of Aristotle.[18] The four principal meanings of the word cause were nevertheless outlined by Aristotle long ago. These are:

(1) efficient cause, or that by which some change is wrought,
(2) final cause, or the purpose for which change is wrought,
(3) material cause, or that in which a change is wrought, and
(4) formal cause, or that into which something is changed.[19]

In terms of the much quoted example of the sculptor, "The material cause of the statue is the marble, the formal cause is the essence of the statue to be produced, the efficient cause is the contact of the chisel with the marble, and the final cause is the end that the sculptor has in view."[20]

In the past few centuries, three of the above four have tended to fall into disuse (and to some extent, into disrepute). The sole survivor—efficient cause—has in the post-Newtonian era acquired rather special connotations.[21] Before the rise of experimental science, the idea of absolute uniformity of causation, while by no means absent from the philosophical literature, was seldom emphasized. Once the goals of the scientist became to explain, to predict, and to control by discovering uniformities in the flux of observable phenomena, the natural tendency was to emphasize one of the two fundamental ideas underlying the idea of cause; namely, similar cause, similar effect.[22] (The other basic idea—

18. Cited in Sorokin 1943:38.
19. The above wording might be considered by classical scholars to be too much of a twentieth-century rewording of Aristotelian ideas. The original reads: "Evidently we have to acquire knowledge of the original causes (for we say we know each thing only when we think we recognize its first cause), and causes are spoken of in four senses. In one of these we mean the substance, i.e. the essence . . . ; in another the matter or substratum, in a third the source of the change, and in a fourth the cause opposed to this, the purpose and the good (for this is the end of all generation and change)" (Aristotle 1908:983).
20. Russell 1945:169; see also R. Taylor 1967:56.
21. For a discussion of the decline of teleological explanations, see Burtt 1951:*passim.* For an indication that this decline has by no means been synonymous with extinction, see Nagel 1961:Chapters 12 and 14; also 1953b:537–558.
22. See, for example, Nagel 1961:4.

that every effect has a cause—considered as self-evident by most writers until recently is now regarded as more of an open question incapable of scientific verification.)[23] The resulting puzzles concerned the meaning of similar, and whether the phrase "similar cause, similar effect" should be prefaced with the word "Always," "Necessarily," or "Probably."

A discussion of possible answers usually begins with a specification of what is meant by necessary and sufficient conditions. Consider the problem of explaining why a match will light when struck. A "causal law" might be formulated to read: Every time oxygen is present (C_1), the match head is dry (C_2) and the match is struck (C_3), then it will light (E). In more general terms,

$$\text{If } (C_1, \ldots, C_n), \text{ then } E.$$

In the match example the first three—the causes—are regarded as the sufficient conditions for the effect. Or in the more precise wording of Mill, "The cause . . . is the sum total of the conditions, positive and negative taken together . . . which being realized, the consequent [or effect] invariably follows" (1851:I, 345). The key word is "invariably." If a given collection of conditions are truly sufficient, they are said to lead necessarily or inexorably or invariably to the effect. That is,

$$\text{If } (C_1, \ldots, C_n), \text{ then } E,$$

is modified to read

$$\text{Necessarily, if } (C_1, \ldots, C_n), \text{ then } E.$$

The word "necessary" unfortunately is used in these discussions in two quite different ways. It may refer to the relationship between sufficient conditions and their effect. Alternatively, it may refer to the indispensability of a particular member of that collection of sufficient conditions. If a given cause is, in this sense, necessary, then whenever it is absent, the effect will not occur. More rigorously, if a given cause (such as oxygen) is common to all possible collections of sufficient conditions that produce the effect in question, then this cause is also a necessary condition in the sense that without it the effect cannot occur regardless of what else might transpire.[24] This second meaning would seem to pose few conceptual difficulties. The collection of causes

23. R. Taylor 1967:57–58.
24. The implicit assumption is, of course, that effects cannot occur unless they are caused.

$(C_1, \ldots, C_n)$ are said to be jointly sufficient for effect E. Other collections may also be jointly sufficient. If E only occurs when it is preceded by one of these collections, and if the cause C_1 is common to all possible collections, then E will never occur unless C_1 occurs. But why, one might ask, should the relationship between antecedent causes and subsequent effect be viewed as being a "necessary" relationship?

To attempt an answer is to broach one of the more complicated issues in philosophy. Before attacking the mountain, one should perhaps dispense with two of the lesser escarpments that dot the landscape of historical debate. The first concerns the problem of the infinite regress. If one of the causes of the Russian Revolution of 1917 was the outbreak of war in Europe in 1914, does a complete explanation of that revolution have to include the causes of World War I, the causes of those causes, and so on? In terms of the format given above, causal analysis can always be extended to include a discussion of the factors producing one or more of the sufficient conditions (such as explaining why the match head was dry). The desirability of extending the analysis in this way is purely a subjective matter. To list the sufficient conditions for an effect is, as it were, to give the first and indispensable round of factors leading to the effect in question. Whether further rounds are required is not a matter of logic but of personal preference. The philosopher's problem is to decide whether the construction of a first round is possible, and if not, why not.

Historians have also frequently debated which rules would justify singling out one or more members in a collection of causes deemed sufficient for an event and designating that subset as "the causes" of the effect in question. The only list acceptable to the philosopher is the complete list. As Mill pointed out, "We have . . . no right to give the name of cause to one of them, exclusively of the others" (1851:I, 340). Debates about the rules for choosing a subset of the total list therefore reflect nothing more than practical considerations and personal preferences, both of which have no bearing on the fundamental philosophical problems.[25]

25. One final preliminary puzzle (not easily resolved) concerns the question of temporal sequence. The usual presumption is that a cause must precede its effect in time, but this idea confronts the difficulty that certain examples—such as a hand moving a pencil—seem to involve simultaneity rather than temporal sequence. For a discussion of the associated difficulties, see R. Taylor 1967:65–66.

Those problems, to repeat, relate to the sentence: Similar causes will necessarily be followed by similar effects. Or translated into the symbols previously used,

$$\text{Necessarily, if } (C_1, \ldots, C_n), \text{ then } E^{26}.$$

What does the word "necessarily" mean?

Before David Hume tackled the problem, the usual presumption was that a cause "produced" or "entailed" its consequent or effect, a presumption sometimes (but not always) founded on the belief that forces were at work analogous to the forces experienced when one pushed or pulled on an object. What Hume pointed out is that our visual impressions allow us to observe constant conjunction—that things of type C are always followed by things of type E—but "we never can observe any tie between them. They seem *conjoined*, but never *connected*."[27] We can see, for example, that the litmus paper is immersed in an unpleasant smelling liquid, but we cannot "see" the acid turning the paper red—or more correctly, that it is the acid that is forcing or entailing or producing the redness in the paper. Put another way, our experience is that every time litmus paper is immersed in acid, it turns red. *Nothing* in immediate experience (visual or otherwise) teaches us that it is impossible for the litmus paper not to turn red. In short, we do not perceive forces, we perceive effects and choose to impute an added ingredient called "force," "necessity," or "entailment" to the visual experience.

If one rejects this imputation because it does not seem to be directly verifiable by our perceptions, the result is a completely revised definition of cause. "Since repetition is all that distinguishes the causal law from a mere coincidence, the meaning of causal relation consists in the

---

26. Translated into the symbols of the philosopher, "The fundamental form of a causal law will be

$$(x)[A(x) \supset Z(x)],$$

that is, for each causal situation if characteristic A is present among the initial conditions then characteristic Z will feature among the subsequent conditions, or, All A-type events are followed by Z-type events" (Lucas 1962:39–40). Translation into another language does not, however, solve the problem, which in this revised formulation is to explain what is meant by the symbol occurring between A(x) and Z(x).

27. "But when one particular species of events has always, in all instances, been conjoined with another, we make no longer any scruple of foretelling one upon the appearance of the other.... We then call the one object *Cause*; the other, *Effect*" (1894:74–75).

statement of an exceptionless repetition—it is unnecessary to assume that it means more. The idea that a cause is connected with its effect by a sort of hidden string, that the effect is forced to follow the cause, is anthropomorphic in its origin and is dispensable; *if—then always* is all that is meant by a causal relation."[28]

Both the historian and the economist should find this a curious statement. Every beginning course in methodology encourages the historian to beware of the fallacy *post hoc, ergo propter hoc*—after this, therefore because of this. Every introductory course in statistics that is taught by economists stresses the danger—indeed, the naiveté—of assuming that correlation (or constant conjunction as indicated by a statistical measure called correlation) is equivalent to causation. The philosopher now seems to be asserting that correlation is all that there is to causation. Moreover, he may argue, none of the findings of sciences contradict this view, including those causal generalizations which, when expressed in equation form, include a specific symbol for the idea of force. A brief review of Newton's contribution to the idea of causation will show why.

The discoveries in question may seem at first glance to lend support to the idea that causes necessarily produce their effect. Newton began by sweeping aside three of the four Aristotelian definitions of cause and focusing his attention upon a particular problem of efficient causation; namely, how bodies move. His next step—in Einstein's words "perhaps the greatest intellectual stride that it has ever been granted to any man to make"[29]—involved (a) reducing all observable phenomena to the positions and velocities of point-masses (providing en route operational definitions for all terms), and (b) discovering how bodies so defined move according to laws fully statable in mathematical form.[30] If one knew the initial state of a system of point-masses at some instant in time (initial state being defined in terms of the positions and velocities of all point-masses in the system), then the mathematical laws would enable

28. Reichenbach 1951b:158.
29. Quoted in D'Abro 1952:54.
30. The mathematical innovations in question consisted of discovering the concept of the differential coefficient and enunciating the Laws of Motion in the form of second-order differential equations relating the acceleration of bodies to the inverse square of their distances from neighboring bodies. For a description of the associated equations and a discussion of the importance of time derivatives in Newtonian mechanics, see D'Abro 1952:Chapter 7; Nagel 1961:278–279; and J. S. Coleman 1968:429–430.

one to predict the configuration of the system at any future point in time.[31] This in turn seemed to constitute nothing less than the first rigorous formulation of the doctrine that similar causes produce similar effects.[32] Small wonder that the determinism implicit in the theory[33] prompted Laplace to suggest that a divine intelligence knowing "all of the forces acting in nature" as well as the positions of all things in the universe could predict the future with absolute certainty.[34]

If Newtonian mechanics appear to lend support to the idea that similar causes are always followed by similar effects, do those mechanics also support the related but stronger assertion that similar causes *necessarily* produce similar effects? The answer depends upon the meaning of force and whether one's knowledge of force can appropriately be regarded as justification for the assertion that a cause necessarily produces its consequent. For Newton, force was the cause of observed changes in motion. (He was prepared to speak of the "power of gravity" and of the certainty of its existence, but concerning the causes of gravity itself he formulated no hypothesis.)[35] *If* one believes that Newtonian force is similar to what one experiences by pushing on a door, and *if* one further believes that the power of the force in question is irresistible, then necessity would seem to have been reinstated into the concept of cause. One obvious difficulty is that Newtonian forces seem to act at a distance—a rather different setting from that associated with leaning

31. One could just as easily postdict the configuration of the system at any previous point in time, making the choice of initial instant entirely arbitrary.

32. This statement as it stands is too strong. Newtonian mechanics permit only an approximate test of the doctrine of strict causality because (a) no observable system is perfectly isolated, (b) observation itself constitutes a violation of whatever isolation the system has, and finally—and predictably—(c) human measurements are always subject to error. "These difficulties were not regarded as fatal to the doctrine, because approximately isolated systems could be found, and our measurements could be so refined that they would not perceptibly disturb the magnitudes to be measured. The situation was expressed by the statement that, in practice, rigorous causality could not be tested, but that no theoretical obstacle barred the way to a rigorous test" (D'Abro 1952:55).

33. "A theory is labeled properly a deterministic one if analysis of its internal structure shows that the theoretical state of a system at one instant logically determines a unique state of that system for any other instant. In this sense, and with respect to theoretically defined mechanical states of systems, mechanics is unquestionably a deterministic theory" (Nagel 1961:285).

34. For a complete citation of Laplace's statement, see Nagel 1961:281 n. 4. For a discussion of the *non sequitur* in Laplace's inference from Newtonian mechanics to perfect foresight, see *ibid.*, p. 282.

35. 1819:II, 313–314. See also Harré 1964:107.

on a door. The more fundamental problem for Newton (and for everyone else) is that "what was observable was a certain relation between acceleration and configuration; to say that this relation was brought about by the intermediacy of 'force' was to add nothing to our knowledge."[36] In the motions of mutually gravitating bodies there is nothing (according to this view) that can be called a cause or an effect. There is merely a formula.[37] Exit necessity, and enter equations only. The equations formalize the observed regularities, but the regularities themselves should not be construed as being symptomatic of, or conditioned by, forces at work in the natural world. Causation is again reduced to constant conjunction or correlation and is not something in addition to constant conjunction.[38]

If this is the correct view of causation—if such ideas as force, necessity, and entailment have no place in the definition of cause—why should one expect conjunctions observed in the past to persist in the future? In more technical language, why should one accept the principle of induction? That principle asserts that "if A has been found very often accompanied or followed by B, and no instance is known of A not being accompanied or followed by B, then it is probable that on the next occasion on which A is observed it will be accompanied or followed by B."[39] The empiricist resists this principle because, as evidenced by the litmus paper example, no matter how many times B has been observed to follow A in the past, nothing in our experience has demonstrated the impossibility of B not following A. In the language preferred

36. Russell 1945:539. Another way of making the same point is to say that we do not have different and independent measures of all three variables in the Newtonian equation: force, mass, and acceleration.

37. See Russell, 1953:395. This is a view to which Samuelson seems to be particularly sympathetic. He cites in its support two outstanding examples from the natural sciences: "Heinrich Hertz said that a belief in Maxwell's theory of light meant nothing more and nothing less than that the observable measurements agreed with the partial differential equations of Maxwell. . . . Poincaré said that the whole content of classical dynamics was summed up in the hypothesis that certain sets of second-order differential equations exhibited solutions that to a good approximation duplicated the behavior of celestial bodies and terrestrial particles" (1963:232).

38. The modern mind has a curious propensity to be satisfied with an explanation couched solely in terms of equations. Because the motions of the planets can be reduced to mathematics does not make the occurrence of those motions—not to mention the observed regularities—one bit less mysterious. "Natural Science describes, so far as it can, *how*, or in accordance with what rules, phenomena happen, but it is wholly incompetent to answer the question *why* they happen" (Hobson 1923:82). In Aristotelian terms, then, mankind does not grasp completely the why of these occurrences.

39. Russell 1945:673.

by philosophers, it is never deductively impossible for a falsifying instance to occur.[40]

Despite these difficulties, most human beings are willing to formulate general propositions using the methodology employed by Newton and every other experimental scientist since the days of Bacon: "Particular propositions are inferred from phenomena, and afterwards made general by induction."[41] One possible reason for their ready acceptance of the principle of induction is pragmatic. Without it all prediction would be impossible. Human experience involves action, and the problem of choosing among possible actions inevitably raises the issue of forecasting. "To date," one can hear the layman saying, "acceptance of the principle of induction has worked out fairly well in the sense that my initial expectations were subsequently fulfilled, at least to some degree, by actual developments."

A second and quite different reason for accepting the principle in question is the argument that, at least in some instances, one can directly perceive or experience causes entailing or forcing or producing effects. The evidence for this assertion is usually taken from those human experiences associated with intervening in the flux of phenomena as an active agent. Indeed, the word "cause" in the sense of "responsible for" can be traced to Greek and Roman technical terms denoting actions accountable for wrongs for which there were legal remedies.[42] To refer again to the example of section 1, one may argue that intervention in the flux of phenomena on the football field includes the immediate experience of force, and then argue—more tenuously but perhaps still persuasively—that this experience is analogous to that of colliding billiard balls and to other situations where the forces at work are not experienced directly. The perceived similarities with experiences in which

40. "It does not seem feasible to construct a deductive justification of induction; that is, a justification by means of a series of deductive inferences from premises which are analytically true" (Lucas 1962:32).

41. Newton 1819:II, 314. "Bacon was the first of the long line of scientifically minded philosophers who . . . emphasized the importance of induction as opposed to deduction. . . . [He] despised the syllogism [and] was virulently hostile to Aristotle . . . everything, he held, should be explained as following necessarily from efficient causes. He valued his method as showing how to arrange the observational data upon which science must be based. We ought, he says, to be neither like spiders, which spin things out of their own insides, nor like ants, which merely collect, but like bees, which both collect and arrange. This is somewhat unfair to the ants, but it illustrates Bacon's meaning" (Russell 1945:543–544).

42. See Nagel 1965:17.

force is directly experienced, so this argument runs, then justify the imputation of force to the latter type of situation. Debates among adherents to this point of view are to be expected concerning which extrapolations are justified. The main bone of contention, however, is whether forces can ever be experienced directly. If they cannot, then questions concerning legitimate extrapolations become irrelevant.

Philosophers appear to be somewhat uncertain on this point. They readily concede that the human experience includes active intervention. What they question is whether any intervention includes the "direct experience" or "perception" of a causal relationship. They note, for example, that between the decision to move my arm and the actual movement of the arm can be found a long chain of intermediation involving nerves and muscles that seems to challenge the claim that in implementing bodily movements one actually "experiences" a direct causal connection.[43] The major problems with this line of attack would seem to be (a) a failure to define what "direct experience" means, and (b) the difficulty of formulating a definition that would discount muscular action for the reasons noted but still legitimate the claim that some experiences, such as visual, are appropriately labeled as direct experiences. To approach the same problem from a slightly different vantage point, if our ideas about causation are to be founded only upon sense experience that is immediate or direct, what sense experience cannot be stigmatized as the product of long chains of intermediation involving nerves and muscles?

If despite these difficulties the attack cited above carries the day—if one accepts the view that (a) causal relationships are never perceived directly, and (b) because of this, the concept of necessity should be eradicated from the idea of cause—then two puzzles come immediately to mind. The first, as already suggested, concerns why one should be willing to accept the principle of induction. (The problem of induction itself is essentially where Hume left it.) The second concerns what should be left in the idea of causation if necessity is thrown out. Examples of constant conjunction are not difficult to find where, despite that conjunction, the relationship between the two conjoined events is not considered to be one of cause and effect. Night regularly follows day; the growth of teeth in infants regularly follows the growth of hair. This

43. See, for example, Russell 1945:669–670.

suggests that something *in addition* to constant conjunction is included in our ideas of causation. What is that something else? At least part of the answer concerns the desire for consistency with the sum total of our previous observations on constant conjunctions. The physicist, for example, can give us an explanation for night following day that incorporates a vast range of observations.[44] The consistency in question is, in general, also much broader than that associated with visual perceptions. In addition to seeing, we feel, taste, smell, and hear. This desire for consistency therefore requires that "our statements about the external world face the tribunal of sense experience not individually, but as a corporate body."[45] When those statements include an explanation of human behavior, that tribunal is usually—and perhaps invariably—supplemented by the evidence of introspection.[46] (The extent to which the evidence of introspection is itself the product of earlier sense experience is another question.)

One therefore confronts two possibilities. In formulating general causal propositions, if one believes that direct causal connections can be perceived at least in certain situations, and if one further believes that this perceived link between cause and effect can legitimately be extrapolated to other situations where the link itself cannot be perceived directly, then necessity is reinstated into the idea of causation. The accepted manner of formulating causal statements is

$$\text{Necessarily, if } (C_1, \ldots, C_n), \text{ then } E.$$

The other alternative is to insist that causal links can never be perceived directly and that the correct wording is

$$\text{Always, if } (C_1, \ldots, C_n), \text{ then } E.$$

If either formulation is accepted, Hume's arguments have not entirely carried the day, insofar as both reflect an acceptance of the principle of induction. Finally, whichever formulation is preferred, that fundamental idea of causation—similar cause, similar effect—seems to have

44. If two different theories cover equally well the relevant observations on conjunction, the human tendency is to prefer the simple to the more complex. That choice, however, reflects "merely a methodological precept, not a law of Nature" (Russell 1953:401).

45. Quine 1953:41.

46. One implication is that objective history, in the sense of history not conditioned by the experience and personality of the historian, is out of the question when the problem is to explain past human behavior.

survived relatively unscathed. The only debate concerns whether the appropriate addition to that idea is the word "always" or the word "necessarily."

The remaining difficulty—and indeed the rock upon which the entire analysis is about to founder—is to decide what is meant by the word "similar." To formulate a causal law explaining the occurrence of an event requires, in the first instance, the ability to classify various different phenomena into a single category labeled "effects of type E_1." This may seem to pose few difficulties if the type of effect to be explained is the lighting of a match. It is considerably less easy for many of the phenomena that the historian would explain, such as social unrest or political revolution. Even in the most simple of cases, the event or effect in question cannot be described completely: "No finitely long statement can possibly formulate the totality of traits embodied in any concretely existing thing."[47] Description can therefore only proceed by abstraction; by ignoring as irrelevent many of the actual circumstances associated with a given event, and settling for, or focusing upon, a minute residual. The obvious danger in this procedure is that in pursuit of homogeneous categories we shall abstract too much: that we shall end up attempting to give a single explanation for what are in fact diverse effects with different associated causes.

Even if all effects could be classified easily into homogeneous sets, problems of the first order would still arise in the attempt to identify and to classify into homogeneous sets the actual causes of the event in question from what is literally an infinite list of possible contenders. Again the process of abstraction is indispensable, both for classification and for weeding out the attendant but irrelevant contenders until the residual can appropriately be regarded as the minimum sufficient conditions for the type of effect under study. In explaining observed motion, for example, we may follow Newton's lead and ignore all attributes of moving bodies except their positions, point-masses, and velocity. The resulting theory then enables us to predict the behavior of such diverse phenomena as the phases of the moon, the occurrence of tides, and the rate at which freely falling dinner plates approach the surface of the kitchen floor.

47. Nagel 1963a:214.

The techniques usually proposed for establishing what can and cannot be ignored as irrelevant tend to be some variant of the following:

(1) If the effect is a discrete event, hold constant all factors suspected of being relevant except one, remove that one, and if the effect fails to occur, then the removed factor is a relevant cause. Alternatively, if the effect still occurs, the removed factor is irrelevant. In more general terms, if the occurrence of $(C_1, C_2, C_3, \ldots, C_n)$ is always followed by E, and if $(C_2, C_3, \ldots, C_n)$ is not followed by E, then C_1 is a cause of E; i.e., is appropriately listed as one of the minimum sufficient conditions for the event E.

(2) If the effect to be analyzed is a variable, such as the pressure of a gas or the price of gold, the same procedure should be followed, although removal or variation in C_1, if the latter is a relevant cause, may now produce either variation in E, or a complete absence of E.[48]

If, for example, all members of a primitive tribe pronounce a spell before striking matches, the relevance of that spell could be tested by asking them to repeat the experiment holding all other relevant variables constant (such as dryness of the match head and the presence of oxygen), but omitting the variable suspected of being irrelevant (the pronouncing of the spell). The same technique could also be applied to other factors, although removal of oxygen in a primitive setting might pose certain practical difficulties.

The implicit article of faith is that similar causes do indeed produce similar effects. The indispensable requirements to test that belief empirically include: (a) the ability to group diverse phenomena into homogeneous categories labeled "Effect of type E_1," "Suspected cause of type C_1," etc., (b) the ability to hold constant all relevant causes except one, vary that one, and observe the results, and finally (c) the ability to repeat the procedure listed under (b) for all causes that are in fact the sufficient conditions for a given effect. Only by such means can we achieve a

48. The name perhaps most commonly associated with elaborating these techniques is that of John Stuart Mill. (See especially 1851:I, Chapter 8.) Others have pointed out that for practical purposes the various possible techniques listed by Mill reduce to some variant of the two noted above. "The function of experiment . . . is eliminative. And the methods of experimental inquiry . . . have precisely that function" (Cohen and Nagel 1934:250).

complete list of sufficient conditions; only with a complete list can we test the validity of the assertion "similar cause, similar effect."

Difficulties associated with achieving homogeneous categories have been touched upon briefly above. Even if all of these were easily resolved, a host of problems would still bedevil our effects to implement the above procedure for all relevant causes. Among these, two are particularly intractable.

The first is created by variations in an unknown causal factor. One might, for example, be unaware that barometric pressure affects the boiling point of water. Experiments conducted at different times and in different locations would therefore yield different results, however much the scientist might try to hold other things constant. This incapacity means that when all known relevant variables are held constant except one, and that one is changed to detect its influence, the scientist can never be sure whether the observed change in the effect is produced by changes in the known factor, or by changes in the unknown factor, or by both. (It also means that one is greatly puzzled by the failure of potatoes to cook in boiling water at high altitudes.)

Even more destructive to our goal of achieving a precise and complete causal law is the possibility of an unknown causal factor that has remained constant, or at least relatively constant, during all previous experimental situations. Before the discovery of oxygen, for example, no one would have listed oxygen as the cause of anything. This failure, in turn, would have seriously impaired all predictions about ignition in situations where oxygen was not present, or was present to a very limited degree. So crucial is this point that it is worth laboring in some detail. The following example is deliberately chosen from physics, a discipline in which many still believe at least some universal generalizations known to be universal can be found. The point to be illustrated is that this is not the case—that even here, in Quine's wording, "All is tentative, all admits to revision." An examination of a problem encountered by Galileo will demonstrate why.

In analyzing observed motion, Galileo chose as his main experimental situation the rolling of smooth spheres down an inclined plane. Part of his good fortune lay in the fact that the influences of a number of relevant variables such as friction and air resistance were negligible relative to the degree of accuracy desired. Their effects could also be assumed away by formulating the final law in terms of objects falling freely in a vacuum, the major conclusion being that under such circumstances, the instant acceleration of those bodies would be constant.[49] Newton subsequently demonstrated that predictions based upon Galileo's law were tolerably accurate only because the mass of the earth and the distance between the falling object and the center of the earth were both relatively constant—or constant, relative to the degree of accuracy desired by Galileo.[50] For all situations in which the ignored variables were not constant, such as those pertaining to the motions of planets, predictions based upon the same law would, in all likelihood, turn out to be grotesquely wide of the mark.

All of these difficulties can be neatly side-stepped if the causal law

Always, if $(C_1, \ldots, C_n)$, then E

(or "Necessarily, if . . . then . . . ") is modified to read

Always, if $(C_1, \ldots, C_n)$ then E *ceteris paribus*,
or other things being equal.

The appended phrase can then be used for such diverse purposes as (a) ensuring constancy in unknown but relevant factors that in practice do tend to vary (e.g., ensuring the constancy of barometric pressure in a law about the boiling point of water that omits barometric pressure), (b) guaranteeing the continued presence of unknown relevant factors that have not varied enough in previous experimental situations to

49. Defining initial position, distance traveled, and initial velocity as S_0, S, and V_0, then Galileo's law suggests the relationship $S = S_0 + V_0 t + \frac{1}{2} g t^2$, where t stands for time and g for a constant.

Acceleration of any falling body is therefore $\dfrac{d^2 S}{dt^2} = g$.

50. If one assumes (as Galileo in effect did) that the distance between two objects (d), the mass of the earth (M), and a gravitational constant (G) are all relatively constant for objects falling near the earth; or $G \dfrac{M}{d^2} = g$ (a constant); then Newton's law of gravitation, $F = G \dfrac{Mm}{d^2}$, can be altered to $F = gm$ (where F is force and m is the mass of the falling object). If one further defines total displacement, time, and acceleration as S, t, and a, respectively, then Newton's second law, or $F = ma = m\left(\dfrac{d^2 S}{dt^2}\right)$, implies that $g = \dfrac{d^2 S}{dt^2}$. To retrace the steps implicit in the previous footnote, this implies that $\dfrac{dS}{dt} = gt + V_0$ (where V_0 is an arbitrary symbol for initial velocity), and $S = \frac{1}{2} g t^2 + V_0 t + S_0$ (where S_0 is an arbitrary symbol for initial displacement). Galileo's law is therefore a special and somewhat imperfect case of Newton's more general formulation.

indicate that something is missing (e.g., guaranteeing the continued presence of oxygen in those laws concerned with the ignition of matches that fail to list oxygen among the relevant causes), and finally (c) guaranteeing the *absence* of known and unknown factors which, if they did occur, would partially or completely counteract the causes listed under "$C_1, \ldots, C_n$" (e.g., guaranteeing the absence of a supernova in causal laws that link increased residential construction to a previous rise in income).

As handy as the phrase "*ceteris paribus*" may seem to be, to append it to any causal law constitutes an admission of defeat. Our goal was to achieve not a subset but rather a complete list of sufficient conditions: "the sum total of the conditions, positive and negative taken together . . . which being realized, the consequent invariably follows."[51] Now it appears that every conceivable list, however long, *cannot be known to be complete.* We may share as an article of faith Mill's belief "that there are such things in nature as parallel cases; that what happens once, will, under a sufficient degree of similarity of circumstances, happen again" (1851:I, 316). That belief unfortunately can never be subjected to an empirical test. We can in practice formulate causal laws that appear to be precise; namely,

If $(C_1, \ldots, C_n)$, then E ceteris paribus.

On close inspection, however, these merely assert that E will follow the occurrence of $(C_1, \ldots, C_n)$ unless something happens to prevent E from following $(C_1, \ldots, C_n)$. In effect, we have not only buried our ignorance in a Latin phrase, but interred with it the problem that we set out to solve.[52]

To sum up: because of the above difficulties, we can *never* in practice hope to bring to the problem of explaining or predicting observed phenomena a "precise" causal law in the sense of a law that lists all of the relevant antecedent conditions which, if fulfilled, the consequent invariably follows. Also inevitably eluding our grasp is the goal of

51. Mill 1851:I, 345.
52. Similar arguments apply to the historical concept of the "ideal type." Laws concerning such types are evolved in exactly the same manner as are causal laws in general; the laws in question are valid only if *ceteris paribus* is appended to them; that appending is subject to all of the criticisms noted above; and finally, despite the validity of all of the criticisms, ideal types (like all causal laws) can often provide a useful if imperfect guide to understanding the past. (See, for example, Gerschenkron 1968:41–42; and Scriven 1956:338.)

identifying necessary conditions in the sense of those conditions common to all possible sets of sufficient conditions. (If we cannot know all possible sets, we can never know the conditions common to those sets.) The force of Quine's assertion that "all is tentative, all admits to revision" (1957:17) is therefore overwhelming, whether the discipline be history, economics, or one of the natural sciences. Or as one economist once quipped to this writer, "Not even physics is physics."[53] This suggests that *all* causal laws of the form

$$\text{Always, if } (C_1, \ldots, C_n), \text{ then } E, \textit{ ceteris paribus}$$

should perhaps be reworded to read

$$\text{Probably, if } (C_1, \ldots, C_n), \text{ then } E.$$

The point of the revision is to underscore the uncertainty of both predictions and explanations based upon those laws. Insofar as their reasoning and explanations rely upon such laws, the economist and the historian cannot hope to achieve the absolute certainty of deductive reasoning. Their mutual problem is to explain observable reality by inferring conclusions or theorems from a set of premises. In causal explanation, at least one of those premises must be a causal law formulated as all such laws are formulated: diverse phenomena are grouped into quasi-homogeneous categories by means of abstraction; the relationships between or among these categories are then assessed for constant conjunction and whatever other elements are included in one's concept of cause and effect, with that assessment incorporating the totality of the examiner's experience; categories passing these tests and judged to be linked in a cause-and-effect relationship are then rendered general by the principle of induction; finally, that general rendering will appear as either

$$\text{If } (C_1, \ldots, C_n), \text{ then } E \textit{ ceteris paribus}$$

or

$$\text{Probably, if } (C_1, \ldots, C_n), \text{ then } E.$$

53. Physicists appear to have similar views. Writing about the methodology of his discipline, Schrödinger noted that "the physicist formulates the more stringent hypothesis that an exactly defined initial state of a physical system whenever it recurs is always succeeded by precisely the same course of events, precisely the same succession of states. Confronted with the question whether this assumption is true we must, however, admit that even with the most precise means of observation it can in principle not be verified; for Nature is given to us only once and never returns to precisely the same state" (1956:204).

All reasoned inferences based upon such premises can never be deductive in form. In deductive reasoning, if p implies q, and p is true, then q is true. If a premise is instead only probable, then all conclusions based upon that premise are also only probable.

The final inference from these thoughts about inference is that a peculiar challenge can no longer be avoided. Our discussion of causation began by focusing on such concepts as necessity, entailment, and the goal of a universal law pertaining to a complete set of sufficient conditions which, if fulfilled, the consequent invariably followed. Now all our thoughts about causation as they apply to observable phenomena and practical experience must apparently incorporate that improbable bedfellow, probability.

4. On Incorporating Probability into Causal Explanations

We may not know "Certainly A is always followed by B," but we may know "Probably A is usually followed by B," where "probably" is to be taken in the sense of "degree of credibility." [Bertrand Russell][54]

A historian . . . can never assert that an effect will always happen but only that it will probably happen. The connection between cause and effect is not necessary but probabilistic. [David H. Fischer][55]

An economic historian interested in finding explanations for specific events has for his goal the ability, given a set of historical data, to predict the likelihood of the most explicit set of admissible outcomes. [John Meyer and Alfred Conrad][56]

Three quotations are hardly symptomatic of universal acceptance, but any time two economists, one historian, and Bertrand Russell evidence rough agreement on any subject, one suspects that the underlying idea must have widespread appeal. The idea in this case defies facile exploration. The terrain before us bears an unfortunate resemblance to that associated with causation: the pinnacles are many, the footing is treacherous, and the entire landscape appears to be shrouded in the smoke of unresolved disputes.[57] One of these—for our purposes perhaps the key dispute—concerns the many different meanings of the

54. Russell 1948:427.
55. Fischer 1970:184.
56. Meyer and Conrad 1957:533–534.
57. For contrasting views of the confusion accompanied by extensive bibliographic citations, see de Finetti 1968; and Black 1967.

word "probability." For all its many nuances, the word as it is used in explanation and prediction seems to have only two major reference points: what is inside the observer's head, and what is outside that head. One exponent of this viewpoint (as will be argued below, one imperfect exponent) is Rudolf Carnap. His views, insofar as they are both crucial and controversial, deserve to be quoted in some detail.

Among the various meanings in which the word 'probability' is used in everyday language, in the discussion of scientists, and in the theories of probability, there are especially two which must be clearly distinguished. We shall use for them the terms 'probability$_1$' and 'probability$_2$'. Probability$_1$ is a logical concept, a certain logical relation between two sentences . . . ; it is the same as the concept of degree of confirmation. I shall write briefly "c" for "degree of confirmation," and "$c(h, e)$" for "the degree of confirmation of the hypothesis h on the evidence e"; the evidence is usually a report on the results of our observations. On the other hand, probability$_2$ is an empirical concept; it is the relative frequency in the long run of one property with respect to another.[58]

Degree of confirmation refers to the relationship between evidence and hypothesis, a concept to which the discussion will return below. "Relative frequency in the long run" apparently refers to some probability that is intrinsic to phenomena quite independent of our knowledge of it.[59] Some of our statements about probability may therefore not refer to our own degree of confidence about predicting or explaining single events, but rather may attempt to relate to this "intrinsic" frequency. The contrast is between statements that read

Probably, if $(C_1, \ldots, C_n)$, then E

as against

Probably, if $(C_1, \ldots, C_n)$, then E will occur Y percent of the time

(or alternatively between "In all probability, all A's are B," as against "In all probability, that portion of A's which are B is X percent").

If frequency is intrinsic to repeated trials of a "similar" event (the very use of that adjective should alert us to homogeneity problems of the sort discussed earlier), how can we gain knowledge of that frequency, and what rules should be followed in estimating what that "true" frequency is? Perhaps the most obvious examples refer to the flipping

58. Carnap 1945:72. For a more extended treatment of the subject by the same author, see 1953:438–455.
59. See, for example, Jeffreys 1955:284.

of a coin or the rolling of a single die. If the same coin is flipped repeatedly and one is asked to guess the number of times that a head will
appear on the uppermost side after the coin has come to rest, the usual
answer is "About 50 percent of the time." Similarly, if we observed that
the results of 100 flips of a given coin were 48 heads and 52 tails we
would not be puzzled. We would be puzzled if we knew in advance that
the coin in question was heavily weighted on one side. If asked to
explain the difference between these two situations, we would begin by
noting that for any given flip of the coin, the total number of possible
outcomes is two. (The possibility of the coin coming to rest upon its
edge will be ignored.) If each of these two possible outcomes is equally
likely, then the probability of either of them occurring is one-half or
50 percent. In more general terms, if a given type of event Z has n
possible outcomes and the characteristic E_1 is common to m of those
outcomes, then if all outcomes are equally likely, the characteristic E_1
should be observed roughly $(\frac{m}{n})$ percent of the time—and (we assume)
exactly $(\frac{m}{n})$ percent of the time in an infinite number of trials. If in fact
a head appears 48 of 100 times, that observed frequency would be
explained by appealing to (a) the total number of possible outcomes,
(b) the idea that all possible outcomes for any given flip were equally
likely, and therefore (c) the number of times heads should be observed
if the coin is flipped repeatedly is "roughly" one-half of the total number
of flips.[60]

On close inspection this type of explanation is both curious and
distressingly vague. The curiosity results from the total absence of
reference to causal factors. Any given outcome is the result of the force
applied to the coin, the turbulence of the air, the shape and elasticity
of objects struck, and so on. We may even believe that with perfect
knowledge of the mechanics involved we could predict *exactly* what
the results would be for any particular flip of the coin. The appeal to
long-run frequency of equally likely outcomes therefore seems to be
necessitated by, and a reflection of, our ignorance concerning what
actually causes each specific outcome. That appeal is logically defensible in explaining or predicting observable phenomena only if accompanied by the knowledge that all of the outcomes in question were or

60. For a discussion of the related belief concerning the probability that the observed
frequency will converge to the intrinsic frequency as the number of trials increases, see
Black 1967:472–473; and Noether 1968:493–494.

will be equally likely. In practice, we cannot "know" this. We can only assert it as an axiom incapable of scientific verification.

This seemingly indispensable axiom is, in turn, the reason why explanations of this type tend to be distressingly vague. The problem is to give a meaningful definition for "equally likely." We might attempt to resolve the issue by retreating into a different wording of the same problem: if the coin is "fair"; if the outcomes are "random"; if the factors determining the actual outcomes do so in an "unsystematic" way. The coin is unfair, or outcomes are nonrandom, or factors determine the outcome in a systematic way if the causal factors at work produce a (long-run) frequency different from that implied if all outcomes are equally likely.[61] Our search for a definition has therefore ended in a circle. Events are equally likely if they have that frequency which they would have if they were equally likely. What we lack is a means of defining "equally likely" independent of an appeal to frequency itself.[62]

These considerations suggest that whether or not a specific frequency is intrinsic to repeated trials of similar types of events, our knowledge of that frequency—and our explanations and predictions which appeal to that frequency—will always remain imperfect for several obvious reasons:

(1) Events can only be classified into homogeneous categories by the method of abstraction discussed earlier. This classification is particularly difficult if it must include a judgment as to whether causal factors were affecting previous outcomes or will affect prospective outcomes

61. *Webster's Dictionary*, for example, gives as one definition of random "having the same probability of occurring as every other member of a set." Gould and Kolb's *Dictionary of the Social Sciences* defines a random sample as "a sample . . . selected from a population in such a manner that each combination of n elements has the same chance or probability of being selected as every other combination" (p. 615). We shall meet yet another variant of this concept of random in the discussion of econometric techniques in Chapter III.

62. Perhaps one of the most outstanding attempts to circumvent these difficulties was made by Richard von Mises, randomness being defined as follows: if a limiting frequency does exist for an infinite number of trials, then "these limiting values must remain the same in all partial sequences which may be selected from the original one" (1939:33). The difficulty is that this requirement of invariance in all partial sequences leads to a contradiction. "The requirement must be modified so that p [the limit of the frequency] is invariant only under a *denumerably* infinite class of partial sequences" (Nagel 1961:334 n. 48). The latter requirement may or may not be judged to yield a meaningful definition of randomness, but the requirement itself clearly deprives that concept of any operational content. (See Carnap 1953:444.)

in a systematic or nonrandom way.[63] (Note, for example, that repeated flips of a given coin cannot be "too similar" with respect to initial position, force applied, etc.; otherwise the same result would be produced every time.)

(2) Our observations in practice always relate to a finite number of trials, not to an infinite number of trials.

(3) Even if we did know the limiting frequency of an infinite series, for purposes of explanation and prediction "we could draw no conclusions whatever about any finite set without some further principle, which cannot be contained in either pure logic or experience; and all applications in practice are to finite sets."[64]

If asked to explain or predict the prevalence of a given characteristic in repeated trials of events judged to be similar in certain crucial ways, we often do appeal to such notions as randomness and equally likely events or to other limiting frequencies which for various reasons we believe to be intrinsic to observable phenomena: the flipping of coins, the rolling of dice, the results of crossing red and white flowers, and so on.[65] Just why we are prepared to believe in the existence of these long-run or limiting frequencies is not at issue here. (The answer would seem, at least in part, to include our previous observations on frequency, acceptance of some variant of the principle of induction, and acceptance of certain additional axioms which may, for some frequency statements, refer to such vague terms as "random" and "equally likely.") What is at issue and worth emphasizing is the extent to which even these types of predictions and explanations are conditioned by the experience, knowledge, and beliefs of the observer. The frequencies themselves may

63. This judgment may be directed toward assessing either what is known or what is not known. "Concerning 'equal probabilities,' it has long been debated whether they ought to be based on 'perfect knowledge that all the relevant circumstances are the same' or simply on 'ignorance of any relevant circumstance that is different,' whatever these expressions themselves may mean. To illustrate, is the probability of heads $\frac{1}{2}$ for a single toss only if we know that the coin is perfect, or even if it may not be but we are not informed which face happens to be favored? The terms *objective* and *subjective*—now used to distinguish two fundamentally different natures that probability might be understood to have—first appeared in connection with these particular, not very well specified, meanings of 'equally probable'" (de Finetti 1968:497).

64. Jeffreys 1955:283.

65. Although Carnap draws a sharp distinction between the two, the case of equally likely outcomes and its implied long-run or limiting frequency ("the ratio of the number of favorable cases to the number of all possible cases") would seem to be a special case of "the conception of probability as relative frequency." (See Carnap 1953:441–442.)

be intrinsic to phenomena and quite independent of our knowledge about them, but statements about frequencies obviously do not have that same independence.

If a coin were about to be flipped 100 times and we were asked to forecast whether heads would appear at least 30 times, we would tend to reply in the affirmative, justifying that forecast by appealing to the type of arguments cited above. If we then discovered that the coin in question was being supplied by a well-known criminal, our confidence would begin to wane. If we also discovered that the brother of the gentleman in question has already bet that heads will not appear more than 15 times, we would tend to revise our forecast even further.

This contrived example merely illustrates a general problem. Seldom do we have no information whatsoever aside from the total number of possible outcomes. Whenever additional information is available, the resulting modification in expected frequencies will vary across individuals precisely because experience, knowledge, and beliefs vary across individuals. Whether our own predictions and explanations of observed frequencies are judged to be reasonable by others will depend once again upon whether the object of inquiry—in this case the frequency—is related to their realm of understanding in some comprehensible and appropriate way. That relating process may refer to any or all of the following: (a) previously observed frequencies, (b) a belief in an intrinsic or limiting or long-run frequency, (c) judgments concerning the extent to which that belief and/or those observations refer to events that are exactly similar, or only partially similar, to the observations under scrutiny, and finally (d) judgments and supporting evidence concerning how expectations should be modified if the observations in question are considered to be only partially similar to the type of events included under (a) and (b). A persuasive explanation of an observed frequency—like all persuasive explanations—is merely an explanation that persuades.

All of the foregoing would seem to have very little do to with causal explanation. The discussion originated because of the realization that causal explanation in all disciplines consisted of subsuming specific facts under generalizations of the form

$$\text{Probably, if } (C_1, \ldots, C_n), \text{ then } E.$$

This in turn raised the question as to what was meant by the word "probability." One of two possible meanings concerns long-run frequencies intrinsic to phenomena and quite independent of human perceptions. As noted above, however, knowledge of such frequencies is profoundly influenced by the perceptions of the would-be knower. Our attention is thereby shifted from what is external to the human observer to what is internal to that observer. This brings us back to causal explanation and the second meaning of probability: "the degree of confirmation of the hypothesis h on the evidence e." The generalization

$$\text{Probably, if } (C_1, \ldots, C_n), \text{ then } E$$

suggests the question: How probable? Subsequent discussion will focus upon two related questions:

(1) Can the "Probably" of a causal generalization be translated into a numerical coefficient that can be viewed as the odds that one would accept, or should accept, in betting that the next time $(C_1, \ldots, C_n)$ occurs, E will also occur?

(2) What are the origins of the degree of confidence with which the above type of generalization is advanced; or if the "Probably" in that generalization can be translated into a numerical coefficient, what are the inputs that lead to the formation of that coefficient?

To begin with the first: suppose an historian believes that if it is cloudy (C_1), then it will probably rain (E). On a particular day he observes stratocumulus opacus that he is prepared to label as cloudy and therefore observes to his wife, "It will probably rain." The latter, being an expert in decision theory, replies with the observation just noted: that the use of the word probable raises the question "How probable?" The husband protests that he has no numerical thoughts whatsoever. His wife responds by asking, "Suppose that I offer you two choices: a gift of one dollar or the chance of making two dollars if it rains and nothing at all if it does not rain. Will you take the bet?"[66] When her husband responds in the affirmative, she points out that this choice implies that he has judged the probability in "It will probably rain" to be at least equivalent to 0.5.

---

66. The smallness of the bet has as its objective the avoidance of problems associated with the diminishing marginal utility of money. The husband's answer might be substantially different if all of the above dollar values were multiplied by a factor of 100 or 1,000. See Black 1967:500. One must also assume that the person choosing between a certain payoff and a gamble does not receive a positive utility from gambling.

The reasoning behind this inference is that *if* the chance of rain is judged to be *exactly* 0.5, then the expected value of the proposed bet is exactly one dollar. This follows from the definition of expected value as the sum of all possible payoffs multiplied by their respective probability of receipt. In this particular instance, if

V = expected value,
$2 = the payoff if it rains,
p = the probability that it will rain,
$0 = the payoff if it does not rain, and
$(1 - p)$ = the probability that it will not rain,

and if p is equivalent to 0.5,[67] then

$$V = (p)(\$2) + (1 - p)(\$0)$$
$$= (0.5)(\$2) + (1 - 0.5)(\$0)$$
$$= \$1.$$

By choosing the bet over the certainty of a one-dollar gift the husband reveals that in his judgment the expected value of the bet exceeds one dollar. This in turn implies that his subjective probability attached to the statement "It will probably rain" exceeds 0.5. If it fell short of 0.5, he would decline the gamble in favor of the certainty of receiving the one-dollar gift.

Even if the husband is patient enough to study closely the above arguments and associated mathematics he may remain unconvinced. "See here," one can imagine him protesting, "surely this suggests an aura of precision that is false. Your betting experiments may be able to reveal some range of probability coefficients associated with my statement 'It will probably rain,' but they cannot narrow that range to a single precise probability coefficient. I would decline your offer of a gift of one dollar in favor of a chance to make two dollars if my forecast is correct (and nothing at all if it is not correct), and I would take the certain one dollar over the gamble if the payoff for a successful forecast were reduced from $2.00 to $1.50—which by your calculus implies that

67. With respect to the specific values given to p, "Considered as a mathematical quantity, a probability is a value that obeys three quite simple rules: it remains between 0 and 1; 0 means impossibility and 1 means certainty; and the probability of an event taking place plus the probability of it not taking place add up to 1.... What are controversial are the identification rules linking these abstract numbers with observations made or makable in the real world" (W. Edwards 1968:39).

the probability coefficient attached to my statement 'It will probably rain' lies between one-half and two-thirds.[68] I nevertheless do not have the foggiest notion which of the two alternatives I should prefer—the certain gift or the gamble—if the payoff for a successful forecast is in the range of $1.60 to $1.80." His wife might then point out that exact precision was never promised in the first place. What was promised, and what has been achieved, is that the "degree of confidence" associated with the statement

<blockquote>Given that it is cloudy, it will probably rain</blockquote>

has now been translated into a range of probability coefficients that at least place boundaries upon that degree of confidence. "Should this betting procedure strike you as absurd," his wife might add, "you should note that every day, faced with similar kinds of uncertainties as revealed by your use of the word 'probable,' you bet with your actions; in this case, by taking an umbrella to the office."

As the husband ponders this one, he notices that lightning is now visible in the west (C_2) and that the motions of the trees indicate a strong wind to be blowing from that direction (C_3). "I tell you what," he ventures. "I have changed my mind and am now willing to take that bet where I receive only $1.50 if it rains." "All this demonstrates," replies his wife, "is that your initial degree of confidence or subjective probability can be changed by further information. Since I can now see raindrops bouncing on the pavement, all bets are off."

The above type of betting experiment can always be used to translate the subjective and vague degree of confidence that accompanies any prediction of the form

<blockquote>Probably, if $(C_1, \ldots, C_n)$, then E</blockquote>

into a range of subjective probability coefficients. In each case the forecaster is asked to choose between the certainty of one dollar and a gamble that features the chance to receive a payoff above one dollar if his forecast is correct and below one dollar if his forecast is incorrect.[69] By choosing (a) the highest payoff that is *not* preferred to the certainty

---

68. Two-thirds is the solution for p if the expected payoff is still equated to the certain payoff of one dollar, but the reward for success is reduced from $2.00 to $1.50. Algebraically, it is the solution for p in

$$\$1.00 = (p)(\$1.50) + (1 - p)(\$0).$$

69. A zero payoff is merely a special case of this general requirement.

of one dollar, and (b) the lowest payoff that *is* preferred to the certainty of one dollar, the forecaster should reveal the range of subjective probability coefficients associated with any given forecast. These in turn are a measure of his degree of confidence or degree of belief.[70]

This process of translating degree of confidence into subjective probability coefficients does not reveal anything whatsoever about how that initial degree of confidence was formulated.[71] A statement which predicts a single event, such as

>   The sky is cloudy, therefore it will probably rain

is difficult to judge as either true or false. Either it will rain or it will not, whereas the above statement refers to the *likelihood* that it will rain. One could judge as true or false such statements as

>   In the past twenty years in this city, rain has occurred
>   on Y percent of the total number of cloudy days.[72]

Awareness of the second will undoubtedly be a key reason for making the forecast in question, although one's knowledge about actual frequency may be no more precise than "very often" or "quite often." The same knowledge is also a key input in the formulation of such general propositions as

>   If the sky is cloudy, it will probably rain,

or

>   Probably, if C_1, then E,

or

>   If C_1, then E *ceteris paribus.*

The means whereby such generalizations are reached on the basis of available evidence have been discussed at length in the previous section.

70. High numbers indicate considerable confidence that the prediction will be correct. A wide *range* indicates great uncertainty as to how available information should be assessed. Concerning the chances of drawing an ace from an ordinary pack of cards, for example, one might have a narrow range of relatively low numbers. The lowness of the numbers, in turn, will reflect considerable confidence that the prediction "An ace will be drawn" will prove to be incorrect.

71. With respect to the mathematical treatment of probability, "the axiomatic approach assumes only that *some* probability $P(A)$ is associated with an event A. The axioms do not say how the probability is to be determined in a given case. Any probability assignment that does not contradict the axioms is acceptable" (Noether 1968:488). The Noether article also provides a discussion of the axioms in question.

72. This assumes that the adjective "cloudy" can be given an operational definition.

How the degree of confidence associated with a particular hypothesis can be translated into a betting proposition has been outlined above. The question to which the discussion must now turn is whether rules can be established that will relate evidence and hypothesis in such a way that the implied degree of confidence becomes the betting odds that a *rational* man *should* accept when faced with specific evidence, *e*, and specific hypothesis, *h*, that hypothesis *h* is correct.

Carnap and others who share this goal suggest that one logical requirement for a rational bettor is his or her insistence on "total evidence". On close inspection this amounts to nothing more than urging the forecaster not to ignore any evidence that is relevant: a requirement that is surely reasonable but perhaps overdignified if modi-fied by the adjective logical.[73] The usual axioms of decision theorists also place boundaries on rational betting behavior that would seem to be eminently reasonable. The axiom of "coherence," for example, asserts that no bet resulting in certain loss is acceptable.[74] Unfortunately, however elaborate these axioms become—and however detailed the "requirement of total evidence" is made—the implied betting odds for any given hypothesis *h* and evidence *e* remain indeterminate. Nor is this surprising. The real problem is to define what rational behavior would mean in this context, and the main argument tendered here is that no meaningful definition is possible. Another contrived example will help to suggest why.

Suppose that a Quaker and a cannibal were asked to forecast what would happen if two men—one very strong and the other crippled in both arms—were marooned on a desert island where food was not in abundant supply. If the forecast of the cannibal differs markedly from that of the Quaker—or if the subjective probability that each one attaches to the prospect of the strong man killing the cripple are markedly different—does it follow that one forecast is more rational than another? Put another way, if both the Quaker and the cannibal are superbly rational beings, should they reach identical forecasts? The obvious difficulty is that the relevant evidence for making predictions of this sort is as broad as the sum total of the experience, knowledge,

73. For all its common-sense appearance, this requirement has been the subject of considerable discussion in the philosophical literature. See, for example, Kim 1967:160; Humphreys 1968:113; Hempel 1962:139; and Scriven 1962:230.

74. "Coherence is equivalent to *admissibility*, according to which no decision is preferable to another that, in every case, gives as good an outcome" (de Finetti 1968:500).

and beliefs of the would-be forecaster. This suggests that no two people *ever* face exactly the same total evidence in such situations. One cannot therefore hope to explore systematically the possibility of achieving an impersonal theory "in the same sense as in ordinary logic: that different people starting from the same data should get the same answers if they followed the rules."[75] People seldom if ever start from exactly the same data.

In terms of the language and symbols of Carnap noted earlier,

The logical theory of probability interprets probability as a logical relation between sentences, namely, as the degree to which stated evidence confirms a proposed hypothesis. It holds, that is, that the probability of a hypothesis on the basis of evidence can be determined purely logically once a definition of "degree of confirmation" is given. The central problem of the logical theory is, therefore, to find such a definition. Since this definition must uniquely determine the probability, c, of any hypothesis, h, on the basis of given evidence, e, the problem may also be put as one of finding a suitable c-function, $c(h, e)$.[76]

The arguments cited above when translated into this language amount to the assertion that no such unique c-function can be found—an assertion which many writers including Carnap appear to accept.[77] This in turn suggests that analysis of probabilistic explanation and prediction in terms of the betting odds that a rational man should be willing to accept is founded upon a nonoperational concept. If this concept is discarded as useless, what can be substituted in its place? The answer would seem to be the betting odds that a given person is willing to accept, with the odds varying across individuals because the evidence that conditions such odds also varies across individuals.

One final problem. The discussion of probability originated with the realization that causal explanations always involve an appeal to generalizations that include an element of uncertainty. The general proposition

If $(C_1, \ldots, C_n)$, then E *ceteris paribus*

in effect asserts that

Probably, if $(C_1, \ldots, C_n)$, then E.

The use of the word "Probably" is required because we can never know

75. Jeffreys 1955:276.
76. Lenz 1956:230.
77. See, for example, Lenz 1956:230–231; Meehl 1958:503–504; Kneale 1951:311.

that the conditions $(C_1, \ldots, C_n)$ do indeed constitute "the sum total of conditions, positive and negative taken together . . . which being realized, the consequent invariably follows."[78]

Our initial consideration of the possible meanings of probability suggested a second reason for using that word quite independent of those relating to the imperfections of human knowledge. The analysis began with the example of flipping a given coin and the associated belief in a long-run frequency reflecting, at least in part, an awareness of our ignorance concerning the manner in which any specific outcome was or will be determined. One might nevertheless insist that certain frequencies are intrinsic to phenomena quite independent of our knowledge of them. Similar causes, according to this viewpoint, do not always produce similar effects. What they do produce is a spectrum of possible effects, each of which may be regarded as occurring with an irregular long-run frequency, or with a regular long-run frequency, or possibly with frequencies that remain unspecified except for the assertion that one of them—the "most likely" outcome—occurs with a much greater regularity than any of the rest.[79]

A variant of one or more of these beliefs is often held by those who would formulate causal propositions about human behavior while simultaneously retaining a belief in free will. (Confusions associated with this viewpoint will be considered briefly in Chapter II.) The implication would seem to be that similar causes (or stimuli), when experienced by similar types of human beings, produce similar responses some of the time. Predictions based upon such generalizations will then be more or less precise—or more correctly, have a high or low degree of confidence associated with them—depending upon the extent to which the most common type of response is regarded as being highly probable or only moderately probable.

78. Mill 1851:I, 345.

79. This general modification in the fundamental idea of causation can assume a variety of appearances. When applied to statistical analysis, for example, Simon suggests the replacing of "the causal ordering of the variables in [a] deterministic model by the assumption that the realized values of certain variables at one point or period in time determine the probability of certain variables at later points or periods" (1953:50). In the language of decision theory, one might "suppose that a decision, a choice of q, does *not* imply a unique transformation, $T(p, q)$ [where $T(p, q)$ is a function of p and q]. . . . Rather a choice of q now yields a set of possible outcomes. Having made the decision q in the state p, sometimes we will observe the resultant state p_{11}, sometimes the resultant state p_{12}, and so on" (Bellman 1961:130).

Notice that the word "knowledge" has not appeared at all in the foregoing paragraph. We cannot empirically verify that the above statements are true of human behavior, but we may believe them to be true. In search of supporting evidence for such beliefs, the social scientist may be tempted to cite the empirical findings of quantum mechanics. At first glance, these findings do seem to be consistent with the belief that (at least for subatomic particles) similar causes produce not a single type of effect but rather a spectrum of possible effects. Analogies drawn between quantum mechanics and human behavior suffer from the obvious difficulty that assessment of their validity must be predicated on a firm grasp of the physics in question, and a firm grasp of quantum mechanics is surely the exception rather than the rule among historians and social scientists. Even with that grasp, the mind apparently is not led inexorably to a belief in "loose" or "imprecise" causal laws. To cite perhaps the most outstanding example, Einstein insisted to his dying day that chance was *not* intrinsic to subatomic phenomena. When corresponding with a physicist who did hold such beliefs he noted, "You believe that God plays dice, and I in the perfect rule of law in a world of something objectively existing which I try to catch in a wildly speculative way. . . . The great initial success of quantum theory cannot convert me to believe in that fundamental game of dice."[80]

If physicists and philosophers are still in doubt about the nature of the "true" causal laws operating in the world of subatomic particles—and the writings of Albert Einstein and Ernest Nagel[81] suggest that at least some of them are—then the social scientist who would buttress his own beliefs concerning the indeterminacy of human behavior by appealing to Heisenberg's uncertainty principle would seem to rest his case upon an unresolved debate. The student of human behavior

80. Quoted and translated from German in Born 1949:122. In a subsequent letter, Einstein added, "I am absolutely convinced that one will eventually arrive at a theory in which the objects connected by laws are not probabilities, but conceived facts, as one took for granted only a short time ago" (Born 1949:123).

81. See especially Nagel 1961:305–316. After surveying the evidence, Nagel concludes that "the statistical content of quantum mechanics does not annul the deterministic and nonstatistical structure of other physical laws. It also follows that conclusions concerning human freedom and moral responsibility, when based on the alleged 'acausal' and 'indeterministic' behavior of subatomic processes, are built on sand. Neither the analysis of physical theory, nor the study of the subject matter of physics, yields the conclusion that 'There is no strict causal behavior anywhere'" (1961:316). One should perhaps add that physicists do not widely endorse Einstein's viewpoint. See, for example, Born 1949:122.

can legitimately argue that both he and the student of high-speed elec-
trons have difficulty in formulating precise generalizations, but that
difficulty, as repeatedly emphasized above, is common to all disciplines.
The social scientist may also argue that while he has difficulty predicting
individual behavior, he can predict with considerable accuracy the
average behavior of a large collection of individuals. That statement,
however, is predicated upon the assumption that the group behavior
in question has a strong central tendency. To the question of whether
such tendencies are much in evidence in economic behavior the discussion will return in Chapter III.

5. Conclusions

The discussion would seem to have come full circle. This chapter
began with the observation that despite the inescapable uncertainties
in human generalizations, those generalizations have been, and will
continue to be, an invaluable guide for human action. Those who listen
to weather reports and study the sky before deciding whether to carry
a raincoat should, on the average, experience fewer soakings than those
who do not. For our purposes, it is the uncertainty rather than the usefulness that is worth underscoring for two quite different reasons. The
first is that if uncertainty is forgotten, barriers to progress can be erected
that are difficult to overcome precisely because of the human tendency
to regard as established truth what is merely a tentative hypothesis.
The pernicious effects of such propensities were well summarized by
Einstein:

Concepts which have been proved to be useful in ordering things easily acquire
such an authority over us that we forget their human origin and accept them as
invariable. Then they become "necessities of thought," "given *a priori*," etc. The
path of scientific progress is then, by such errors, barred for a long time. It is
therefore no useless game if we are practising to analyse current notions and to
point out on what conditions their justification and usefulness depends, how they
have grown especially from the data of experience. In this way their exaggerated
authority is broken. They are removed, if they cannot properly legitimate themselves; corrected, if their correspondence to the given things was too negligently
established; replaced by others, if a new system can be developed that we prefer
for good reasons.[82]

82. From an obituary article on Ernst Mach, quoted in Schilpp, ed. 1949:175–176.

That phrase of Quine's—all is tentative—is therefore both the philosopher's final judgment and the revisionist's call to arms. It remains the quintessential guardian against the ossification of knowledge and the stultification of a discipline.

For yet another reason the uncertainty of knowledge in all disciplines is worth emphasizing. Only with this awareness can one perceive the unity of method in the causal explanations of all disciplines. That unity turns upon two assertions. The first is that causal explanation consists of subsuming specific facts under generalizations of the form

$$\text{If } (C_1, \ldots, C_n), \text{ then } E.$$

The second is that because knowledge is uncertain, all such causal generalizations must be prefaced with the word "Probably." To the reader who considers the latter point a trivial concession or a trivial insight, confusions that will be criticized in subsequent chapters should appear to be all the more startling. Many economists and philosophers bring to the problem of causal explanation the ideal of subsuming facts under universal generalizations—the universal nature of the generalizations then permitting a deductive explanation of the facts. This particular intellectual baggage must be jettisoned from the start. If it is not, it can be the seedbed of multiple confusions concerning both the nature of causal explanation and the unity of method in the causal explanations of all disciplines.

To the philosopher, the foregoing may well appear to be a reckless assault across perilous ground against the wrong peak.[83] Our goal, however, was not so much one of logic as one of methodology: to understand how general propositions are formulated and applied, rather than how they should be formulated and applied. Of little interest is the optimal behavior of that amorphous being, the rational bettor. Of consummate interest are the bets implied by the degree of confidence with which a given historian or economist advances a general proposition. Our objective has been not so much one of discovering the logical relationship between hypothesis, h, and evidence, e—although such a discovery would be only too welcome—but rather to analyze the mental processes that lead to specific causal statements. That practice should be revealed to be imperfect is not, per se, a subject of concern, at least

83. See, for example, Black 1967:477.

not within the confines of the present chapter. To the implications of those imperfections the discussion will return elsewhere.

The above discussion and examples have been directed, in the main, to the problems associated with making a prediction on the basis of an imprecise generalization of the form

$$\text{Probably, if } (C_1, \ldots, C_n), \text{ then } E.$$

The historian must have long since wondered what all of this has to do with his craft which, insofar as it concerns causal analysis, is directed toward explaining what has already taken place. What is the appropriate role for a generalization that asserts

$$\text{Probably, if } (C_1, \ldots, C_n), \text{ then } E,$$

when the C's and E in question are known to have already occurred? This and related topics will be the subject of Chapter II.

II Causal Explanation in History

> History is Humanity's knowledge of itself, its certainty about itself. It is not "the light and the truth," but a search therefor, a sermon thereupon, a consecration thereto.
>
> —Johann Gustav Droysen[1]

> The field of history is cluttered up with inherited habits of thought and themes of long standing which altogether render it nearly impenetrable. . . . Actually, the whole area is pervaded, and overshadowed, by a curious blend of concrete ad hoc insights, and ill-fitting generalities.
>
> —Siegfried Kracaver[2]

1. The Nature of the Problem

The preceding chapter focused upon one idea and the meaning of four words. The idea was "similar cause, similar effect"—the central tenet of efficient causation. The words were necessary, sufficient, similar, and probable. The subject matter of the historian is human behavior of the past, or in the imagery chosen by Marc Bloch during those dark days of Nazi supremacy, "The good historian is like the giant of the fairy tale. He knows that wherever he catches the scent of human flesh, there his quarry lies" (1953:26). If that is the quarry, the question is how this tenet and its associated four words must be modified to facilitate pursuit.

Historians are unlikely to provide the answer. They evidence a marked reluctance to grapple with the issues, either among themselves or in concert with philosophers of history. Not until 1962 did the two groups meet at an American conference specifically devoted to such problems,[3] and even on that occasion exchanges were hardly symptomatic of an entente cordiale. Bernard Bailyn spoke for perhaps the majority of his profession. He had, he confessed, "never once felt it necessary to work out precise answers to such questions" in order to advance his

1. Droysen 1893:49.
2. Kracaver 1969:60.
3. The occasion was the Fifth Conference of the New York University Institute of Philosophy in May 1962. See Hook, ed. 1963:ix.

work in history, nor did he expect that closer scrutiny of such questions would improve his ability to write history.[4] Whether such attitudes have been salutary or debilitating is not at issue here. What is at issue, as suggested in the previous chapter, is to understand the mental rules being employed when an historian says, "Now that's what I call a satisfactory causal explanation."

Causal analysis of human behavior is not quite the same as causal analysis of colliding billiard balls. The obvious difference is that billiard balls do not have internal response mechanisms that mediate between external stimuli and resulting overt action. Humans do. The first order of business is to decide how this internal response mechanism should be characterized. The second is to decide how that response mechanism modifies the central tenet and associated ideas of causal explanation.

2. On Dispositions

Introspection will invariably confirm the notion that desires are frequently experienced that have no overt manifestations. Those desires can and do influence our actions, but the desires themselves are different from, and usually antecedent to, the actions. They have, as it were, a life of their own independent of our overt behavior. In attempting to characterize our own internal response mechanisms, or the response mechanisms of others, we use a variety of words: purpose, motive, personality, to mention only a few. The word preferred for purposes of this discussion is disposition. One should hasten to add that philosophers still argue about the meaning of this word.[5] (It cannot even be found in the index of the 1967 edition of the *Encyclopedia of Philosophy*.) What follows will closely parallel the views of a central figure in that debate, W. V. Quine.[6] At the outset the reader should be cautioned that while defining "disposition" is useful for subsequent analysis, accepting the definition offered here is not crucial to the main argument. What is crucial is acceptance of the notion that generalizations are used to explain human behavior and that in those generalizations can be found a reference to dispositions—however they should be defined. But this is to anticipate the arguments of section 4.

---

4. Bailyn 1963:94. For evidence of similar propensities on the other side of the Atlantic, see Stern, ed. 1956:14.

5. For a compact survey of the associated debates, see Quine 1973:Chapter 1.

6. *Ibid.*; also Quine 1966:48–56.

We often speak of salt as being soluble, or Mr. X as being irascible. Both words seem to promise that something will happen to salt, or to Mr. X, if subjected to certain stimuli. There is, as Quine points out, an evident affinity between the idioms of cause and disposition. "The disposition is a property, in the object, by virtue of which the circumstances c cause the object to do a" (1973:8). The problem is to give meaning to the phrase "by virtue of." The answer—or at least Quine's answer—is that all dispositions are promissory notes for explanatory mechanisms. The word "mechanism" is important. The implied view of causation is not merely one of correlation, but one of correlation resulting from mechanisms at work in the phenomena being scrutinized. The word "promissory" suggests that whether or not the note is redeemable at the moment, the expectation is that at some point it will be redeemable. Solubility has been redeemed, although only the chemist is likely to know the explanatory mechanisms involved. Words that refer to human dispositions, such as intelligence or irascibility, have not yet been redeemed, nor is it clear what form that redemption is likely to take.[7]

To review, any recourse to dispositional terms tends to signal two things: the user's belief in a promisory note for an explanatory mechanism, and the user's incapacity to specify what that mechanism is. Use of the word "soluble," for example, indicates—at least in my case—an incapacity to explain the dissolving of salt in water in terms of the mechanisms so familiar to the chemist. If the chemist were also incapable of redeeming this particular promissory note, it would indicate an incompleteness in his science. The same two signals are conveyed whenever we speak of human dispositions, although in this instance we lack an expert comparable to the chemist.

Unredeemed or not, some reference to promissory notes of this sort is unavoidable in any causal explanation of human behavior. The historian begins with the effect—the action of his historical character—

7. "Solubility is the capacity to dissolve in water; intelligence is the capacity to learn, or to solve problems. Whereas chemists have redeemed the solubility idea by uncovering the explanatory traits, the intelligence idea is still as unredeemed as it can be. We do not even know whether to seek the explanatory traits in the chemistry of the nerve cells or in the topology of the nerve net or in both or somewhere else. Intelligence today is where solubility was centuries ago. Still I think it is a promissory note. I do not think we would use the word 'intelligent' if we did not think there was an unidentified but some day identifiable causal agency or mechanism that sets one man above another in learning and in the solving of problems" (Quine 1966:52–53).

and searches for the cause, in part by searching for stimuli external to his agent. Without hypotheses concerning dispositions, this search for relevant stimuli becomes a hopeless task. The list of possible contenders is literally infinite: every event that occurred prior to the action in question. What matters in that list will vary across individuals depending upon their dispositions. Some revolutionaries take up arms in defense of ideals. Others are more responsive to the prospect of economic gain. One cannot therefore hope to search for relevant stimuli without some thoughts concerning the dispositions of the human actors involved.

Acquiring knowledge about the dispositions of others is far from easy. The relevant evidence includes (a) statements by the agent, (b) statements by others about the agent, (c) the observed actions of the agent, and finally (d) the sum total of our own knowledge, beliefs, and experience concerning human behavior, including the evidence of introspection. All four are imperfect guides to the truth.

Invariably used, and perhaps most compelling of all, is the evidence of introspection. If we wish to explain the behavior of Mr. X, we instinctively ask ourselves how we would have behaved in X's situation. As John R. Hicks notes with respect to research in his own field, "The way in which the economist develops his hypothesis is by asking himself the question: 'What should I do if I were in that position?' It is a question that must always be qualified by adding: 'if I were that kind of person'" (1969:6). The historian proceeds in a similar fashion.

Two inferences follow. If the evidence of introspection is a crucial input in the formulation of hypotheses concerning the dispositions of others, and if those dispositional hypotheses are in turn crucial inputs in all causal explanations of human behavior, then for this reason alone causal explanation in history is at least partly subjective in the conventional sense of that word: "determined by and emphasizing the ideas, thoughts, feelings, etc. of the artist, writer, or speaker." The dispositional hypotheses that the historian formulates about his characters are profoundly influenced by his own "ideas, thoughts, feelings, etc."; or more generally, by the type of person he is.[8] He is therefore not only a prisoner of his own age—a point that historians frequently

8. For example, men lacking in subtlety themselves will tend to portray historical characters as unsubtle. The physicist whose name dominates Chapter I was, surprisingly, one such historian. "When men did at times obtrude into his histories, Newton almost unconsciously imputed simple motives to their actions. His kings are automatonlike

concede[9]—but also a prisoner within the confines of his own knowledge, beliefs, and past experience, which is a considerably smaller cage. That no two people share exactly the same cage follows from the realization that no two people can be expected to have exactly the same knowledge, beliefs, and past experience.

The other inference from Hicks's statement about the search procedures of an economist concerns that crucial qualification "if I were that kind of person." We usually believe that although we are to some extent like X—the person whose actions we would explain—we are not exactly like X. Exclusive reliance upon the evidence of introspection to formulate dispositional hypotheses concerning X therefore will not do. We need some technique for establishing the extent to which X is and is not "like us," as well as some technique for modifying our dispositional hypotheses about X once those differences have been established.

One obvious source of evidence is the agent's statements about himself—his letters, memoirs, conversations, containing his own ideas about who he is and why he behaved as he did in certain situations. To the continual bedevilment of the historian, this type of evidence also has its defects. The revolutionary preoccupied with lining his own pockets is unlikely to broadcast that fact to his contemporaries. The Boston merchant whose challenge to British authority stemmed from a mixture of idealism and self-interest is inclined, in his memoirs, to emphasize the former and suppress the latter. Those memoirs may also be flawed by genuine ignorance. So prevalent is this latter phenomenon that we often stigmatize professed motivations with the label "rationalizations," to rationalize being "to devise superficially rational, or plausible explanations or excuses for one's acts . . . usually without being aware that these are not the real motives."

One could, of course, downgrade the evidence of introspection, ignore all statements by the agent, and focus only upon his or her overt behavior. The attempt to infer dispositions from actions alone encounters two problems. One is the threat of a tautology. If we explain

agents in the acquisition of power and the extension of dominion. When on rare occasions he examines them more closely they invariably operate in terms of the seventeenth-century balance of power principles. . . . Royal lust for acquisition is based on 'vanity' and other such staples of contemporary literary psychology" (Manuel 1963:137).

9. See, for example, E. E. Edwards, ed. 1938:52; Gershoy 1963:70; Marwick 1970: 20–21.

a given act by a disposition which is inferred from that act alone, we would be hard pressed to distinguish operationally between the agent's disposition to act in a certain way under certain stimuli and the fact that he or she did so act. Put another way, consistency is guaranteed (rather than demonstrated) if the disposition is inferred from the act and the act is explained by the disposition so inferred.[10]

The other difficulty with exclusive reliance upon overt behavior to infer dispositions is that any given act is usually consistent with a distressingly broad spectrum of possible dispositions. Was Brutus, for example, a crass opportunist or the noblest Roman of them all?

The solution for all of the above difficulties—though imperfect—is to make the evidence that enters into the framing and testing of any dispositional hypothesis as broad as possible. That evidence should include statements by the agent, statements by others about the agent, and whatever can be discovered about the agent's past, including his previous behavior in a variety of situations. Also relevant—indeed, crucial—is that potpourri of experience, recollections, beliefs, and vague generalizations about human behavior internal to the would-be explainer. To confront any dispositional hypothesis with such a broad tribunal does not, of course, promise anything beyond consistency (or at least the best consistency possible) between hypothesis and relevant evidence. But that, as repeatedly emphasized in Chapter I, is all that any causal explanation can ever hope to be.

We are left with a curiosity. More correctly, we have arrived at conclusions suggesting that all causal explanations of human behavior have a curious structure. One begins with the framework of Chapter I, with causes and effects now referring to external stimuli and human actions, respectively. The new and indispensable causal inputs—dispositions—upon close inspection appear to be only promissory notes for explanatory mechanisms that are unredeemable at the moment, and even the form of prospective redemption remains obscure. Indis-

10. This problem is characterized by Quine as follows: "If there is no distinguishing between a thing's disposition to act in a certain way in certain circumstances and the mere fact of its so acting in those circumstances, then whatever the thing may do can be laid to a disposition, by defining the circumstances narrowly enough.... Why not attribute a man's every act to an innate disposition? True, if the circumstances in which he now acts in a certain way are circumstances in which he once failed so to act, we seem to have grounds for denying an innate disposition; but the trouble is that any circumstances whatever can be said to be of an unprecedented kind by defining the kind narrowly" (1973:5).

pensable, however, they remain. Without them, the search for relevant external stimuli is virtually impossible.[11]

3. On Free Will

Two broad assaults might be launched against any attempt to apply the framework of Chapter I to the problems of causal analysis in history, even if the preceding arguments concerning dispositions are accepted. The first is the claim that no generalizations in history are possible, with its corollary (from those who still believe that causal explanation in history is possible) that no generalizations are needed. The dubious merit of these claims will be examined in more detail in the next section.

The second assault might seem at first glance to be more subtle and therefore more difficult to repulse. The desire to explain human behavior, this argument runs, flies in the face of the sense of freedom that accompanies the willing of an action. If human beings are always free to will their acts, how can one hope to give a causal explanation of the acts so chosen? This apparent dilemma can be resolved merely by noting that freedom of action consists in the action having been willed. Whether or not the will is causally determined is a separate issue. To postulate that human action can be at least partially explained is only to imply that the choices dictated by the will (or more broadly, by dispositions) can be predicted, at least with some degree of accuracy. This is entirely consistent with the agent preserving a sense of freedom when choosing as predicted.[12]

4. On The Role of Generalizations in Causal Explanation of Historical Events

It is a truth perpetually, that accumulated facts lying in disorder begin to assume some order when an hypothesis is thrown among them. [Herbert Spencer][13]

11. This view, if accepted, challenges the basic premise of those who would treat causal explanation in history as distinct from causal explanation in general because "reasons" for human behavior are not the same as causes. See, for example, Brodbeck 1962:266; Margolis 1970:187; Gunnell 1968:194, 197; Abelson 1963:168–171.

12. As is true with so many of these philosophical problems, the opinions of Quine are worth quoting in some detail: "Hobbes, Hume, Russell, and many others have seen the matter clearly: causal determination of one's actions does not preclude his having willed them.... Freedom of action consists in the action's having been willed, and the will itself can be as causally determined as you please. Hence the possibility of moral training" (letter from W. V. Quine to the author, April 16, 1973).

13. Quoted in Conrad and Meyer 1964:3.

By and large [American historians] have retained the concept of "causes", while rejecting the idea of "laws." [H. Stuart Hughes][14]

a. Are Generalizations Indispensable?

Facts, as David Hume pointed out long ago, do not speak for themselves. The historian may share with Marc Bloch "the thrill of learning singular things" (1953:8) and not share with the social scientist the desire to formulate general laws. These preferences per se, however, do not license the claim that causal explanations of past events are possible with no reliance upon any generalizations.[15] If accumulated facts, in Spencer's phrasing, always start out lying in disorder, what can one throw among them to effect some kind of order if not some kind of generalization? A central point of Chapter I bears repeating. Facts as they appear to the human observer are conjoined, never connected. The human observer supplies the connection by subsuming them under generalizations. If a fact is truly unique in the sense that it cannot be subsumed under any generalization, then it follows that a causal explanation of that fact cannot be given.

One philosophical red herring must be dispensed with at this point. All facts do have unique aspects. If nothing else, no two facts share the same time and space coordinates. This is as true for two eclipses of the moon as it is for two assassinations. The natural scientist begins exactly where the historian begins—with facts that are singular in the sense that no two are identical in every respect. They can only be explained in a causal framework if they can be subsumed under a generalization, they can only be subsumed if they are made "similar," and they can only be made similar if features not common to all can be abstracted out or dismissed as irrelevant. To claim that a given fact is "truly unique" is therefore either to claim what is trivially true for all facts or to claim that abstraction is not legitimate. The criteria for assessing legitimacy will be considered at length below. At this point some

14. H. S. Hughes 1960:24.
15. As the Hughes quotation noted above suggests, the view that generalizations are expendable and/or unavailable for historical explanations is comparatively widespread. See, for example, Aron 1961:31; Elton 1970:129; Gardiner 1952:30, 51; Oakeshott 1966:143, 154. The view that generalizations are required for causal explanation in history is also widely held, especially among philosophers of history. See, for example, Carr 1961:82; Davidson 1967: 701; Degler 1963:211; Hexter 1971:44; Kracaver 1969:94; Nagel 1961:555; Reichenbach 1951a:124.

clarification would seem in order concerning the type of generalization used in causal explanation of human behavior.

b. Causal Analysis of Human Behavior: What Type of Generalization?

The above arguments can be easily summarized. The central tenet of causal analysis is "similar cause, similar effect." Causal explanation of specific events is only possible if those events are subsumed under a generalization of this form. If the phenomenon to be explained is human behavior, then the form of this generalization must be modified to read, "Similar stimuli, experienced by people with similar dispositions, will result in similar actions." This in turn raises the same two questions considered at length in Chapter I:

(1) Should this generalization be prefaced with the word "Necessarily," "Always," or "Probably"?

(2) What is meant by "similar"?

c. On Sufficient Conditions

Our starting point is once again the framework of Chapter I. The causes of an effect are the complete set (not a subset) of those conditions which, if fulfilled, the consequent will follow. Debates concerning the rules for choosing a subset therefore reflect nothing more than practical considerations and personal preferences. Consciously or unconsciously, all historians bent upon causal analysis are participants in such debates. They voice their opinions, if nowhere else, in those segments of their writings that tender a list of causes for a given historical event. No list of causes, however long, can ever be a complete list—a logical point that most historians readily concede. Their only recourse is therefore to explain historical events in terms of a subset of the total.

Not surprisingly, different historians have chosen to focus upon different subsets.[16] Unexceptional antecedents are usually ignored in favor of the extraordinary and the unexpected. Catalytic events are emphasized by some and ignored by others in favor of "long-run," "deeper," or "more fundamental" causes—the latter merely reflecting a preference for other subsets. Particularly appealing to the student of human affairs is that subset focusing upon causal factors subject to

16. For a general discussion of the problems of choosing a subset, as well as some examples of subsets chosen by historians, see Bloch 1953:191–192; Gardiner 1952:99–112; Nagel 1961:573 n. 17, 582–588; Dray 1964:Chapter 4; Fischer 1970:183–186.

human manipulation, a perspective that blends easily into moral appraisal in terms of who gets the credit or who is to blame. Any subset of causes is relevant only insofar as its elements are in some way related to the occurrence of the effect to be explained. The next problem is to decide what the nature of that relationship is.

d. On Necessary Conditions

Two key points made in Chapter I bear repeating, one relating to the meaning of necessary, the other relating to the use of *ceteris paribus*. The word "necessary" is used in two different senses in causal explanation. One sense refers to indispensability. A necessary condition is that cause common to all possible sets of sufficient conditions. Without it, the effect cannot occur. The other sense refers to the relationship between antecedent causes and their effect. If that relationship is viewed as being "necessary," or if that relationship is formulated as

$$\text{Necessarily, if } (C_1, \ldots, C_n), \text{ then } E,$$

then causes are being viewed as leading inevitably to their effect.

Historians on occasion do refer to their causes as necessary conditions, although why they should be willing to use this term is something of a puzzle. If all sets of historical causes, however long, are appropriately viewed merely as a subset of the total, then these causes alone can hardly be viewed as leading inevitably to the effect. If all possible sets of sufficient conditions cannot be known—and surely they cannot—then conditions common to all possible sets also cannot be known. Whichever of the two senses of necessary the historian has in mind, he would seem to have no business using this word to connote completeness on the one hand or indispensability on the other. And yet the word is used. Is such practice ever justified?

e. "Contingently Sufficient" and "Contingently Necessary"

Conditions can be made sufficient by appending (explicitly or implicitly) the phrase "*ceteris paribus*" to *any* subset to encompass the fulfilling of all other unspecified conditions in the total set of sufficient conditions. In like manner, *any* single member of a set of sufficient conditions can be made necessary in the sense of indispensable by appending *ceteris paribus*, the Latin phrase now being used to exclude all other substitutes for the causal factor in question. Both uses of *ceteris paribus* are, of course, variations of a verbal dodge denounced in Chapter I. To say that $(C_1, \ldots, C_n)$ are contingently sufficient for E, *ceteris paribus*, is merely to say that they will be followed by E unless something else happens to prevent their being following by E. To say that C_1 is contingently necessary for E, *ceteris paribus*, is merely to say that without C_1, E will not occur unless something else happens which does enable E to occur. The phrase "contingently sufficient" therefore has no meaning beyond that subset of causal factors which the historian chooses to emphasize. "Contingently necessary" has, in logic, no meaning whatsoever. It may nevertheless be used by an historian to convey the results of his own counterfactual speculations concerning the availability of substitutes. Of this, more in Chapter IV.[17]

f. The Meaning of "Similar"

Macaulay would seem to have labored the obvious when he insisted that if chronicles were written with no abstraction whatsoever, "the Bodleian library could not contain the occurrences of a week" (1880:65). Philosophers make the same point in different language: "No finitely long statement can possibly formulate the totality of traits embodied in any concretely existing thing."[18] The Bodleian, it seems, is ill-equipped to handle the occurrences of a single hour. All history requires abstraction, whether it be the chronicle, which does not attempt to explain events, or the narrative, which does. Both begin by attempting to establish what happened, often referred to as "the facts of the case." (One has only to listen to two eye-witness accounts of the same accident to realize that the word "facts" connotes an aura of objectivity and veracity that belies the tentative and adjudicative aspects of all historical descriptions.) The narrative, insofar as its goal is causal explanation, does have a special need for abstraction that raises a special problem. A simple example will help to illustrate why.

Suppose that a match is struck against the side of the table and ignites in a perfectly normal manner, except that a peculiar-smelling smoke accompanies ignition. If asked to explain that smell, we are puzzled. If asked to explain ignition, we are not. In the latter case, we would simply

17. Surprisingly enough, the use of such dubious terminology in historical analysis has been endorsed by at least two leading philosophers of history. See Nagel 1961:559–560; Scriven 1964:408.
18. Nagel 1963a:214.

subsume the facts of the case under a generalization that links the effect (ignition) to various causes (striking, the presence of oxygen, and so on). Notice that our ability to explain depends upon the acceptability of our abstracting away specific characteristics that we cannot explain. The above is useful if the question relates only to the ignition aspects of the event. It is quite useless if the bundle of characteristics "ignition and peculiar-smelling smoke" is, in some sense, an irreducible bundle. It follows that if the event to be explained is, in the language of the historian, a seamless web characterized by an irreducible richness and complexity—if one cannot legitimately ignore some of those characteristics while attempting to explain the rest—then no causal explanation is possible unless the entire bundle can be subsumed under one or more generalizations. The larger the bundle, the more difficult subsumption is likely to be.

Lest the requisite abstraction procedure sound unduly complex and/ or devious, consider the case of a man in red trousers who abandons the sinking *Titanic*. The historian surely would not insist that these two characteristics were an irreducible bundle: that if he could not explain both abandonment and the color of the man's trousers, then he could not explain why a man would get off a sinking ship. Events in our everyday life, or in history, are seldom viewed as being a seamless web. We can and do proffer causal explanations of some characteristics while readily conceding our inability to explain all characteristics. Were it otherwise, explanation would be impossible. As the philosopher reminds us, "No finitely long statement can possibly formulate the totality of traits embodied in any concretely existing thing."[19] If we cannot describe all characteristics, we can hardly hope to explain them.

Historians who concede that generalizations are used in their explanations of past events often claim that many of these generalizations are "time-specific" or "transitory" regularities. One frequently used example is, "In the seafights of sailing vessels in the period 1653–1805, large formations were too cumbersome for effectual control as single units."[20] This is not unlike the argument that a generalization about striking matches is "space-specific" in the sense that it applies to the surface of the earth but not to the surface of the moon. The error—easier to see in

19. *Ibid.*
20. See, for example, Dray 1963:122–124; Joynt and Rescher 1961:156.

the case of striking matches—is that generalizations of the sort "similar cause, similar effect" have neither time nor space subscripts. They suggest that whenever and wherever $(C_1, \ldots, C_n)$ are found, then E is likely to occur. The problem with the surface of the moon is *not* that it has particular space coordinates, but that some of the antecedent conditions required if matches are to light when struck are not present in those particular space coordinates. The same point can be made about the control of seafights. The generalization noted previously is too compact: it leaves implicit many of the factors that link sailing vessels, fighting at sea, and large formations. If as many as possible of these were carefully elaborated, the point would be more apparent that what matters is not the dates 1653 to 1805, but rather the fulfilling of antecedent conditions which at other times were not fulfilled. The regularity is not transitory. It is timeless. What may be transitory is the fulfilling of those conditions to which the regularity applies.

The historian to this point is surely far from satisfied. A philosopher may argue, he might say, that causal explanations are possible only if discrete events can be subsumed under generalizations. My problem as a working historian is that almost no generalizations fit exactly the phenomena that I would explain. If I proceed to make my event identical with other events to which a generalization applies, I end up abstracting too much: characteristics are thrown out which I believe to have made a difference in the causal processes under scrutiny. This demand to explain by subsuming under generalizations that apply to homogeneous sets I can therefore almost never meet. My sets are never all that homogeneous, or as Patrick Gardiner has expressed the problem for me, "The 'things' or events with which history deals . . . overflow the edges of any precise classification" (1952:58).

This challenge the philosophers of history must meet, although curiously enough, few have attempted to deal with it directly. The starting point might be to ask the historian why he believes that certain characteristics of an event did make a difference to the causal process under scrutiny. Or in more general terms, how does an historian know what is and what is not a cause?

g. The Historian as Lawyer

Most historians concede that their craft does involve a search for similarities. One finds, for example, Marc Bloch insisting, "Like any scholar, like any mind which perceives at all, the historian selects and sorts. In short, he analyzes. And, to begin with, he seeks out the similarities in order to compare them" (1953:144). The requisite search procedures are suggested by G. K. Clark's description of the questions that he puts to himself in the course of his own historical research: "Does that action, as reported, remotely resemble any other actions of which I have reliable knowledge? ... Does the suggested motive correspond with human motives as I have known them in myself or other people?" (1967:29).

Historical research may itself suggest generalizations, such as Lord Acton's linkage of corruption to power, or Charles Beard's (or Marx's) insistence on the role of economic self-interest in determining human behavior. The basic difficulty, as noted previously, is that most generalizations are at best "suggestive" in the sense that the historical events to be explained partly do, and partly do not, fit the categories to which the generalizations apply. If generalizations are indispensable for causal explanation and yet few if any aptly fit the events that the historian would explain, how is causal explanation possible at all?

The answer—or at least the answer tendered here—is that the methodology of the historian must be viewed as being more analogous to that of a lawyer than to that of a physicist. Both lawyer and judge—in this case, historian and reader—have a vast store of generalizations concerning human behavior of varying degrees of precision. Most of these, as Isaiah Berlin reminds us, are not "sufficiently clear, sharp, precisely defined to be capable of being organized into a formal structure which allows of systematic mutual entailments or exclusions" (1954:54), but then neither are most of the generalizations that we use to predict or explain human behavior in our everyday lives. Generalizations there must be. Without them all facts continue to lie in disarray. But this is not to say that only those generalizations applying to homogeneous sets that exactly describe the facts of a given case are what we permit ourselves to bring to problems of causal explanation. We do not usually insist upon duplicating the thought processes of the physicist as he thinks about things physical when we attempt to think about human behavior. The historian's craft is merely a subset of this more general tendency.

Like a lawyer arguing from precedents, the historian attempts to explain the facts by appealing to those generalizations judged to be of some relevance, but seldom of perfect relevance. Unlike the lawyer, the historian rarely feels compelled to cite many of the generalizations involved, preferring instead to leave to the reader the task of supplying most of the relevant ones from his own storehouse of information. Psychologists have been reproached for seldom confronting their "wobbly laws of personality" with the concrete person.[21] The historian's bias is just the opposite: to focus upon the concrete person and avoid specific reference to the wobbly laws. The result is an explanation that emphasizes details more than controlling generalizations even though the details remain incomprehensible unless subsumed—however imperfectly—under some generalization. The article of faith held by both historian and reader is that a meaningful causal explanation can be suggested by one and assessed by the other even if the generalizations are not articulated by either party.[22]

A number of puzzles now drop into place. Given that no two people are likely to have exactly the same set of generalizations concerning human behavior, nor are likely to link imperfect generalizations to observed facts in exactly the same way, disagreements concerning the adequacy of a given causal explanation would seem inevitable. These disagreements are likely to remain unfocused because the reasons for them are likely to remain largely unarticulated. When a particular causal explanation is challenged, this preference for leaving generalizations unstated helps to explain why the historian tends to respond by reciting more facts. The same preference also helps to explain the vagueness in much of the language used to describe those facts. The would-be lawyer hopes to appeal to the maximum number of judges by a technique ably described by one of the practitioners: "[Historians] deliberately choose a word or a phrase that is imprecise and may turn out to be ambiguous, because of its rich aura of connotation. Without compunction they sacrifice exactness for evocative force."[23] Definitions tend to be avoided. As noted by another distinguished practitioner, when an historian does choose words, "Almost his only guide, even in the use of his key words, is personal instinct. He arbitrarily expands, restricts, distorts the meanings—without warning the reader; without

21. Allport 1962:407.
22. This failure to make generalizations explicit has, on occasion, been criticized by historians themselves. See, for example, Bogue 1968:11; Salsbury 1971:38.
23. Hexter 1971:18–19.

always fully realizing it himself."[24] In sum, not only do "the 'things' or events with which history deals . . . overflow the edges of any precise classification,"[25] but the terms in which these things are described are often consciously chosen to preserve if not enhance that imprecision. Such literary propensities are unlikely to appeal to the likes of Descartes or Bertrand Russell, but they are accepted and even deemed desirable by the majority of those who read and write history. And a satisfactory explanation—for an historian, as for everybody else—is merely an explanation that satisfies.

One puzzle remains. This entire analysis is imperiled by the seemingly innocuous claim that "the historian is capable of understanding directly, and not by means of laws, a sequence of facts."[26] What does it mean to understand something "directly"? The historian may have in mind the type of knowledge Isaiah Berlin had in mind when he referred to the "I know" of "I know what it is to be hungry" (1960:27). This type of knowledge is neither inductive nor deductive but "immediate." But how can it be used to explain the behavior of other human beings? Put another way, when others use the word hungry, how do we know that they are referring to the same phenomena as we refer to when we use that word? If the knowledge of our own immediate experience is to be related to others, this would seem to require an attempt to perceive similarities and (equally important) the manner in which those similarities are related, one to another. This in turn suggests a groping toward generalizations and toward inductive inference from generalizations, however imperfect the effort and the end result.

Much of what historians appear to have in mind when they refer to their causal assertions as the product of "imagination" or "intuition" is the perception of similarities not heretofore perceived. Arnold Toynbee provides a classic description of the process. His reading of Goethe's "Prologue in Heaven" suggested that in the interaction between God and Mephistopheles there was "the flint and steel by whose mutual impact the creative spark is kindled" (1958:22). This behavioral assertion concerning the origins of creativity was then extrapolated to entire civilizations: "The working of challenge-and-response explains the otherwise inexplicable and unpredictable geneses

24. Bloch 1953:175–176.
25. Gardiner 1952:58.
26. Aron 1961:31.

and growths of civilizations, ... [and also] their breakdowns and disintegrations."[27]

The Toynbee example is instructive on two counts. It well describes an extrapolation procedure that might be labeled "in search of similarities." It also demonstrates that not all newly perceived similarities will appeal to all of the historian's readers all of the time. Toynbee's popular appeal was enormous, whereas his appeal to his professional colleagues was almost nil. In the search for new similarities, in the novel extrapolation of old generalizations, the demarcation line between the venturesome and the rambunctious, between the insightful and the fanciful, is drawn by each writer—and each reader—according to his or her own predilections.

The historian may object at this point that he is using intuition in the conventional sense: "the immediate knowing or learning of something without the conscious use of reasoning." Whether original perceptions—those "firefly flashes of historical insight" as Toynbee put it (1958:20)—are the product of conscious or unconscious reasoning, or the product of "immediate experience" and no reasoning whatsoever, is not the central issue. What matters is the process that determines whether initial insights will be accepted or rejected, first by the historian who originates them and later by the reader who scrutinizes them. To restate the above argument: new causal insights cannot be "understood directly"; they must be related to the totality of previously held information by (a) checking for similarities with other data and (b) referring to generalizations that link those similarities in various imperfect ways, be they generalizations of long standing or newly suggested by the historical material.

Implicit in the previous paragraphs is a tentative answer to the question noted long ago: How does an historian decide what is and is not a cause? Historians themselves may be tempted to answer this question in terms of their search for "controls," by which they mean the search for factors present in one of two or more historical circumstances judged to be similar in other ways. For example, the historical record may show that emigrants fled one area in large numbers and not another, even

27. A quick sketch of Toynbee's general hypothesis is provided by Dray: "Civilizations develop in response to a challenge of adversity, grow through a series of responses to successive challenges, each arising out of the response to the last, break down through eventual failure to respond to a repeated challenge, and disintegrate into a dominant minority and an internal and external proletariat" (1964:91).

though both were subjected to "similar" religious upheavals. The factors that "explain" why they left one area and not the other should be present (at least in concert) in the first area and not the second. This is, of course, an attempt to implement Mill's Method of Difference within the confines of available historical evidence. The difficulty with this procedure is that the list of differences between any two regions will always be, quite literally, infinite. How does the historian decide which of these are worth checking to see if they were present in one area and not in the other? From what sources does he derive the belief that certain factors, roughly of type A, may be followed by certain human responses, roughly of type B?

One of the more cogent replies comes from one of the more self-conscious of contemporary historians. It is worth quoting in some detail:

Men and women constantly judge what they consider to be probable by tests which they use naturally and automatically without knowing clearly what they are doing, or why they are doing it. Probably the best way to understand this process is to try to realize what touchstones one uses oneself when one has to judge what is probable or possible. If one is honest with oneself it will I think be clear that they are provided by a curious assortment of mental bric-a-brac which has been collected at different times in life. There is one's own personal experience sometimes consciously remembered, sometimes wholly or partially forgotten, but none the less powerful for that. There are the experiences, and the prejudices, of the groups with which one has passed one's life. There is the knowledge of the world one has acquired by reading, possibly by reading straightforward descriptions of things and events, possibly by reading fiction. There may be some sort of philosophy which claims to explain what the world is like, and there are likely to be life-long prejudices pretending to be a philosophy. No doubt behind these things there will lurk deep-seated psychological factors of which one is unconscious. Yet though the mass of factors which influence one's sense of what is probable may be very heterogeneous, there is one thing common to them all. They are all in some way peculiar to oneself. What may present itself as the commonsense judgement of all sensible men may very well be heavily coloured by what is in one's own mind and no one else's.[28]

This would seem to describe with tolerable accuracy the process whereby most people, and not just historians, attempt to explain human behavior. From such diverse sources we formulate generalizations of varying degrees of precision concerning similarities of varying degrees of specificity and then attempt, in any given circumstance, to relate both

28. Clark 1967:30. For an example of this procedure at work, see Gershoy 1963:70–72.

to the specifics of observed human behavior. Small wonder that we resist, as the historian resists, the demand to lay bare all of the generalizations and all of the evidence that constitute the intellectual underpinnings of our causal explanations of human behavior.

One final point. Common sense, as the previous quotation suggests, is neither a perfect guide to the truth nor to what others believe to be the truth. The world apparently is not flat, although the constant testimony of common sense suggests otherwise. Notions common to men of our own age have not always been equally prevalent in the past, as the historical record constantly attests. To cite but one example, "'Common sense' . . . would refuse to accept the idea that Emperor Otto I could have signed, in favor of the Pope, grants of territories which could never be made good, since both belied his former actions and were ignored in those that followed. Since his grant was incontestably authentic, however, we are forced to believe that his mentality was different from ours and, more particularly, that there was in his time a gap between words and deeds which surprises us today."[29]

A further problem—or at least a questionable methodological precept—is lurking in the conventional definition of common sense: "the unreflective opinions of ordinary men; good sound ordinary sense . . . not dependent on special or technical knowledge." The technical knowledge frequently absent from the historian's analysis of human behavior is that offered by the psychologist. The plea to study psychology is seldom heard, and then only faintly from a minority of the avant-garde. The fashionability of this neglect is curious, unless one can justifiably conclude that none of the findings of modern psychology can usefully supplement "good sound ordinary sense" in the study of the past. To reach such a conclusion would seem to require extensive knowledge of the very discipline that is spurned. And yet the neglect persists. Exclusive reliance upon common sense does have one strong argument in its favor. If a causal explanation of human behavior appeals, implicitly or explicitly, to generalizations common to the majority, then the likelihood of it being acceptable to any given reader is relatively high. This is not, however, the probability that historians have in mind when they characterize their causal explanations as probable or even highly probable.

29. Bloch 1953:80–81.

h. Probability in Historical Explanation

Chapter I concluded with a puzzle. If all generalizations, however amorphous or explicit, are of the form

$$\text{Probably, if } (C_1, \ldots, C_n), \text{ then } E,$$

what possible meaning can the word "probably" have if E has already occurred? The answer is almost as simple as noting that causal analysis can be applied to explanation as well as to prediction. Explaining yesterday's assassination within a probabilistic framework is no more curious than explaining yesterday's weather within the same framework. The word "probably" in the above generalization refers to the relationship between antecedent conditions and subsequent effect. To give a causal explanation of an historical event by subsuming that event under this type of generalization is merely to assert that the specifics of the case are an instance of a general regularity, or more correctly, an instance of what one believes to be a general regularity. An adequate explanation relates "the object of inquiry to the realm of understanding in some comprehensible and appropriate way."[30] In historical explanation, the relating process consists of suggesting that causes and effect, both of which have already occurred, can be subsumed under a probabilistic generalization. The appeal to generalizations of this sort does not give us a sense of inevitability—that E "had" to occur—but it may remove our surprise or puzzlement by pointing out that once $(C_1, \ldots, C_n)$ did occur, the subsequent event E was probable, or even highly probable.

Most historians appeal to generalizations, as noted previously, by emphasizing specifics and leaving to the reader the task of supplying most of the relevant regularities. The end result is nevertheless expected to be a probabilistic explanation. A few quotations from historians are perhaps worth citing to give the reader a sense of how practitioners of the craft view the product of their labors.

What is a causal explanation? It is an attempt to explain the occurrence of an event by reference to some of those antecedents which rendered its occurrence probable. This definition is ambiguous as to the number and nature of the antecedents.[31]

30. Scriven 1962:202.
31. Fischer 1970:183.

When the historian asks himself about the probability of a past event, he actually attempts to transport himself, by a bold exercise of the mind, to the time before the event itself, in order to gauge its chances, as they appeared upon the eve of its realization.[32]

It can never be shown from evidence that, for instance, the weakness of central authority in Germany and the splintered political organization of the country's territories ... produced the particular effects which these situations are agreed to have had on the Reformation. But neither need this be demonstrated since all that is demanded of such causes is that they should have produced a situation in which the actual course of events became possible, encourageable, or (if one so wishes) even very likely.[33]

The historian may believe in probabilistic generalizations (and hence insist upon a probabilistic form to his causal explanations) for two rather different reasons. The first concerns the limits of his own knowledge. For all the reasons sketched above—most notably, the difficulties of establishing similarities by abstraction and those associated with listing the complete set of relevant causes—the historian must concede that even if the universe of human behavior is governed by precise causal laws, his knowledge about that universe is always less than perfect, and consequently his statements explaining behavior must always be couched in tentative or probabilistic terms. The historian may also believe that the "true" universe is probabilistic in structure. That is, he may postulate (as an article of faith) that even if we had perfect knowledge, we would find with respect to human behavior that similar causes are not always followed by similar effects. He can never know this to be true, but he may well believe it to be true. And beliefs, as well as awareness of imperfections in our knowledge, condition the type of causal explanation that we are prepared to offer and to accept.

5. Causal Explanation in History: A Summary Statement

Historical explanation is to a large degree arrangement of the discovered facts in patterns which satisfy us because they accord with life as we know it and can imagine it. [Isaiah Berlin][34]

The problem raised by Isaiah Berlin's quotation might be put as a question: How can historical facts be so arranged that the end result

32. Bloch 1953:125.
33. Elton 1970:144.
34. Berlin 1960:24.

does indeed satisfy us? The answer tendered here with respect to causal explanation is that the *only* possible way of arranging facts to yield *any* causal explanation is to subsume those facts under a generalization. The central tenet of efficient causation *is* a generalization: similar cause, similar effect. When the effect to be explained is human behavior, the controlling type of generalization must be modified to read: similar stimuli, experienced by people with similar dispositions, will result in similar actions. This revision is necessitated by an awareness that response mechanisms internal to the human actor intermediate between external stimuli and overt behavior. Characterizing those response mechanisms with the word "disposition" signals both a belief in a promissory note for an explanatory mechanism and an inability to redeem that note; that is, to specify what that mechanism is.

Recourse to generalizations of the sort noted raises the same two basic problems considered in Chapter I:

(1) Should this revised generalization be prefaced with the word "Necessarily," "Always," or "Probably"?

(2) What is meant by "similar"?

With respect to the first of these, several points concerning the role of necessary and sufficient conditions in historical analysis, while perhaps obvious, are worth underscoring. Given that all sets of causal antecedents proffered by an historian are incomplete, it follows that the fulfilling of any subset of relevant causes cannot be viewed as being sufficient for, or leading inexorably to, the effect. Given that all possible sets of sufficient conditions for an historical effect cannot be known, it follows that conditions common to all possible sets also cannot be known, the latter being "necessary conditions" in the sense that only with them can the effect be realized. A subset of sufficient conditions can be made "contingently sufficient" by appending *ceteris paribus* to the subset, the Latin phrase being used to signify the fulfilling of all other relevant and unspecified conditions. Any given causal factor can be made "contingently necessary" also by appending *ceteris paribus*, with the Latin phrase now being used to preclude the occurrence of all possible substitutes for that given causal factor. Neither phrase has meaning in logic, although "contingently necessary" will be found in Chapter IV to play a special role in counterfactual speculation.

The second of the two questions noted above—What is meant by "similar"?—invariably raises a puzzle that might be summarized as follows: no causal explanation is possible unless specific events are subsumed under a generalization, and yet few if any generalizations seem to "fit" exactly most of the events that the historian would explain. Two resolutions are possible. One is to insist that causal explanation is impossible. The other is for both historian and reader to accept as adequate the results of imperfect subsumption of historical facts under generalizations deemed to be at least partially relevant.

The historian may be convinced that he understands the causal processes at work—that he has it, as the Spanish say, in the inkstand—but when putting pen to paper, he seldom details much more than the facts of the case for several obvious reasons. One is that the generalizations leading to his understanding—or to his belief in his understanding—are usually many in number and of varying degrees of precision. To put them all down on paper would be laborious and (given the vagueness of many) quite possibly embarrassing. To put down the supporting evidence for each one—often as broad as the sum total of his experience with other human beings—would be even more laborious and (given the frequently disorganized and tenuous aspects of that evidence) quite possibly even more embarrassing. More important, the historian usually believes that such labors would be redundant for those readers who share roughly comparable generalizations and fruitless for those who do not. Finally, given that those who share his generalizations are unlikely to share exactly the same set, the historian has a propensity to couch his explanations in imprecise and evocative terms, not only to stimulate the imagination of his reader, but also to give to his explanations the widest possible appeal. Following the 1923 Tokyo earthquake, the Japanese government wired Charles Beard, "Bring your knowledge of disaster."[35] The historian extends to his reader a similar invitation: Come and bring your knowledge, experience, and beliefs, especially your generalizations linking stimuli, dispositions, and human action. I shall supply the facts.

All of the above arguments lead to a conclusion that answers a question noted previously. The relationship between antecedent conditions and observed action in all causal explanations in history is probabilistic.

35. Quoted in Hofstadter 1956:360.

The causes must be viewed not as leading inexorably to the effect, but rather as making the effect in question more probable, or at best, highly probable.

This conceptual framework may be rejected by two different audiences for very different reasons. Those who insist that no generalizations are needed for the understanding of causal processes in history must be asked: If facts, as David Hume noted, are never connected but only conjoined, and if connection can only be supplied by the human observer, how can that connection be supplied if not by subsuming specific events under some kind of generalization? The confident insistence that the causal processes of history can be "understood directly" may seem to the philosopher reminiscent of the type of brashness that prompted a stranger to address the Duke of Wellington as Mr. Smith, provoking (in Wellington's case) the reply: "If you can believe that, you can believe anything."

The philosopher may well have harsher words to say. All historians who do attempt causal explanation, he may charge, bring to their subject matter a panoply of evocative phrases disguising threadbare underpinnings of ill-formed generalizations. From brick and mortar such as these, how can one fashion any causal explanation whatsoever? The historian's reply—or at least Isaiah Berlin's reply implicit in the quotation noted at the outset—is to emphasize that in everyday life most human beings are satisfied to offer and to accept causal explanations based upon exactly this type of underpinning.[36] Generalizations concerning human behavior are imperfect. Evidence in support of those generalizations is also imperfect. And yet that evidence does lead to those generalizations, which in turn lead to causal assertions about the world of human behavior. You may well fault me, the historian might say, for all these imprecisions, but in my frailty I hardly stand alone. Reliance upon such imperfect materials to fashion imperfect causal explanations is a commonplace of daily discourse. If causal explanation of human behavior is to be possible at all, it can only be achieved in these terms. Or at

36. Berlin, for one, has been quite explicit about the parallel: "We account for the French Revolution or the character of Napoleon or the behavior of Talleyrand as we would account for the behavior of our own contemporaries and events in our lives, public and private, with the same rich, scarcely analysable mixture of physiological and psychological, economic and biographical, aesthetic and ethical, causal and purposive concepts, which provide what we regard as normal and sufficient answers to our normal questions about how and why things or persons act as they do" (1954:51–52).

the risk of overdignifying my methodology, my final word can only be the plea of Luther: "Here I stand, I can do no other."

6. Other Views of Causal Explanation in History

Under the amorphous heading "Methodology of History" are a variety of amorphous questions. The very persistence of one—What is history?—is perhaps the most conclusive evidence of a failure to resolve some of the more fundamental issues of the discipline. Another general question under the same heading is: What is explanation in history? All of the foregoing, and all of what follows, relate only to a special case of this more general question. Our problem has been, and will remain, what is causal explanation in history? The debate concerning acceptable answers is centuries old, but since World War II that debate has taken several curious twists. The objective of this section is to outline briefly the positions of the major participants in recent developments and then to explain, using the framework of section 5, why their positions are curious, if not incorrect.

a. "Verstehen," Dilthey, and Collingwood

Published posthumously in 1946, R. G. Collingwood's *Idea of History* reflects a variety of intellectual influences, of which perhaps the dominant is a school of though linked to the German philosopher Wilhelm Dilthey and the word *verstehen*.[37] Literally translated, this word means to comprehend or to understand. For Dilthey and others of his school, the word has a more specific meaning. The understanding in question concerns human behavior only; the means whereby that understanding is accomplished involves the linking of what is internal to the historian with what is internal to the character whose behavior he would explain. The problem is to specify how that linkage is effected. One common characterization is "empathic understanding,"[38] empathy being used in its usual sense: "the projection of one's own personality into the personality of another in order to understand him better." This leaves unanswered two questions:

(1) What is it that the historian wants to understand better?

(2) How can he project his own personality in order to gain that understanding?

37. For a survey of this school, including the precursors of Dilthey, see Abel 1948.
38. See, for example, Hempel 1942:44; Scriven 1964:412–413.

Different historians offer different answers to both questions. Indeed, the debate concerning what *verstehen* means and how it is to be implemented is so ill-defined that it is far from clear who is and is not a member of this school of thought.[39] That both Dilthey and Collingwood are members does seem to be generally accepted, although even between these two men fundamental disagreements exist. Dilthey, for example, claims that the objective of history "is to seek out the mind"[40] of the historical characters, with "understanding [being] an intellectual process involving the highest concentration."[41] Collingwood seems to maintain a similar position: "Historical knowledge is the knowledge of what mind has done in the past. . . . [The object of history] is an activity of thought, which can be known only in so far as the knowing mind re-enacts it and knows itself as so doing" (1956:218). Apparent agreement disappears, however, once one understands what each man means by the word "mind." For Collingwood the activity of the mind relates to intellectual operations only. History is therefore the study of those operations. Dilthey's concern is with human experience in the widest sense of that word. History is therefore the study of emotions and intentions as well as thinking and reasoning. His willingness to lump all of these under the one word "mind" is merely a semantic preference that can mislead the unwary reader.[42]

The major source of confusion lies elsewhere. The word "empathy" implies the projection of self into the personality of another. As noted in section 2, the unadulterated projection of self will not do (although with his narrower focus, Collingwood may find the associated problems less burdensome than Dilthey[43]). As John Hicks has already point out, if we begin by asking, "What should I do if I were in that position?" we must immediately add, "if I were that kind of person" (1969:6). Once the historian concedes that the unmodified projection of his own personality is unacceptable, he must specify the procedures whereby acceptable modification can be achieved. How do we gain knowledge of the dis-

39. See, for example, Aron 1961:31, 45; Berlin 1960:21; Elton 1970:133; Gunnell 1968:178; Rickman 1967:405; and Winch 1967:283.
40. Quoted in Hodges 1952:287.
41. Hodges 1952:335.
42. This characterization of Collingwood's ideas follows the more conventional interpretation of such writers as W. H. Walsh (see, for example, Walsh 1960:49–50). Another view, suggested by Louis Mink, is that Collingwood's position is really much closer to that of Dilthey than this conventional view implies (1968a:Chapter 6).
43. See, for example, Walsh 1960:51–52, 91–93; Gardiner 1952:117.

positions of others and knowledge of how people with those dispositions are likely to behave? The answer would seem to involve the perception of similarities and the organization of those similarities into generalizations of varying degrees of specificity. If the historian grants this latter point, he denies the basic methodological precept of both Dilthey and Collingwood, that one can "pass directly" from the facts to an understanding of those facts with no reliance upon any generalizations.

Some of the more noted exponents of using generalizations in historical explanations have attacked the *verstehen* methodology for yet another reason which has itself a curious twist. The evidence of introspection, they suggest, is at best "heuristically useful."[44] The historian's empathic identification with his characters "does not, by itself, constitute knowledge"; rather it "is pertinent to questions concerning the *origins* of his explanatory hypotheses but not to questions concerning their validity."[45] The question at issue here is whether this dichotomy between evidence that suggests hypotheses and evidence that tests hypotheses is incorrectly drawn or at least overdrawn.

The relegation of introspective evidence to the first category is surely questionable from the standpoint of the readers of history. Their assessment, as previously noted, requires that any hypothesis about human behavior face simultaneously a vast tribunal of knowledge, experience, and beliefs, including the evidence of introspection. Is the writer of history in a markedly different position? In assessing the merits of his own hypotheses the historian confronts a variety of external evidence—the findings of his own historical research—and a variety of internal evidence—that vast tribunal residing between his ears. An hypothesis may be suggested by either type of evidence, but if it is to be accepted—if it is to be judged consistent with the sum total of relevant evidence and put into print—then the test for consistency must surely include both external and internal evidence. The historian is therefore constantly shuttling between external and internal evidence, both in search of hypotheses and in an effort to check new hypotheses for consistency with all of the relevant evidence available to him. Any of that evidence may be "heuristically useful"; all of it is brought to bear to establish validity.[46]

44. See, for example, Abel 1948:216–217; Hempel 1942:44–45; Nagel 1961:484–485.
45. Nagel 1961:484.
46. Consider, for example, the following description by a practicing historian of procedures used: "Evidence is found which cannot be explained in terms of prevailing

What of the importance of introspection and empathy in this process? Most historians would respond, "crucial to the point of being indispensable." If they share with Beer (as most do) the belief that they "can make progress towards recreating another mind of another time in its own terms" (1963:26), they are likely to share with Theodor Mommsen the conviction that "anyone who is unable to empathize with Ennius and Horace, with Petronius and Papinian will forever talk of Roman life as a blind man of color, however accurate his pragmatic inquiry into the source may be" (1956:194). Put another way, historians do not expect the definitive history of Casanova to be written by a eunuch.[47]

Buried here is a subtle problem ultimately incapable of conclusive resolution. It is raised (and then ignored) by Patrick Gardiner: "Extraordinary behavior by another person may be intelligible to a normal person provided that it bears some likeness—even if this is remote—to what he himself on occasion has done" (1952:132). The question is how much likeness is enough. If the historian himself is not psychotic, to what extent can he hope to understand and explain the behavior of someone who is? If all of the evidence of introspection in such cases were totally irrelevant, then all historians could presumably give an equally good, or equally bad, explanation by referring to what Hempel calls "the principles of abnormal psychology" (1942:44). What Hempel seems to miss when he insists that the evidence of introspection is not a necessary ingredient for satisfactory explanations (1942:44) is that almost never—and possibly at no time—are we in a position of feeling that the human actor whose behavior we would explain is totally unlike us; that is, that the evidence of introspection is totally useless. To put

---

notions; then, instead of discarding the evidence, one is forced to entertain new hypotheses; finally, by working backward from the ideas, one discovers hitherto neglected aspects within the movement. My own position was developed precisely in this way. Starting the research with the preconceptions of previous writers, including the retrogressive framework, I began to note what at the time seemed contrary straws in the wind: an Alliance in Nebraska endorsing Coxey's army, a militant labor leader praising the proclamation of a Kansas Populist governor, and a Socialist Labor Party organizer complaining that Populism stole potential recruits. Slowly the details fell into place. The process is described here to show that my interpretation, however controversial, grows directly out of the evidence itself. It was reached inductively, and not deductively" (Pollack 1962:11). Hypotheses were apparently suggested to Pollack by the historical evidence itself, but one would hardly regard that evidence, for that reason, as being *only* heuristically useful.

47. Modern psychology in some of its earlier phases attempted to dismiss as irrelevant the evidence of introspection, but more recently that dismissal has been questioned and, in the main, itself dismissed as unwarranted. See Nagel 1961:476–477.

the matter as a question: What kind of behavior by what kind of human actor would we expect could be explained equally well by a Martian and by an historian?

b. Hempel and Deductive-Nomological Explanation

Perhaps more than any other name, that of Carl Hempel has dominated the literature concerned with historical explanation in the postwar years[48]. His seminal article dates from 1942, its title signaling his main concern: "The Function of General Laws in History." That function he later summarized as follows:

> If E describes a particular event, then the antecedent circumstances described in the sentences $C_1, C_2, \ldots, C_k$ may be said jointly to "cause" that event, in the sense that there are certain empirical regularities, expressed by the laws $L_1, L_2, \ldots, L_r$, which imply that whenever conditions of the kind indicated by $C_1, C_2, \ldots, C_k$ occur, an event of the kind described in E will take place. Statements such as $L_1, L_2, \ldots, L_r$, which assert general and unexceptional connections between specified characteristics or events, are customarily called causal, or deterministic, laws.[49]

Explanation is therefore to be nomological, that is, "it accounts for a given phenomenon by reference to general laws" (1964:13). Those laws, in turn, must be universal generalizations (1942:35). In terms of the framework of Chapter I, they assert that

Always (or necessarily), if $(C_1, \ldots, C_n)$, then E.

The resulting explanation is therefore deductive in form: if the premises are true, then the conclusion is necessarily true. Hence the name "deductive-nomological."

According to the arguments developed in section 5, Hempel is half right. His insistence that causal explanation requires subsumption of specific facts under a generalization reiterates a plea repeatedly made above. His requirement that those generalizations be universal in form is unacceptable for reasons elaborated in Chapter I. All causal laws, insofar as they state our knowledge about the world around us, must be

---

48. The main ideas concerning the nature of historical explanation to be discussed here did not originate with Hempel, as he himself was quick to point out. For a discussion of his precursors, see Dray 1970:1–3; Donagan 1959:428; Scriven 1959b:443 n. 3; Hempel 1962:98 n. 2.
49. Hempel and Oppenheim 1948:139.

probabilistic in structure; that is, they must be expressed in the form[50]

$$\text{Probably, if } (C_1, \ldots, C_n), \text{ then } E.$$

This in turn implies that in practice causal explanation can *never* be deductive in form. If one of the premises of an argument is not a universal generalization but only a probabilistic generalization, then even if the premises are true, the conclusion is not necessarily true. Causal explanation in history therefore turns upon inductive inference rather than upon deductive inference.

Historians sensed this difficulty from the start.[51] For that matter, so did Hempel. The examples concerning human behavior used in his original article described tendencies only, rather than universal generalizations (1942:40–41). He explicitly conceded that "it seems possible and justifiable to construe certain explanations offered in history as based on the assumption of probability hypotheses" (1942:41). Causal explanations actually advanced by historians he labeled as "explanation sketches" in need of "filling out" (1942:42). Despite this awareness of key difficulties, Hempel not only failed to specify how filling out could be accomplished (aside from the trite provision of more "empirical research"[52]), but more important, he left totally unexplored the logical implications of his own point that generalizations used in historical explanation could legitimately be probabilistic in form. In sum, after decimating with effective counterexamples his own universal generalization that all causal explanations must rest upon universal laws, he

50. One of the major points made in Chapter I was that there are no *known* sets of sufficient conditions, or (in language not used there but sometimes used by philosophers) there are no *known* closed sets. The example of Galileo's law was used to demonstrate that an observed regularity could not be equated with such a set. Newtonian mechanics subsequently demonstrated that Galileo's formulation held to a fair approximation because relevant variables unknowingly assumed to be constant were in fact roughly constant for terrestrial experiments. Curiously enough, Hempel cites Galileo's law repeatedly as an example of a universal generalization even when conceding—sometimes on the same page—that Newtonian mechanics demonstrated the incompleteness of Galileo's formulation (1964:11; 1948:136).

51. See, for example, Fischer 1970:xi; Beer 1963:7–8. This may also shed light on Hughes's quotation at the beginning of section 4, if American historians, in "rejecting the idea of 'laws,'" mean only to imply the rejection of universal generalizations.

52. Furthermore, he seems to concede that filling out need not produce a universal generalization: "Many an explanation offered in history seems to admit of an analysis of this kind: if fully and explicitly formulated, it would state certain initial conditions, and certain probability hypotheses, such that the occurrence of the event to be explained is made highly probable by the initial conditions in view of the probability hypothesis" (1942:42).

continued to write as if his central tenet were totally unscathed.[53] The article concludes that for every explanation, "the criterion of its soundness is . . . exclusively whether it rests on empirically well confirmed assumptions concerning initial conditions and general laws" (1942:45), general laws having been previously defined as universal hypotheses (1942:35).

c. Hempel and Statistical or Probabilistic Explanation

In later articles Hempel attempted to remedy these defects. As he himself summarized both the key problem and his proposed solution:

Some of the covering laws are of probabilitistic-statistical form. In the simplest case, a law of this form is a statement to the effect that under conditions of a more or less complex kind F, an event or "result" of kind G will occur with statistical probability — i.e., roughly: with long-run relative frequency—q; in symbolic notation:

$$P_s(G, F) = q.$$

If the probability q is close to 1, a law of this type may be invoked to explain the occurrence of G in a given particular case in which conditions F are realized. [1963:144]

If by nomology one means "of, relating to, or in accordance with laws," and if one does not insist that the laws in question be universal generalizations, then one might fairly characterize Hempel's second type of explanation as inductive-nomological.[54] Facts are to be explained by being subsumed under laws, those laws are probabilistic in form, and thus the inference based upon them is inductive rather than deductive.

One of the puzzles left unresolved by the quotation cited above is which of the two types of probability considered in Chapter I is being considered by Hempel. The answer is both. Since Hempel readily concedes his debt to Carnap in these matters (1963:145; 1962:137, 145), a key quotation from the latter bears repeating:

53. In subsequent writing Hempel attempted to redeem the validity of his initial approach by noting the difference between a logical issue and an epistemological one; the first being concerned with "the claim made by a given law-statement" and the second with "the degree of confirmation or probability, which it possesses on the available evidence" (1964:15). The problem with this defense is that the evidence should and does influence the claim. If that evidence never justifies more than a probabilistic claim, then Hempel's deductive-nomological format is irrelevant for both the scientist and the historian.

54. It is not entirely clear if Hempel would accept this label. See, for example, 1964:13; and 1968:116–117.

Among the various meanings in which the word 'probability' is used in everyday language, in the discussion of scientists, and in the theories of probability, there are especially two which must be clearly distinguished. We shall use for them the terms 'probability$_1$' and 'probability$_2$'. Probability$_1$ is a logical concept, a certain logical relation between two sentences . . . ; it is the same as the concept of degree of confirmation. I shall write briefly "c" for "degree of confirmation," and "$c(h, e)$" for "the degree of confirmation of the hypothesis h on the evidence e"; the evidence is usually a report on the results of our observations. On the other hand, probability$_2$ is an empirical concept; it is the relative frequency in the long run of one property with respect to another. [1945:72]

The previous quotation from Hempel suggests that the probability in his statistical or probabilistic laws should reflect long-run frequency. When those laws are used to explain a given event, they confer a degree of inductive support (or Carnap's probability$_1$) equal to the statistical probability or equal to relative frequency in the long run. To take Hempel's example of flipping a coin, if the hypothesis is that in ten flips a head will appear at least once, then our "degree of belief" in this particular hypothesis is conditioned by our views concerning long-run frequency. As Hempel puts it, "For the simple kind of argument under consideration here, it is clear that the value of the logical probability should equal that of the corresponding statistical probability"[55]

What is the appropriate relationship between the two if the argument is not simple? In his principal article exploring the nature of statistical explanation, Hempel restricts his examples to such events as the flipping of coins, the rolling of dice, and the drawing of balls from an urn (1962). The insights gained from such examples are little help to the would-be explainer of human behavior. The historian and the social scientist seldom can refer to observed frequencies, let alone to long-run frequencies. As historians themselves have repeatedly emphasized, "Statistical laws . . . cannot apply because historical events are never sufficiently alike to form the basis of a statistical conclusion. The historian does not deal with identical units sufficient in number to produce a probability approximating to a certainty; he deals with units (people, facts, events) of a similarity sufficient to permit limited generalizations, but no more."[56]

    55. Hempel 1962:145; see also 1962:129, 135.
    56. Elton, 1970:131. Philosophers of history have, on occasion, made the same point. "There is next to no statistical material bearing on the relative frequency of occurrence of the phenomena of special concern to students of human affairs. Historians are therefore compelled, willy-nilly, to fall back upon guesses and vague impressions in assigning weights to causal factors" (Nagel 1959:384–385).

Hempel is once again on the brink of irrelevancy. His plea for the use of universal generalizations to derive deductive-nomological explanations the historian can never heed. His tracing of the origins of probabilities underlying inductive-nomological explanations to long-run frequency ignores what was characterized in Chapter I as the homogeneity problem. The central tenet of efficient causation Hempel describes as "same cause, same effect" (1962:105; 1964:12), rather than as "similar cause, similar effect." If all events could be classified readily into homogeneous sets, then the main factor conditioning Carnap's degree of inductive support would be observed frequencies and the relationship of these observations to our beliefs in long-run frequencies. The very word "similar" suggests the need to examine issues which, when explored in any detail, lead inexorably to the conclusion that *all* generalizations about empirical reality must be probabilistic in structure. And that is as true for Galileo and Newton as it is for Toynbee and Trevelyan.

What of the other puzzles for historians left unanswered by Hempel's original article? How can an "explanation sketch" be "filled out," and if properly filled out, will the resulting explanation be "sound"? Hempel does suggest that ideally the degree of inductive support conferred upon an explanation by associated evidence and generalizations should be "high," by which he means "close to one," but he recognizes that no criteria can be marshaled to specify how close is close enough (1962:130, 144; 1963:144; 1964:14; 1968:117). As for the soundness of the best of the statistical or probabilistic explanations, Hempel never seems to abandon his original stringent criterion: that to be sound an explanation must include the deduction of the effect from causal laws that are universal generalizations.[57] By this criterion, no causal explanation of human behavior can ever be sound, but then neither can any of the causal explanations of the natural scientist. Or to repeat the economist's quip from the previous chapter, "Not even physics is physics."

d. Dray and Rational Explanation

William Dray is perhaps the most prominent among recent challengers to Hempel's pre-eminence in this field. The theory expounded

---

57. Hempel's criteria for soundness are broader than this single requirement. The criteria are listed in 1948:137–138.

in his 1957 book *Laws and Explanation in History* in the space of five
years earned him the reputation—at least among some historians—as
"the historian's philosopher."[58] That theory he summarized as follows:

> When an historian sets out to explain an historical action, his problem is usually
> that he does not know what reason the agent had for doing it. To achieve under-
> standing, what he seeks is information about what the agent believed to be the
> facts of his situation, including the likely results of taking various courses of
> action considered open to him, and what he wanted to accomplish: his purposes,
> goals, or motives. Understanding is achieved when the historian can see the
> reasonableness of a man's doing what this agent did, given the beliefs and purposes
> referred to; his action can then be explained as having been an "appropriate"
> one. [1963:108]

The resulting explanation is considerably more curious than this
quotation would suggest. Dilthey and Collingwood wanted to make
contact with the "mind" of historical characters. In a very real sense,
Dray does not care whether contact is made or not. He terms a rational
explanation that calculation which the agent would have made *if* the
agent had attempted to make a calculation. Whether the agent actually
did this is, for Dray, quite beside the point.

As Hempel was quick to point out (1963:155–158), this approach
offers no causal explanation unless a linkage can be established between
Dray's calculations and the actual disposition of the agent at the time
that he acted. Hempel therefore proposed (1963:155) that Dray's
formulation be modified to read: "Agent A was in a situation of kind
C. A was a rational agent at the time. Any rational agent, when in a
situation of kind C, will invariably (or: with high probability) do X."
Therefore: "A did X." The result is, of course, a nomological explanation: specific facts are subsumed under a generalization that links
stimuli, dispositions, and actions.

This may seem to be merely a quarrel over personal preferences.
Hempel prefers explanations that subsume facts under generalizations.
Dray does not. As the latter put it, "Sometimes all we really want to
know, when we ask for an action to be explained, is how it could have
seemed rationally possible or 'all right' to do it" (1963:120). We do not

---

58. Krieger 1963:137. At the same conference another historian noted that "for a
long time Hempel's position has been dominant, but with the appearance in 1957 of
William Dray's *Laws and Explanation in History* some serious doubts have been raised
as to the applicability of the covering law model to history" (Degler 1963:205).

want to know, or at least Dray does not want to know, whether the action actually was the product of a rational calculation.

The crucial issue is not this simple. It turns, not surprisingly, on the definition of rational. If that word is narrowly defined, Dray's methodology collapses into near irrelevancy. If it is broadly defined, the result is an explanation closely approximating that advocated in section 5.

Dray frequently uses such words as "calculation" or "deliberation" when describing those processes that constitute the focus of his rational explanation (1963:111; 1970:122, 141, 150). On these occasions he seems to imply that history is to be the study of intellectual operations directed to problem solving under uncertainty—or more correctly, historical explanation is to consist of those calculations that the agent would have made if the agent had made calculations, with the action to be explained being consistent with the calculations proffered. To view human actions exclusively in these terms is to take to history a view that is narrow to the point of being myopic. Whether the event be the storming of the Bastille or the Second Continental Congress, whose actions could the historian adequately explain with no reference whatever to passion, distress, stupidity, or ineptness? Even if one tolerated a history of the American Revolution that was written in terms of an upheaval "in which all scholarly, refined, and conservative persons might have unhesitatingly taken part,"[59] would one further tolerate behavioral explanations couched exclusively in terms of careful calculations directed toward the achievement of clearly specified goals? Napoleon—hardly a conservative but certainly a calculator—readily conceded that "there is nothing so rare as a plan," and the Russian whose monumental novel was based in part upon Napoleon's actions expressed similar sentiments: "Out of all the immense number of tokens that accompany every living phenomenon, these historians select the symptom of intellectual activity, and assert that this symptom is the cause. But in spite of all their endeavours to prove that the cause of events lies in intellectual activity, it is only by a great stretch that one can agree that there is anything in common between intellectual activity and the movement of peoples."[60] To study human behavior solely in terms of the calculations of rational problem solving is not only to

59. S. G. Fisher 1902:9.
60. Tolstoy 1931:1106.

confine the historian who would paint a picture to a single color, but to deprive his palette of all those subtleties made possible by modern psychology. The end product may well satisfy Dray, but it is likely to be dismissed by most historians most of the time as grotesquely inadequate.

On occasion Dray does write as if he has in mind a much broader definition of rational explanation. All that is required is to show that the agent's actions "made perfectly good sense from his own point of view" (1963:109), and the criteria for making good sense seem to be anything but rigorous: "It is enough that what provides the agent with a reason for acting be a *rationally* necessary condition—that is, that it be shown that without it, he had no reason to do what he did" (1963:129).

Consider the type of altercation that is the common currency of any game of ice hockey. If in a moment of anger I strike my friend on the opposing team because he has just subjected me to a particularly unreasonable body check, that striking at its moment of implementation would no doubt make perfectly good sense from my point of view: it releases an inner tension and reminds my friend that body checks of a certain type cannot be allocated in my direction without his experiencing undesirable consequences. Is this a "rational explanation"? Not only does it "make perfectly good sense from my point of view," but if reasons of the sort just noted are ruled out, "I would have no reason to do what I did." The general problem raised by this example can be put very simply: very few actions do not make sense—that is, appear to be nonsensical—to the agent at the time he undertakes them. If we abandon the connotations of ratiocination implicit in the word calculation and attempt to explain actions in terms of the agent's perceptions and dispositions when faced with certain external stimuli, then we have taken a giant step toward the type of explanation outlined in section 5. In making that step, however—in moving from explanation in general to causal explanation in particular—we must insist that the analysis attempt to focus upon only those factors that were operative, and we dismiss as irrelevant what Dray seems willing to accept (1963:114; 1970:124–126): rationalizations after the fact that have nothing to do with the agent's true reasons for acting as he did.

One other problem may or may not concern Dray. He notes, but does not unequivocally support, Scriven's point that "particular occurrences 'rattle around' in statistical explanations."[61] Whether or not that rattling disturbs Dray, it clearly does disturb Michael Scriven. To avoid it, he offers "normic" explanations.

e. Scriven and Normic Explanation

Scriven begins with a definition of soundness for causal explanations that is reminiscent of the criteria advocated by Carl Hempel: "One set of facts cannot be a watertight explanation of another fact unless we can guarantee they are adequate to produce it—and the only kind of guarantee that connects facts is a law. Failing such a law, we cannot be certain our explanation is adequate" (1959b:444). Not surprisingly, Scriven is caught on the horns of the same dilemma that impaled Hempel. Causal explanations are not adequate unless they are watertight, they cannot be watertight unless the generalizations under which facts are subsumed are universal in form, and universal generalizations are scarce to the point of being nonexistent.

Scriven's solution is to propose a generalization that is neither universal nor probabilistic, but "normic." Beginning with such examples as "Power corrupts" and "The American bourgeoisie normally reacts with hostility to those on whom it is dependent" (1959b:465), he attempts to derive a generalization that is both watertight and immune to counterexamples:

One might term the study of normic statements . . . the logic of *guarded generalizations*. . . . The normic statement says that *everything* falls into a certain category *except* those to which *certain special conditions* apply. And, although the normic statement itself does not explicitly list what count as exceptional conditions, it employs a vocabulary which reminds us of our knowledge of this, our trained judgment of exceptions. . . . Now if the exceptions were few in number and readily described, one could convert a normic statement into an exact generalization by listing them. Normic statements are useful where the system of exceptions, although perfectly comprehensible in the sense that one can learn how to judge their relevance, is exceedingly complex. [1959b:465–466]

Because normic generalizations are (according to Scriven) at least implicitly watertight, the problem of rattling around is solved. "The

---

61. Dray 1963:119. Dray would seem to be as aware of the key issues as Scriven is. His failure to take a firm stand on the problems about to be considered may reflect his failure to take a firm stand on whether or not the "covering law" approach has any merit. On occasion he advocates abandonment of the latter; on occasion he writes as if his method of rational explanation is only an alternative to the covering law approach. See, for example, 1963:132; 1970:19, 32, 88, 118, 134, 154–155.

normic statement tells one what had to happen in *this* case, unless certain exceptional circumstances obtained; and the historical judgment is made (and open to verification) that these circumstances did not obtain. An event can rattle around inside a network of statistical laws, but it is located and explained by being so located in the normic network" (1959b:467).

The basic error in this approach to causal explanation of human behavior should be readily apparent from all that has gone before. However few the exceptions, a normic statement cannot be converted into "an exact generalization," if by an exact generalization one means (as Scriven seems to mean[62]) a universal generalization. The central thrust of Chapter I was to demonstrate that we can never bring to causal explanation of observed phenomena universal generalizations known to be universal. For historian and scientist alike, the generalization under which facts are subsumed must always be probabilistic in form. The obvious implication is that individual events *always* rattle around in the resulting explanation, and there is no way to silence that rattle. Or to abandon Scriven's metaphor, we can never conclusively prove that E *had* to follow the occurrence of $(C_1, \ldots, C_n)$. We can only say that when $(C_1, \ldots, C_n)$ occurred, the subsequent occurrence of E was probable.

The discussion would seem to have come full circle to the starting point of Chapter I. To face the limits of one's own knowledge requires at bottom an act of courage. That knowledge, insofar as it relates to causal explanation of human behavior, will always have its tenuous aspects. However discomforting such uncertainty may be, it cannot be removed by semantic dodges that disguise our ignorance. The ignorance remains, but it is hardly total ignorance. Using procedures outlined previously, we can and do offer and accept imperfect causal explanations of observed phenomena, including human behavior. We can hardly claim, in Droysen's phrasing, to have achieved "the light and the truth," but neither can we claim the total failure of the blind. If Emerson could bear with a theory of the world that was "a thing of shreds and patches," why should the historian prove unequal to a similar task?

62. See 1959b:444, 462, 466; 1963:344–347.

7. Summary and Conclusions

An obvious tension exists between the quotations cited at the outset of this chapter and the methodology sketched in section 5. In attempting causal explanation of human behavior, how can the historian pursue the goals of Droysen and combat the frailties cited by Kracaver while relying upon generalizations that must always be, in some sense, ill-fitting?

The philosophers considered in section 6 offer depressingly little guidance. Collingwood and Dilthey emphasize the self-evident in stressing the importance of introspection and advocate the impossible in urging the complete abandonment of generalizations in favor of "direct understanding." Hempel also advocates the impossible in urging the use of universal generalizations to derive deductive explanations. As for his exploration of statistical-probabilistic explanation, not only does he fail to consider homogeneity difficulties central to the indeterminacies in historical explanations, but he continues to write as if all those explanations were somewhere between unsound and in need of filling out without specifying how soundness or filling out can be achieved. William Dray's methodology of rational explanation remains obscure because his definition of rational remains obscure, as does the linkage between his calculations and the causal processes actually at work in historical phenomena. To avoid the "rattling around" of individual events in probabilistic explanations Michael Scriven proposes the use of "normic" explanations which, on close inspection, are merely universal generalizations with the exceptions not clearly specified. The competent historian knows that his explanations always rattle around. He understands the importance of introspection, recognizes the impossibility of acquiring universal generalizations, and distrusts explanations of human behavior couched exclusively in terms of deliberate calculations aimed at achieving precisely specified goals. For guidance in pursuing his appointed tasks he must apparently look elsewhere.

What aid, if any, can he garner from the social sciences? They can, of course, provide a progressively longer list of progressively better defined generalizations, which all students of human behavior can bring to their subject matter. In their insistence upon making assumptions precise and generalizations explicit the social scientists may render a second service. To expect all generalizations to be made explicit in most historical explanations is, as emphasized in section 5, to ask too much. This does not, however, negate the urgency of laying bare some of them, particularly those most crucial to the causal processes at work, and/or those most original to the historian who relies upon them. Between elephantine profundity and sprightly persiflage, between the Scylla of spurious precision and the Charybdis of vacuous innuendo, the historian navigates as best he can. From the sciences deemed social—or from those studies of human behavior tenuously deemed scientific—he can perhaps acquire a handful of insights and a salutary admonition.

At least one historian appears to welcome both: "Insofar as empirical social research can drive historians to criticize their assumptions, to expose their premises, to tighten their logic, to pursue and respect their facts, to restrain their rhetoric—in short, insofar as it gives them an acute sense of the extraordinary precariousness of the historical enterprise—it administers a wholly salutary shock to a somewhat uncritical and even complacent discipline."[63]

Economics, as the most rigorous of the social sciences, might be expected to administer the most authoritative, shock. This is a not unreasonable characterization of a central goal of what has become known as "the new economic history." Before elaborating and assessing the techniques whereby it has attempted to administer those shocks, we must gain some familiarity with the methodology of that social science whose application will constitute the core of those attempts. To what extent is economics a science, and to what extent can it claim to offer precise causal explanations of economic phenomena?

63. Schlesinger 1962:768.

III Causal Explanation and Model Building in Economics

For that part of economic doctrine, which alone can claim universality, has no dogmas. It is not a body of concrete truth, but an engine for the discovery of concrete truth, similar to, say, the theory of mechanics.

—Alfred Marshall[1]

1. Definition of the Subject

The Droysen quotation with which the previous chapter began had an aura of antiquity. History was to be not merely a search for the truth, but "a sermon thereupon, a consecration thereto." How sharply this contrasts with Marshall's view of economics. Its theories are, he suggests, merely engines to aid in the search for "concrete truth." If these engines are not unlike the theory of mechanics in their guiding function, are the truths to which they lead of similar mechanistic precision? And what would the owner of the engine analyze? To attempt an answer to the first question is the main objective of this chapter. The obvious starting place is with the second, which rephrased might read: What is economics?

Definitions of the subject are almost as numerous as practitioners of the craft. They range from Marshall's brief but vague "study of mankind in the ordinary business of life" (1952:1) to Samuelson's less brief but more enlightening commentary: "Economics is the study of how men and society end up choosing, with or without the use of money, to employ scarce productive resources that could have alternative uses, to produce various commodities and distribute them for consumption, now or in the future, among various people and groups in society. It analyzes the costs and benefits of improving patterns of resource allocation" (1973:3). About the core of the discipline there is relatively little disagreement. Economics is concerned with production and distribution—as Marshall suggests, about as ordinary a business as mankind has. Production is generated by the interaction of the forces

1. Marshall 1925b:159.

of supply and demand. The determinants of supply—those various bundles of goods and services that might feasibly be created—are the same for all societies: the available factors of production (which economists group under the four broad categories of land, labor, capital, and enterprise) plus the available technology which dictates how these factors can be combined to create different bundles of goods and services. Which bundle will be created from among all those possible depends upon demand. Just whose demand will be of influence has varied across time and space, depending upon the extent to which choices can be dictated by the lord of the manor, or by the bureaucrats of a central planning agency, or by all members of society according to wealth owned and willingness to spend it. The economist's central questions, however, always remain the same: What? How? and For Whom?

Although the core of economics is reasonably well defined as the study of the interaction of productive factors with human wants, the margin remains a subject of dispute. In tracing out the causal linkages that determine what gets produced and for whom, at what point should the economist, *qua* economist, cease his labors? For a minority, the answer is cut and dried: "It is precisely at that point at which in the course of his reasoning [the economist] finds himself in contact with some phenomenon *not* economic, with some physical or mental fact, some political or social institution. So soon as he has traced the phenomena of wealth to causes of this order, he has reached the proper goal of his researches."[2] The majority of economists would probably note the difficulty of defining with precision "some phenomena not economic," and not a few would regard the above-mentioned boundaries as an intolerable intellectual strait jacket. The charge that economists have too narrowly defined their discipline has become in recent years a rallying cry for those who call themselves radical economists. Their specific allegations will be considered briefly within the broader framework of assessment developed in section 8.

The remaining problem for this section is to define both microeconomics and macroeconomics. Here too the end result will have its tentative and inconclusive aspects. The Greek words "macro" and "micro" are frequently used to designate those subdivisions of a

2. Cairnes 1888:54.

discipline concerned with large and small units, respectively. When used as prefixes to the word "economics," the implied division of the discipline would appear to be self-evident.[3] Microeconomics should be the study of economic decision making by the smallest possible unit of analysis: the household or individual consumer (whose behavior influences demand) and the firm or producer (whose behavior influences supply). Macroeconomics should be the study of aggregate behavior within larger units—regions, nations, or groups of nations. The problem with the above division as it stands is that general equilibrium, which involves the study of certain kinds of aggregate behavior, is generally regarded as being part of microeconomics. The latter is distinctive as the one study of aggregate behavior carefully built up from postulates about individual decision making. A curiosity of economics is its failure to relate in any precise manner its theories about individual behavior to almost all of its theories concerning aggregate behavior. General equilibrium theory is the one exception. The article of faith, as James Tobin has expressed it, is that "economies are subject to laws of motion which are largely independent of the details of their internal structure" (1970:44). But why has it been so difficult to relate the study of large units to the study of small units? And what success has each field of study achieved in providing Marshall and others of similar inclinations with an engine of analysis? To these and related issues the discussion will return below. Two final preliminary matters concern the purposes for having an engine and what the general nature of that engine is. These are the topics for sections 2, 3, and 4.

2. A Contrast in Objectives: The Economist vs. the Historian

Economics is a social science. The word "social" implies that it involves the study of humanity ("the reasoned history of man" was how Marshall chose to put it [1925a:299]); the word "science" implies the objectives of explanation, prediction, and control. These objectives can only be achieved by developing conceptual schemes that organize and unify the flux of observable phenomena. The economist is therefore a man in search of generalizations, a man preoccupied with the typical or the average, not with the unique. As one theorist turned historian

3. Fritz Machlup traces the introduction of these terms into economics to the work of Ragnar Frisch in the 1930's (Machlup 1967:103).

formulated his priorities: "It will be the group, not the individual, on which we shall fix our attention; it will be the average, or norm, of the group which is what we shall be trying to explain. We shall be able to allow that the individual may diverge from the norm without being deterred from the recognition of a statistical uniformity. This is what we do, almost all the time, in economics."[4]

The economist might pause to consider the implications of his goal of control. Chapter I suggested that two broad views of efficient causation were possible, the first emphasizing a maximum of consistency with observed correlations but denying any thoughts about mechanisms; the second insisting that efficient causation consisted of observed correlations plus a belief in mechanisms creating or producing those correlations. The majority of humanity would seem to subscribe to the second view. This is not to suggest that the first view and the priority of control cannot be reconciled, but it does suggest that the associated intellectual stance may seem curious to the majority of social scientists. The failure to understand that some economists debate methodological issues from precisely this stance has been an ongoing source of confusion in the methodological literature. Of this, more in section 7.

To return to our own priority of comparison: the goals enunciated in the first paragraph are in marked contrast with those enunciated in Chapter II. The historian is concerned with the unique, not the average, with explanation, not prediction and control. To achieve causal explanation he requires the use of generalizations—if facts cannot be subsumed under some generalization then a causal explanation of those facts cannot be given—but the *raison d'être* of his research is not to discover generalizations. The economist believes otherwise. The very term "social science" implies that the goal of its practitioners *must* be to discover generalizations and, where possible, organize them into larger consistent systems. Small wonder that those with doctoral degrees in economics who subsequently turn to history bring to the second discipline priorities that are judged atypical by more conventional disciples of Clio. Historians have not infrequently protested that new barbarians have invaded an old field with little more than a yardstick and the bed of Procrustes disguised as economic theory.

4. Hicks 1969:3.

Invasion there has clearly been. Whether its main contribution has been distortion or enlightenment will be the subject of Chapter V. The remaining preliminary task of the present chapter is to explore the nature of that bed—or to return to the more fortunate metaphor of Marshall, to explore the nature of the engines that the economist brings to the analysis of all economic phenomena, past, present, and future.

3.   Causal Explanation in Economics: A Preliminary Overview

The economist has the same article of faith or central tenet as does the historian bent upon causal explanation of human behavior: that similar stimuli, experienced by people with similar dispositions, will result in similar actions. This raises the same three questions considered at length in Chapter II:

(1) What is meant by "disposition"?

(2) What is meant by "similar"?

(3) Should the resulting generalizations be prefaced with the word "Necessarily," "Always," or "Probably"?

To begin with dispositions, economists usually presume that economic decision makers are, in some sense, rational. The historian begins with observed action and searches for evidence that will indicate associated disposition and relevant stimuli. The economist, at least within the confines of microeconomics, postulates the disposition, combines this behavioral assertion with other postulates, and then attempts by deductive inference to derive conclusions that can subsequently be used to explain observable reality. The procedures of microeconomics will be detailed in section 5. (The treatment of dispositions in macroeconomics will be discussed in section 6.) Our problem at this juncture is to determine what an economist means by rational behavior.

Two different assertions tend to be intertwined in the associated debates. The first concerns the manner in which decisions are made; the second the priorities or objectives that underly that decision making. The first of these usually reduces to little more than the twin assertions (a) that each economic decision maker has preferences which he or she can order, and (b) that the chosen ordering is always consistent or transitive, by which is meant that if A is preferred to B and B to

C, then A is preferred to C.[5] The behavioral postulate concerning actual choices made is usually some variant of the assertion that more is preferred to less in matters economic, or as Mill expressed one of those variants almost a century ago, "Man is a being who is determined, by the necessity of his nature, to prefer a greater portion of wealth to a smaller."[6]

The resulting abstraction, *homo oeconomicus*, is clearly that: an abstraction. From a range of critics has come the predictable accusation that economists have abstracted too much, that man is neither a careful calculator nor is he driven exclusively by the desire to maximize material welfare.[7] The economist's reply begins with the observation that his discipline never promises exactitude, but only useful first approximations. Is this approximation likely to be useful? The answer depends upon how closely the explanations and predictions based upon such premises fit the facts. The fate of much of economics will turn upon that judgment. The edge that this particular social science seems to have over other social sciences can be, to no small degree, attributed to the simplicity of its dispositional postulates and the quantitative nature of observed effects which those dispositions ostensibly produce. To the problem of judging its success in predicting and explaining, the discussion will return below. The final two questions for this section, as noted previously, are (a) what is meant by similar in the economist's generalization "Similar stimuli, experienced by people with similar dispositions, will result in similar actions," and (b) should this generalization be prefaced with always, necessarily, or probably?

The answer to the first is the same for an economist as for anyone else bent upon causal explanation. Diverse phenomena must be grouped into quasi-homogeneous sets, those sets must then be linked in a cause-and-effect relationship, and that linkage cannot be viewed as being "tight" unless the set of causes can be viewed as a complete set,

5. Other assumptions for consumer behavior include nonsatiation and continuity. See, for example, Dorfman 1964:46–47.

6. Mill 1874:138–139. Mill was well aware that this represented an abstraction, often requiring qualification. See, for example, pp. 137–141.

7. Perhaps the most often quoted accusation in this context is Thorstein Veblen's, economists being charged with viewing humanity exclusively in hedonistic terms: "The hedonistic conception of man is that of a lightning calculator of pleasures and pains, who oscillates like a homogeneous globule of desire of happiness under the impulse of stimuli that shift him about the area, but leave him intact" (Veblen 1898:389).

known to be complete. The economic theoretician begins, as it were, at the other end—with pencil and paper and abstract symbols, rather than with the flux of observable phenomena. Within the confines of pencil and paper, the construction of a deductive causal explanation is eminently feasible. One need only postulate that the set of causes being considered is the entire set, and the result is a universal generalization that can be employed with other premises to lead the would-be reasoner by the force of logic to whatever conclusions are deductively implied by those premises. Economics is, however, an empirical discipline and not merely a branch of mathematics or logic. We want, as F. H. Hahn and R. C. O. Matthews suggest, "theories that can be used as a plumber uses a spanner—not simply abstract systems."[8] The ultimate touchstone for any theory is therefore always the same: How useful is it in explaining, predicting, and controlling observable economic phenomena? This is not to deny that theorizing cut loose from observed phenomena may yield new insights that will subsequently prove useful in explaining the world around us. In the house of Adam Smith and Alfred Marshall are many mansions including—appropriately—that of the pure theorist. What is denied to all those who would turn from abstract systems to explaining observable reality is the deductive certainty guaranteed by universal causal generalizations. The reasons for that denial have been emphasized repeatedly in Chapters I and II. Reality is organized with difficulty into quasi-homogeneous sets labeled causes of type C_1, of type C_2, and so on. Sets of causes, however long, cannot be viewed as being known to be complete. The inescapable implication is that generalizations employed to explain observable phenomena must always be probabilistic in structure; that is, of the form

Probably, if $(C_1, \ldots, C_n)$, then E.

8. Hahn and Matthews 1964:888. As self-evident as this priority may seem to be, the modern theorist—ever pressed to ignore it—would perhaps do well to heed the cautioning of a great theorist from an earlier day: "I conceive no more calamitous notion than that abstract, or general, or 'theoretical' economics was economics 'proper.' It seems to me an essential but a very small part of economics proper: and by itself sometimes even—well, not a very good occupation of time. The key-note of my *Plea* is that *the* work of the economist is 'to disentangle the interwoven effects of complex causes'; and that for this, general reasoning is essential, but a wide and thorough study of facts is equally essential, and that a combination of the two sides of the work is *alone* economics *proper*" (letter from Alfred Marshall to F. Y. Edgeworth, Aug. 28, 1902, reproduced in Pigou 1925:437).

The economist can, of course, convert this generalization into the seemingly precise or universal generalization

Always, if $(C_1, \ldots, C_n)$, then E, *ceteris paribus,*

where the Latin phrase is once again appended to signify the fulfilling of all other unspecified sufficient conditions. This phrase is used repeatedly by the economist in partial equilibrium analysis to designate his awareness that some factors in the total set of relevant causes are being held constant. The point to be emphasized—which is too often missed by economists—is that even if all of the factors knowingly held constant in *ceteris paribus* were allowed to vary and the effects of those variations were incorporated into a more complex causal generalization, the end result would *not* be a universal generalization. Thus, for example, general equilibrium analysis, while impounding fewer factors in *ceteris paribus* than partial equilibrium analysis, still invariably impounds some, such as consumer tastes and the institutional framework. The economist also uses *ceteris paribus* to calculate the partial derivatives of his economic model. That is, he knowingly holds constant all but one of the causal variables in the model in order to study the relationship between changes in that one cause variable and resulting changes in the effect variable. The connection between this use of *ceteris paribus* and the usage discussed in Chapter I is that to the economist's *deductive* model—whatever its form—must always be appended *ceteris paribus* to encompass the fulfilling of all other causes *not* specified in the model itself. The economist therefore does well to divest himself of the ideal of realizing in practice deductive explanations based upon universal generalizations. He is perhaps more easily misled as to the feasibility of realizing this ideal because of the technique just cited. From constant employment of the phrase "*ceteris paribus*" to impound *some* of the relevant sufficient conditions, practitioners may be deceived into believing that *all* of the relevant sufficient conditions could be specified if that were required. The basic argument here and elsewhere is that a complete set known to be complete cannot be specified.

These arguments in turn answer the last of the three questions noted above. All causal generalizations in economics, insofar as they refer to observable reality, must be prefaced with the word "Probably," not with the word "Always" or "Necessarily." The preoccupation of the discipline with the average or typical rather than with the unique gives to the word "probably" a rather different focus from that which it has in history. For the economist, what is crucial is the ability to explain or predict the behavior of the typical or average economic decision maker. His use of the word "probably" therefore relates to his expectations concerning a large collection of individual cases, and his main concern is that group behavior have a strong central tendency. The historian's concern is that available evidence about the disposition of a specific human actor will enable him to explain why that individual was likely to behave as he or she actually did behave when confronted with certain stimuli. To the extent that generalizations concerning individual behavior tend to be less precise than those concerning group behavior, the second will have a more difficult task than will the first.

4. Model Building in Economics

As noted in Chapter I, attempts to define a model and to distinguish a model from a theory run afoul of the multiplicity of uses to which both words are put in economics in particular and the social sciences in general. Giving a precise and all-encompassing definition would seem to be less crucial for our purposes than exploring the relationship between model building on the one hand and causal explanation on the other.

The starting point is with causal generalizations. In economics these most commonly relate to causes and effects that admit to variation. The generalizations therefore attempt to summarize how variations in one factor or set of factors will affect variations in another. The model builder tends to translate these causal assertions into mathematical functions. Thus, for example, the assertion "consumption expenditure (E) is a function of income (Y)" would be translated into

$$E = f(Y).$$

This translation adds nothing to the original causal assertion. It merely expresses the same idea in a more compact language, relating an independent variable (the cause) to a dependent variable (the effect).[9]

9. Subsequent discussion will ignore all problems of simultaneity. The concern of economists with such problems would seem to be partly the result of data limitations (for example, consumption may be a function of income previously received but data

The point is perhaps worth laboring that a causal structure is implanted in the model at the outset. The origins of the ideas so implanted, as repeatedly stressed elsewhere, are as broad as the knowledge, experience, and beliefs of the would-be model builder. These ideas therefore cannot be characterized as a priori in the sense of being prior to any experience, although they are prior to whatever testing is envisioned for the particular model being constructed.[10]

The great strengths of model building as a supplement to causal analysis have been hinted at in the preceding paragraphs. Assumptions are made explicit, thereby eradicating confusions that result from the changing of assumptions in mid-argument.[11] A system of causal generalizations can be checked for internal consistency and for conclusions that are not intuitively obvious at the outset. The result is not designed to replace all of the common laws of common sense with a *code économique*. It is often well suited for organizing a collection of generalizations and seeking out supplementary ideas implied by them. The historian's absence of enthusiasm for this engine of analysis is hardly surprising. Reluctant to specify any generalizations, he is unlikely to welcome a device that calls for the specification of a consistent set.

Different attempts to classify models defy a ready summary, but here too our purposes allow us to avoid complexity. The important distinction in subsequent discussion is between models that include only universal generalizations (and hence permit deductive inference) and those that include probabilistic generalizations (thereby permitting inductive inference only). Broadly speaking, the pure theorist is preoccupied with the first while the would-be practitioner is restricted

---

are collected on both variables only for large blocks of time) and partly the result of the dominant position of comparative statics in most economic theory. In practice, economic causes and effects would seem generally to have a time dimension, with causes preceding effects, rather than all occurring at the same time.

10. The *Oxford Dictionary*, for example, distinguishes several possible meanings for a priori, including "previous to any special examination" and "prior to experience; innate in the mind." Economists on occasion seem to confuse the notion of being prior to the particular experience of testing a given hypothesis with the notion of being prior to any experience.

11. It does not follow that because assumptions are made explicit they are therefore transparent. "This distinction cannot be overemphasized. Even though the list of items which we have posited have been written out *in extenso*, the obscurity of their statement may leave us largely unaware of their full meaning" (Baumol 1966:95).

to the second. With no universal generalizations available to the latter, his preoccupation could hardly be otherwise.

Construction of the first type of model, often termed construction by the axiomatic method, begins, as this term suggests, with axioms or postulates. Where causal assertions are involved (and they are almost always involved in the models of economics), they are made in the form of universal generalizations. In the language of Chapter I, they state that

Always, or necessarily, if $(C_1, \ldots, C_n)$, then E.

Their universal nature then permits deductive inferences based upon this type of generalization and whatever other postulates are included in the model. The choice of axioms or postulates tends to be dominated by the aesthetic of Occam's Razor. A given conclusion is to be derived from the weakest possible set of axioms, and the discovery of an even weaker set from which to derive the same conclusion is regarded as a positive achievement. A more careful scrutiny of this technique in operation will be attempted in section 5.

The second type of model is very much a creature of the twentieth century. Ever present in the economist's priorities is the desire to relate theory to observed fact. A growing dissatisfaction with the success of that relating process expressed itself in a variety of ways, including the founding in 1930 of the Econometric Society with the avowed purpose of transforming economics from a qualitative-deductive discipline into a quantitative-empirical one. The requirements were then, and still remain, broadly three. Models must begin by specifying suspected causal relationships between independent and dependent variables; the symbols of the models must then be related to the empirical data thrown up by the economic system; and finally, that data must be combined with statistical techniques to make more specific the general tendencies specified by the model at the outset. Causal assertions appear as probabilistic generalizations, not as universal generalizations. Variables whose behavior is to be analyzed or explained by the model are termed "endogenous." Those regarded as being determined by factors outside the model are termed "exogenous." The crucial distinction from the standpoint of causal analysis is that exogenous variables can influence endogenous variables, but not vice versa. In practice this neat compartmentalization is seldom met. Again the presumption is that the neglected influences (of endogenous on exogenous variables) are not significant. The problem is then to determine how little influence is little enough. To these and related issues the discussion will return in sections 6 and 8.

One cannot overemphasize that this tying of a model to reality—this relating of symbols on a piece of paper to the flux of observable economic phenomena—is a complicated and ongoing challenge. The symbols appear homogeneous. Reality is not. A joining of the two is therefore only possible with abstraction harnessed to "an intricate system of basic definitions, classifications, and rules of measurement."[12] Macroeconomic models, for example, often include as a key variable the symbol M which stands for the money supply. In the American economy of today can be found demand deposits, currency in circulation, savings and time deposits, traveler's checks, commercial paper, and various other "near money" assets. In acquiring data that corresponds to the symbol M, should the economist include only demand deposits plus currency in circulation, or these two plus savings and time deposits? Or should he revise his model to include several monetary variables instead of just one? Available options are always the same: to lump diverse phenomena into a single set presumed to be homogeneous, or if the associated abstraction appears to be excessive, to expand the number of sets (that is, the number of separate variables in the model). That now familiar problem is again upon us: How can one decide how much abstraction is too much?

The associated puzzles will be explored in the remaining sections of this chapter. To anticipate, much of the answer will turn upon the purpose for having a model in the first place. If the only objective is to specify tendencies—if, for example, the economist wishes to forecast only the *directional* impact of a change in the money supply upon the average level of prices—then a highly abstract model may be quite satisfactory. Specification of tendencies only, however, may not be good enough. The president of the Federal Reserve Bank of St. Louis suggests why:

It is not sufficient for an economist to tell us that a slower growth in money will eventually result in a slower rate of price increase. As a policymaker, I would like to have better information as to the specific open market transactions that

12. Leontief 1958:104.

would achieve, with a high probability, a desired growth of money. I am also vitally concerned with the time distribution to be expected with regard to changes in prices and output for a given change in the rate of growth of money. Then I want to know how some tangible results can be expected with regard to prices and output, and how the pattern will appear in the data subsequently reported.[13]

In short, the priorities of the policy maker may call for precision in both the amount of the expected change and its time distribution. A tall order, one might conclude, and a tall order it remains. To anticipate further, economics has achieved considerable success in forecasting directional tendencies, but only limited success in forecasting exact magnitudes. To a consideration of the related failures the discussion will return in sections 6 and 8.[14]

5.   Causal Explanation and Model Building in Microeconomics

Political economy, in particular—being concerned pre-eminently with quantities—has a special tendency to become on its inductive side statistical, just as on its deductive side it tends to become mathematical. [J. N. Keynes][15]

a. Objectives

Microeconomics is not exclusively deductive, nor is macroeconomics exclusively inductive. The former has its applied studies, the latter its pure theory. Microeconomics is nevertheless dominated by deductive models and macroeconomics by inductive-empirical studies. For this reason, the exploration of deductive model building will be the main preoccupation of this section, with inductive model building the main preoccupation of the next.

The puzzle that for a long time has been the central focus of microeconomics is exchange value—the ratios at which different commodities and productive factors exchange for one another. Within Western economies dominated by the market system, this priority is evidenced by the ascendancy of such questions as why observed market prices are what they are, what causes them to change, and what the relationship is between market prices on the one hand and production and distribution on the other. To conceive of microeconomics (at least in the West)

13. Francis 1973:9.
14. Two of the more fashionable forms of current model building, simulation and operations research, will be ignored in subsequent discussion. Readers unfamiliar with either topic can find useful introductory surveys in Orcutt 1970 and Theil 1970.
15. J. N. Keynes 1891:337.

without these questions is no more feasible than imagining *Hamlet* without the Prince of Denmark.

In seeking answers, the economist has two very different goals. The first is quite modest: to forecast the directional impact upon prices and quantities if a particular causal factor were to change. In the case of the price and quantity of wheat, for example, the analysis might concern the directional impact of such factors as a fall in the price of harvesting machinery, or an increase in wheat subsides, or a rise in farm wage rates. To answer such questions, all that is required are the conventional supply and demand curves of introductory price theory—curves that postulate a behavioral relationship between prices charged and the amount individuals want to consume (the demand curve) and between prices charged and the amount producers wish to supply (the supply curve). (The beginning student of economics who has been puzzled by the intellectual energy devoted to demonstrating that, in the main, demand curves are negatively inclined might attempt to answer the directional questions posed above without that assumption.)

The second goal is far more ambitious. The crucial issue turns not upon establishing tendencies but rather upon establishing marginal equivalences—or as micro theorists occasionally put it, that marginal everything equals marginal everything else. That issue arises because of the desire to assess the extent to which resource allocations and associated production within a market system are efficient. Narrowly defined, efficiency concerns conditions of supply, in which case the problem is to decide whether the market system produçes the largest possible output from available inputs. If the human dimension is added, then efficiency also includes the study of consumer choices and is often described as that situation in which it is impossible to make one person better off without making another worse off. Translated into the jargon of economics, the first concerns the extent to which market prices reflect real opportunity costs; the second the extent to which a competitive equilibrium is a Pareto optimum.

To answer such questions the economist must engage not in an infinite regress, but in a regress of one step. Analysis must begin not with supply and demand curves, but with those causal factors that underly or determine supply and demand curves. The engine of analysis most commonly brought to such questions is the neoclassical model of competitive markets—for all its hard knocks in recent years, still the most powerful engine of analysis in all of economic theory.

The adequacy of this model in achieving these objectives is the controlling theme for the remainder of this section. The stakes are very high. Practitioners who evidence an absence of concern for the fate of competitive theory overlook the fact that their calculations and recommendations would often make little sense if observed market prices did not reflect, to a tolerable degree of accuracy, real opportunity costs for the entire economy. So central is this point—and so neglected—that it bears repeating: the calculations of practitioners, *including historians*, would often make little sense if observed market prices did not reflect, to a tolerable degree of accuracy, real opportunity costs for the entire economy.

The model will be elaborated briefly in section 5b, criticized in 5c, and attempted rebuttals to those criticisms described in 5d. To the more general issues raised by the latter two the discussion will return in sections 7 and 8.

b. The Neoclassical Competitive Model: An Example of Deductive Model Building

Arnold Toynbee recounts a conversation with Sir Lewis Namier in which the latter observed, "Toynbee, I study the individual leaves, you the tree."[16] The micro theorist might be tempted to make the same observation to his macro counterpart. The analogy would not, however, be quite correct, insofar as micro theorists study a particular set of aggregation problems labeled general equilibrium. The foundations for such studies—or at least that foundation which is the neoclassical model—reduces to a set of assumptions concerning individual producers and consumers. Unlike the historian who searches for evidence concerning the dispositions of specific human actors, the micro theorist postulates the dispositions for his two problem-solving units. The consumer (or household) is assumed to be driven by a desire to maximize utility; the producer (or firm) by the desire to maximize profits. To these basic dispositional postulates several other assumptions are added, the most important of which are the following:

(1) Consumers have transitive and stable preference sets which they can order, perfect knowledge, and derive satisfaction only from specific goods consumed independent of the consumption pattern of others.

(2) Producers have perfect knowledge, produce standardized goods,

16. Quoted in Kracaver 1969:110.

and have no ability to affect directly observed market variables such as price.

(3) As consumers consume more of any good they experience diminishing marginal utility (or a diminishing marginal rate of substitution with other goods).[17]

(4) As producers expand production of a given commodity they encounter diminishing returns or rising unit costs.[18]

These four assumptions imply two well-defined functions: a utility function and a profits function. Combined with the initial disposition assumptions concerning the desire to maximize, they permit the economist to treat the problem solving of both producers and consumers as one of maximizing subject to constraints. The consumer is viewed as maximizing utility subject to the constraints of market prices and the money he or she has to spend; the producer as maximizing profits subject to the constraints of market prices and production techniques available. From these few postulates the economist can deduce a set of marginal equivalences which are nothing more than the working out of the mathematics of maximization subject to the constraints noted.[19] These inferences can then be used to pursue the goals outlined in section 5a. The root idea is one of equilibrium: that only when these marginal equivalences have been achieved will equilibrium be achieved.[20]

c. Criticism of the Neoclassical Model

The major criticisms of the neoclassical competitive model concern the lack of correspondence between one or more of the above assumptions and the underlying economic reality that the model would explain.

17. The latter formulation is preferred by most economists because of their belief that utility is an ordinal, not a cardinal, concept.
18. More rigorously, assumptions (3) and (4) concern the convexity of preferences and production and consumption sets, with interchangeability of set summation assuring the last condition cited in both assumptions (1) and (2) plus the absence of externalities.
19. Much of the contrast between introductory and advanced microeconomics would seem to consist in establishing the same conclusions with more elaborate mathematics and weaker assumptions. Thus, for example, instead of assuming a form for the utility function, one can assume that (a) "total expenditure must add up to income," (b) "there must be no money illusion: the relationships must be homogeneous of degree zero in income and prices," and (c) "the Slutsky condition must be satisfied: the matrix of elasticities of substitution must be symmetric" (Stone 1966:22).
20. To this statement the theoretician would want to add qualifications concerning the speed of adjustment and the stability of equilibrium.

Concerning the behavior of consumers, the principal charges are:

(1) Consumers do not maximize utility. Such factors as habit and inertia modify their willingness to weigh carefully the prospective satisfaction from different bundles of goods.

(2) Consumers do not have perfect knowledge. Many feasible choices remain unknown, and the prospective outcome of many known choices remains uncertain.

(3) The satisfaction derived from a given bundle of goods is not independent of the observed consumption pattern of others.

(4) Tastes are not entirely independent of the productive system, but can be manipulated by advertising that has negligible informational content.

Concerning the behavior of producers, the principal charges are:

(1) Producers do not attempt to maximize the single variable profits. In the era of large corporations with management divorced from ownership, decision makers in the firm are also concerned with such variables as growth and total sales.

(2) Producers cannot maximize profits because their information systems will not indicate the marginal inequalities indicative of imperfect maximization.

(3) Producers, like consumers, do not have perfect knowledge. Their decision making is therefore continually modified by the costs of acquiring information and the desire to avoid risk.

(4) Firms often produce differentiated products rather than standardized products, resulting (when there are many firms) in monopolistic competition.

(5) Firms are often so large relative to the total market size that other firms react directly to their actions, resulting in oligopoly.

d. The Response to Criticism: Rebuildings and Rebuttals

Reactions to the above criticisms have, in the main, taken two quite different forms. The first, predictably, is manifest in various attempts to modify the neoclassical model so that the assumptions used will correspond more closely to the reality observed. The second, perhaps also predictably, has taken the form of defending the continued use of the neoclassical model as is.

To describe adequately all of the attempted modifications would be the appropriate subject of a book. Among the most important are

(a) revisions of the concept of profit maximization, (b) the incorporation of uncertainty into the postulated decision making, and (c) the derivation of a new type of theory to analyze situations of recognized interdependence. The third of these is associated with the names of John von Neumann and Oskar Morgenstern and their novel contribution to economics: game theory (1944). Authorship of innovations under the other two headings is more diffused. The incorporation of uncertainty into decision making generally has proceeded by recasting producers as maximizing expected profits and consumers as maximizing expected utility. Expected value is usually defined as the product of the value of an outcome multiplied by the probability of that outcome being realized. Efforts to modify the postulate of profit maximization have tended to proceed under two general headings: managerial theories of the firm and behavioral theories of the firm. The first accepts the concept of maximization but attempts to add to the objective of profits (that is, incorporate into the objective function) such variables as growth and total sales. The behavioral school would make the constraints on maximization correspond more closely to those experienced within the firm. Decision making is therefore portrayed as being conditioned by such factors as rules of thumb, limited knowledge, and risk aversion.[21]

For all their efforts and associated ingenuity, the would-be rebuilders have achieved but limited success. Game theory is still of little relevance in describing or predicting most business behavior in situations of recognized interdependence,[22] and superior alternatives (at least for most practical situations) are virtually nonexistent. So poverty-stricken is the theorizing about oligopoly that as recently as 1970 Martin Shubik concluded, "There is no oligopoly theory,"[23] and two years later one of the cofounders of game theory added that "economic theory . . . has virtually nothing to say where the contribution of certain market types

21. A survey of defects and/or proposed modifications can be found in Cyert and Hedrick 1972; Cyert and March 1963:Chapter 2; Silberston 1970; H. A. Simon 1959 and 1962.
22. David Miller, for example, concludes that game theory is not very relevant in explaining most of observed competitive behavior, although the more closely a given situation approximates a two-person zero-sum game, the more likely it is to be relevant (1963:265; see also 274 and 304).
23. Shubik 1970:412. This sweeping condemnation is subsequently qualified by Shubik: "There are bits and pieces of models: some reasonably well analyzed, some scarcely investigated." His final judgment, however, remains harsh: "Oligopoly . . . is more of a name than a coherent body of theory" (pp. 412, 406).

to total economic activity is bound to be high: few sellers encountering few and many buyers, in physical goods industries and even more so in service industries."[24] Many of the other attempted modifications—to broaden the concept of maximization beyond profits, to make the constraints upon maximization correspond more closely to those encountered within the modern-day firm, to allow for differentiated products in a *Theory of Monopolistic Competition*[25]—have all suffered from the same crucial defect. Theories incorporating these modifications lack clear-cut implications for aggregate pricing behavior, and prices, as noted at the outset, remain the central puzzle of microeconomics.

Defenders of the neoclassical competitive model begin with the point just noted. If the objective is to predict aggregate pricing behavior and if proposed alternatives cannot offer any clear-cut predictions, then the superiority of the neoclassical model is assured—at least for this particular purpose. As Machlup puts it, "The model of the firm in [neoclassical] theory is not, as so many writers believe, designed to serve to explain and predict the behavior of real firms; instead, it is designed to explain and predict changes in observed prices . . . as effects of particular changes in conditions (wage rates, interest rates, import duties, excise taxes, technology, etc.)" (1967:9).

This particular counterattack by defenders of the conventional model would seem above reproach. Their other main counterattack is not. Critics of the neoclassical model tend to launch their assaults from the same vantage point: that the assumptions of the conventional model are markedly at variance with observed economic reality. The defenders would deprive them of this vantage point by three quite different arguments. In summary form, these are:

(1) The argument that unrealism results from abstraction, that abstraction in formulating generalizations is inevitable, and therefore unrealism is unavoidable. As noted repeatedly in Chapters I and II, the argument is correct but trivial. The question is what assessment procedures should be used to decide how much abstraction is too much.

(2) The argument that the more abstract a theory is, the more general it becomes, and therefore unrealism is a positive good. This argument ignores the purpose for having a theory in the first place. If a general

24. Morgenstern 1972:1187.
25. Chamberlin 1933.

theory fulfills those goals less well than a specific and detailed theory, the latter will obviously be preferred to the former.

(3) The argument that it is impossible (or "largely" impossible) to test assumptions except by testing the predictive powers of the theory of which they are a part. This argument is misleading on one count and wrong on another. As emphasized in previous chapters, all aspects of a theory or hypothesis are made to face the collective tribunal of all our knowledge, experience, and beliefs deemed to be relevant. To insist that assumptions not be scrutinized in this manner is absurd. To insist that inconsistencies revealed by that scrutiny are always tolerated if a theory predicts well is misleading. The key issue is whether our goal is merely to predict, or instead, to predict and control. If it is the latter, and if the assumptions hypothesize absurd dispositional mechanisms linking stimuli to overt action, then the theory and its assumptions may well be jettisoned despite a superior prediction record. (These last points and related issues are explored in more detail in section 7.)

What then remains? The answer would seem to be most of the defects cited in section 5c. Despite such defects, the economist can, in many situations, pursue with confidence one of the goals of microeconomics noted at the outset. That goal, to review, concerns the forecasting of the *directional* impact on price and quantity of such causal factors as a change in input prices or output subsidies. These forecasts can be based upon the neoclassical model, or much more simply, upon conventionally shaped supply and demand curves.[26] The other two objectives cited in section 5a concern the extent to which

26. Fritz Machlup, one of the most vigorous exponents of using the neoclassical model in certain situations, summarizes those situations as follows: "The simple marginal formula based on profit maximization is suitable where (1) *large groups* of firms are involved and nothing has to be predicted about particular firms, (2) the effects of a *specified change* in conditions upon prices, inputs, and outputs are to be explained or predicted rather than the values of these magnitudes before or after the change, and nothing has to be said about the 'total situation' or general developments, and (3) only *qualitative answers*, that is, answers about directions of change, are sought rather than precise numerical results" (1967:31). The supply assumptions of the neoclassical model do imply a nonnegative slope for the supply curves of firms. The demand assumptions, however, are consistent with either positively inclined or negatively inclined demand curves, unless supplemented by the assumption that the income effect is positive (that is, if prices remain unchanged and income rises, then the demand for a given commodity will also rise). The minimum assumptions required to derive negatively sloped demand curves are much less stringent than those of the neoclassical model. For example, Gary Becker has shown that negatively sloped demand curves can be derived from a variety of irrational behavioral postulates (1962).

the workings of the economy produce, to a tolerable degree of approximation, the marginal equivalences implied by the neoclassical competitive model. Critics emphasize that the assumptions of this model are widely at variance with most of observed economic reality. Defenders reply that assumptions always diverge from reality. The crucial issue is therefore whether the observed divergences seriously impair the achievement of the marginal equivalences implied by the neoclassical model. On this issue both sides are almost totally silent. To demonstrate that efforts to modify the neoclassical model have been largely unsuccessful is *not* to prove that the defects which motivated those efforts are unimportant. What it does prove is that the defects remain.

The result is rather curious. A cornerstone of microeconomics, both theoretical and applied, is the belief that the marginal equivalences of the neoclassical model are achieved, to a tolerable degree, in whatever economic situation is being analyzed. To date, that belief—for all its importance—is largely an untested hypothesis.[27]

6. Causal Explanation and Model Building in Macroeconomics

a. Objectives

The objectives of macroeconomics become apparent once the term is defined. A first approximation, as noted in section 1, is the study of global aggregates. A second approximation is required because general equilibrium is usually viewed as part of microeconomics. The compromise is to confine macroeconomics to those studies of global aggregates not carefully built up from theories of individual decision making. The negative twist to that definition would seem to reflect not so much the wishes of macro theorists as the limits of micro theories. If the latter could offer precise implications from which theories of aggregate behavior could be constructed, no economist would be likely to turn his back upon such possibilities.

When macroeconomics is defined in these terms, two dominant issues

27. A number of attempts have been made to estimate the extent to which certain marginal equivalences do not hold, most notably the equivalence between price and marginal costs implied by the neoclassical model. None of these, however, are very comprehensive, and all suffer from the profound difficulties of obtaining accurate price and cost data in an economic world of conglomerates, multiproduct firms, and secret rebates. For a survey of attempts made and associated defects, see Scherer 1970: Chapter 17. For an indication of how a classic debate can remain unresolved because of the poverty of empirical evidence, see Peterson 1965; and Kaysen 1965.

emerge. The general problem, as noted, is to analyze both the absolute level and variations in global aggregates—usually aggregate measures of economic activity for a given national economy. Explanations that focus upon short-run changes tend to be demand-oriented. Productive capacity is taken as roughly fixed, and causal analysis concerns those factors that determine the extent to which that capacity is utilized. For the study of long-run changes, the procedure is reversed. Problems of demand sufficiency tend to be ignored, and causal analysis concentrates instead upon conditions of supply. Under the first heading can be found the monetarist-Keynesian dispute over the determinants of inflation and unemployment; under the second all of contemporary growth theory. The remainder of this section will be concerned only with the former; specifically, with problems of constructing a model to explain, predict, and control short-run fluctuations in such national aggregates as employment, income, and the average level of prices. Two of the simpler variants of growth models will be considered in Chapter V.

b. Econometrics and Inductive Model Building

Even under the general heading of short-run macroeconomic models, two broad approaches must be distinguished. The first, associated with the name of Wassily Leontief, is input-output analysis. The related model details the interrelationships of different productive sectors, its primary purpose being to trace the likely responses of those sectors to different patterns of final demand. The model and its uses in the new economic history will be sketched in Chapter V.

The other principal type of short-run macroeconomic model begins with the priorities of explanation, prediction, and control and with observed fluctuations in aggregate economic activity within a given nation. The challenge is to build a model that will permit policy makers to moderate those fluctuations. Historically, the rise to prominence of such models is associated with a constellation of stimuli, most notably the searing economic experience of the 1930's, the impetus given to model building by Keynes's *General Theory*, economists' desire to make their field more empirical, and the rapid evolution of such indispensable tools as national income and product accounts, electronic computers, and statistical theory—the last of these harnessing the previous two to permit pursuit of the objectives cited.

The general requirements for constructing such models have been outlined in section 4. To review, these include: (a) the specification of suspected causal tendencies to be incorporated into the model; i.e., the relationships between dependent and independent variables,[28] (b) the relating of the theoretical constructs of the model to observed data, and (c) the use of that data and statistical techniques to make more specific the general tendencies specified in step (a). The third step is the special focus of this section.

Consider the case of an economist who wishes to analyze total expenditures within the United States economy in terms of the determinants of the behavior of various types of spenders, such as consumers and investors. He begins with his suspicions concerning the dispositions of these people and the implications about relevant stimuli. The procedure has nothing to do with scientific method and everything to do with his views concerning what makes human beings behave as they do in economic matters. Like the historian, the economist consults the sum total of his knowledge, experience, and beliefs deemed relevant to the type of human behavior that he would explain, including the evidence of introspection—perhaps especially the evidence of introspection.

His resulting generalizations linking cause and effect will be probabilistic in structure; that is, of the general form

$$\text{Probably, if } (C_1, \ldots, C_n), \text{ then } E.$$

Since most or all of the factors that he would examine are variable quantities, this generalization is usually reformulated to read

$$E = f(C_1, \ldots, C_n) + U; \cdot$$

or in words, the dependent variable (E) is a function of various independent variables $(C_1, \ldots, C_n)$ plus an error term (U). Thus, for example, consumption expenditure might be viewed as being determined by income received, assets held, and so on. The meaning of the error term will be considered in more detail below.

Recall the priorities implied by the statement of the president of the Federal Reserve Bank of St. Louis cited earlier. To control fluctuations

28. Independent variables may be exogenous or endogenous variables that are dependent variables in other equations. Not all equations of a model express a causal relationship. At least some are likely to be identities; that is, equations that define the relationship between different symbols.

in business activity, what is desired is not a model indicating general tendencies, but rather a model that makes the nature of those tendencies more specific. That is, the policy maker wants to know the likely numerical relationships between variations in causes and resulting variations in effects. Meeting that demand is equivalent to removing the brackets on either side of $(C_1, \ldots, C_n)$ and giving the associated function a precise mathematical form.

Suppose for the sake of simplicity that this form is expected to be linear. Then the relatively imprecise

$$E = f(C_1, \ldots, C_n) + U$$

can be transformed into the more precise

$$E = b_0 + b_1 C_1 + b_2 C_2 + \cdots + b_n C_n + U.$$

The remaining problem is to find the values of the constant term b_0 and parameters $(b_1, \ldots, b_n)$, where b_1 indicates the sensitivity of E to variations in C_1; b_2, the sensitivity to variations in C_2, and so on. Econometric techniques can be used at this point to uncover those estimates of $(b_0, \ldots, b_n)$ that are consistent with both the hypothesized causal relationships and available data on dependent and independent variables. The technique that dominates most applied econometric work of this sort is regression analysis. The technique itself and the reasons for viewing estimates derived by its use as yielding good approximations for $(b_0, \ldots, b_n)$ are the appropriate topics for an introductory textbook in econometrics. Our focus will be confined to the last term (U) in the equation cited above.

At first glance, this term may seem to be a numerical variant of the verbal dodge repeatedly condemned in Chapters I and II. As noted in those chapters, the generalization

Probably, if $(C_1, \ldots, C_n)$ then E

can be transformed into the seemingly precise

Always, if $(C_1, \ldots, C_n)$, then E, *ceteris paribus*,

where the Latin phrase is appended to encompass the fulfilling of all other relevant sufficient conditions. On close inspection, however, the second merely asserts that $(C_1, \ldots, C_n)$ will be followed by E unless something else happens to prevent their being followed by E. In a similar manner, the equation

$$E = b_0 + b_1C_1 + b_2C_2 + \cdots + b_nC_n + U$$

seems to assert that the parameters $(b_1, \ldots, b_n)$ will describe the sensitivity of E to changes in $(C_1, \ldots, C_n)$ unless something else happens to change that sensitivity.

The reasons for including the error term (U) are broadly three. The primary reasons relate to a variant of a point made repeatedly in earlier chapters; namely, the inevitable incompleteness in our knowledge of causal generalizations. In regression analysis, this incompleteness concerns both the omission of relevant variables and the possibility of incorrect specification of the functional form which relates the effect variable to those cause variables that are included. (For example, the true relationship may be quadratic, while regression analysis assumes that it is linear.) Now that the generalizations under scrutiny link variations in numerical magnitudes, the third reason for including an error term is to give cognizance to the fact that data are subject to random measurement errors.

The first and third always ensure that the term (U) is present. The difficulty, as already suggested, is that once the variable (U) is included, the resulting generalization may appear to be a tautology. The assertion that a relationship holds subject to some error is always true. The equation can be converted into a meaningful empirical statement only by asserting something about the nature of that error term.

The conversion process begins with the notion that the error terms are, in some sense, random. The sense most commonly referred to is that of independence: that error terms are independent of the cause variables (or independent variables) and also that each error term is independent of all other error terms.[29] With these assumptions in hand the economist can interpret the equation thrown up by his econometric technique of regression analysis as portraying an estimate of the average causal relationship. The average, however, is usually not by itself very interesting. What the economist usually desires is some indication of how likely actual results are to vary from that average. Put another

29. Thus, for example, in a time series study of annual aggregate consumption spending covering a thirty-year period, the assumption would be that the error term of each year is independent of all other twenty-nine error terms.

way, the numerical values of $(b_1, \ldots, b_n)$ produced by regression analysis are estimates indicating the average sensitivity of E to variations in $(C_1, \ldots, C_n)$, but knowledge of the average sensitivity is unlikely to be helpful unless accompanied by a confidence interval—an upper and lower bound that is likely to include the actual or "true" sensitivity. Estimation of a confidence interval, in turn, is possible only with some assumption concerning the distribution of the error terms. The most common assumption is that the error terms are normally distributed with a mean of zero and a constant variance.[30] This in turn may be derived from a broader definition of randomness. If the error terms can be appropriately viewed as the result of a multitude of unsystematic influences, then (by the central limit theorem) the distribution of the error terms should approximate the normal distribution.

The net result of regression technique plus the assumptions noted[31] is a set of numerical estimates for $(b_0, \ldots, b_n)$ plus a confidence interval on each of these estimates. If, for example, the cause in question is a change in income and the effect is the resulting change in consumption spending, and if the estimate of b_1 (the amount by which consumption should increase when income increases by one unit) is a positive 0.8, several inferences follow: (a) the average sensitivity indicated by the data is $(+0.8)$; (b) if the confidence interval expressed at the 95 percent level is (± 0.12), then the data and assumptions suggest that one should be 95 percent certain that the interval $(+0.68)$ to $(+0.92)$ includes the "true" relationship; and finally, (c) given that the bounds just noted are well above zero, the relationship between consumption and income is statistically significant in the sense that it is most unlikely that the true relationship is zero, or that the two variables are unrelated.

Three points are worth laboring. The first is that the entire procedure is essentially inductive. One begins with an hypothesis: the causal relationship built into the statement

$$E = b_0 + b_1 C_1 + b_2 C_2 + \cdots + b_n C_n.$$

Regression analysis then provides a test of whether available data are

30. The assumption that the variance is finite is also crucial, but by assuming that the distribution is normal one has already assumed that the variance is finite.

31. To review, the main assumptions are that the individual errors (U_j) are random variables, independent of $(C_1, \ldots, C_n)$ and independent of each other, and are normally distributed with a zero mean and a constant variance.

consistent with that hypothesis. If the hypothesized relationship between a given cause and its effect is found to be in the direction initially postulated (for example, that a positive change in C_1 results in a positive change in E) and if the econometric procedures indicate that this relationship is significantly different from zero, then the originally hypothesized causal relationship has survived a particular type of numerical test. As is true of all inductive inference, to demonstrate that the hypothesis is consistent with a particular type of evidence (in this case, the evidence of available data) is not to prove that it is true, but it does make that hypothesis more probable.

The second point to note is that everything in the preceding paragraph refers to the question of whether there is *any* linkage between a suspected cause and a given effect. About this particular question we usually have strong suspicions long before resorting to a statistical procedure that helps to confirm them. The more interesting question, as noted at the outset, is whether one can estimate the numerical sensitivities linking cause variables with the effect variable. The coefficients $(b_1, \ldots, b_n)$ estimated by regression analysis cannot, for practical purposes, be viewed as being precise estimates of those sensitivities. They can be viewed, in concert with their associated confidence intervals, as that range of estimates within which the true numerical sensitivity is likely to fall *if* all of the assumptions of regression analysis are factually correct.

Finally, and perhaps most important of all, the confidence intervals thrown up by econometric techniques are no better than the assumptions used to derive those intervals. Most of the time—perhaps all of the time—the practicing economist is conscious that the assumptions in question are only approximately true, *which means that he can only hope that the associated confidence intervals are approximately correct.* To cite but two of the more crucial problems, the user of regression analysis generally remains uncertain as to how closely the world that he would explain approximates (a) the assumption that the causal relationships were specified correctly in the first place (including the assumption built into the linear equation that the relationships are additive), and (b) the related assumption concerning the error terms; namely, that all of the significant influences on E have been included in $(C_1, \ldots, C_n)$ and the remaining errors "are sufficiently close to the *systematic* lack of system which we call 'random.'"[32] These indeterminacies combined with confidence intervals that are often quite broad to begin with in many cases preclude regression analysis from answering the questions that the economist initially hoped it would answer. A consideration of one of the key disputes concerning appropriate national policy will illustrate the associated dilemmas.

c. The Keynesian-Monetarist Debate

Econometrics has been the tool that has dominated postwar model building, but a tool without advocates might well have gone unused. Macroeconomics did not originate with Keynes's *General Theory*, nor was Lord Keynes in his day the sole exponent of macroeconomic model building. Both qualifications make all the more puzzling the force with which this single book broke upon the economics profession in 1936.[33] Nor was this simply one more storm in the academician's teacup. At stake was nothing less than the mitigation of business cycle fluctuations—so long endemic to capitalist economies, so pernicious in their effects as the decade of the 1930's demonstrated with a vengeance.

From the moment of its unveiling the Keynesian model was regarded as an imperfect engine of analysis in need of immediate repair. Subsequent restructuring emphasized multidirectional causation more than unidirectional in equation systems that tended to abandon the comparative statics of Keynes for dynamic analysis. The number of equations and number of relevant variables were expanded to reflect more accurately those influences suspected of being important in determining economic behavior, especially portfolio selection and aggregate spending by consumers and investors.

Attempts to apply some variant of the Keynesian model now span more than three decades, beginning with Jan Tinbergen's pathbreaking work in the 1930's and perhaps culminating in the 1960's with the joint effort of twenty-five economists that produced the Brookings model of several hundred equations. Measured against the original objectives of explaining, predicting, and controlling fluctuations in aggregate economic activity, the achievements of even the largest of

32. Kuznets 1957:549.
33. One measure of that force is Harry Johnson's summary judgment, made twenty-five years after first publication: "The stimulation given by the *General Theory* to the construction and testing of aggregative models may well prove to be Keynes's chief contribution to economics in the longer perspective of historical judgment" (1961:13).

recent models have been comparatively modest. The authors of the Brookings model, for example, were modest to a fault. "No claims are advanced for the particular model used here . . . this model is tentative and in need of improvement."[34] Their reviewers tended to agree: "Predictions and simulations with a new econometric model should be used primarily to uncover weaknesses in the model, not to generate conclusions regarding the structure of the economy which might be misused by policymakers. The simulations indicate that several equations in the Brookings model appear to be in need of immediate repair."[35]

Partly because of the limited success of even the most elaborate of Keynesian models, a modern version of the old Quantity Theory of Money became progressively more popular in the 1960's. Dissatisfied with the Keynesians' emphasis on income-expenditure relationships, members of this revived monetarist school chose to emphasize what Quantity Theorists have always emphasized: that the main determinants (although not necessarily the only determinants) of the aggregate price level and money income are previous changes in the stock of money. Associated models tended to be simple in structure, with few equations (sometimes only one) in which the transmission mechanisms whereby changes in money affected the price level remained, by and large, unspecified. The ensuing debate between Keynesians and monetarists is difficult to summarize, partly because of its technical nature, partly because members of a given school hold differing views among themselves. Much of the disagreement reduces to different assertions about relative sensitivities: of the demand for cash balances to changes in the rate of interest, of interest rates to price changes, of wages to a disequilibrium in the labor market, to mention only a few.[36]

34. Fromm and Taubman 1968:123.
35. R. J. Gordon 1970:519.
36. In recent years the Federal Reserve Bank of St. Louis has tried in its monthly *Review* to compensate for the scarcity of summary statements by modern Keynesians and monetarists. For an outline of the key areas of disagreement, including those relating to the sensitivities and lag structure of empirical relationships, see Teigen 1972; Rasche 1972; and L. C. Anderson 1973. The disagreements in question go well beyond issues relating to empirical relationships. One member of the St. Louis Federal Reserve staff summarized his reactions to the above statement as follows: "The difference is more fundamental. It is rooted in the opposing judgement about the self-adjusting capacities of the private sector and the dominant source of disturbances which attenuates the self-equilibrating capacity of the economic system. The Monetarists view the economic system as a dynamically stable system in the absence of a substantial short-run variability

The failure to resolve most of these debates is symptomatic of the limitations of the tool that has become central to model construction. Regression analysis is often a powerful device for demonstrating that a postulated causal relationship is insignificant (that is, that the estimated sensitivity of E to variations in C_1 is not significantly different from zero). It is often useful in establishing the directional nature of a causal relationship (that is, whether, when cause C_1 increases, effect E is likely to increase or to decrease). It remains a relatively blunt instrument for discriminating among competing hypotheses when much of that competition, as suggested, relates to relative sensitivities, or to the size of parameters linking independent and dependent variables.

The policy maker of the 1970's therefore confronts two competing models, neither of which predicts extremely well, and both of which predict with about the same degree of imprecision. The forecasts of these models are viewed, at best, as being first approximations to be modified by a host of information in ways that are difficult to formulate systematically.[37] Nor is this situation expected to change in the immediate future. Surveys of the current state of macroeconomic model building by econometricians refer to plateaus having been reached, or to the limited prospects for dramatic new breakthroughs, or to uncertainties concerning whether the rewarding modus operandi of the future will feature more aggregation or more disaggregation.[38] The Brookings Institution itself noted, "Where large models—particularly the Brookings model—go from here is not clear. Many economists think the technique has advanced about as far as it can in the light of the continuing structural changes in the economy and the limitations of data" (1972:9).

The Brookings observation about data limitations and structural

---

in the stock of money whereas the Keynesians tend to view it as essentially unstable. Two opposing approaches to the stabilization policies emerge from these competing diagnoses. Whereas the monetarist conception calls for the provision of a stable and predictable monetary framework to facilitate the coordination of the plans of diverse transactors, the Keynesian diagnosis leads to a more activist pursuit of discretionary (and variable) monetary and fiscal policies to continuously offset the ever-emergent inter-transactor coordination failures" (letter from Jai-Hoon Yang to the author, July 5, 1974).

37. For recent judgments by academicians supporting the policy maker's reluctance to rely upon unadulterated model forecasts, see Ackley 1970:96; R. A. Gordon 1965:374; Phelps Brown 1972:2; Worswick 1972:80; and Paul A. Samuelson's views quoted in Brookings Institution 1972:5.

38. See, for example, Kuh 1965:365–366; Nerlove 1965; Klein 1971; and Tintner 1966.

shifts would seem to understate the difficulties. Tobin's article of faith—that aggregate models could be built without much attention to the constituents of the aggregates (1970:44)—raised the puzzle of why aggregate models were not constructed from micro theories about individual decision making. Why cannot the most mathematical of the social sciences bring to the analysis of that decision making what Bertrand Russell (or at least the younger Bertrand Russell) envisioned could ultimately be brought to such problems: "a mathematics of human behavior as precise as the mathematics of machines" (1956:20)? Many of the economist's difficulties relate to his limited ability to model both the objectives and the ignorance of those human actors whose choices he would explain. Whatever their objectives, decision makers invariably confront the type of problems considered in Chapters I and II; the problems of lumping reality into quasi-homogeneous sets and linking those sets in cause-and-effect generalizations that can be used to forecast the results of alternative choices. The imprecision of the forecasts reflects, to a large degree, the imprecision in the generalizations. The uncertainty accompanying each individual's choices raises the question as to whether aggregate behavior can be expected to have strong central tendencies. In the case of investment spending, for example, choices made are largely a function of expected returns, but about the determinants of those expectations the economist still knows very little. If the objectives and ignorance of each would-be investor are difficult to model, why should the aggregate behavior of all investors be capable of being precisely depicted in a mathematical function that indicates not only the directional linkages between causes and effect, but also, within comparatively narrow limits, the numerical sensitivities of those relationships?

Until microeconomics can provide precise building blocks for macro theory the need for Tobin's article of faith will remain. If macroeconomic theories devised with this article of faith cannot discover strong central tendencies for aggregate behavior, then econometric tools are unlikely to resolve most of those debates concerning the sensitivity of that behavior to various stimuli. Well within our grasp is sufficient knowledge to avoid the worst ravages of cyclical fluctuations that typified the interwar period. Still eluding our grasp is that model of such proven precision that its use to guide national policy would ensure the eradication of most of the lesser ravages of the business cycle.

7.   Friedman vs. Samuelson: Confusions in a Misleading Debate

This section considers the position of two of the major combatants, although by no means the only combatants, in a series of methodological disputes by and for economists. The placement is deliberate. Partly it reflects the belief that with the framework heretofore developed, the confusions in these debates drop easily into place. Partly it reflects the conviction that those confusions are so pervasive that any consideration of the associated debates is appropriately viewed as an appendage or afterthought to a more general discussion of methodological issues in economics.

As Hempel's seminal article on "The Function of General Laws in History" produced a storm of protest from historians, so Friedman's essay on "The Methodology of Positive Economics" (1953:1–43) evoked a storm of protest from economists. In both cases the author's views continue to be the starting point and/or controlling influence for most methodological discussion in that discipline to which his essay was directed. In neither case would this position of pre-eminence seem to be justified.

Friedman's article is difficult to summarize, primarily because it argues several positions simultaneously. The author is, first and foremost, a debater determined to persuade. For the sake of simplicity only two main arguments will be traced, hereafter referred to as the simple Friedman and the complex Friedman.

The crucial question in both cases concerns the relationship between the assumptions of an hypothesis (or a theory) and the means whereby that hypothesis can be tested. The simple Friedman seems to argue that the only test of *both* the hypothesis *and* its assumptions is the ability of the hypothesis to predict. This position is then buttressed by a variety of arguments, the most important of which are:

(1) Unrealism in the sense of abstraction is unavoidable in the formulation of assumptions (1953:32).

(2) Unrealism in the sense of abstraction is a positive good because the more abstract a theory is, the more general and comprehensive it becomes (14).

(3) The only test of whether assumptions are too unrealistic is whether or not the theory that employs those assumptions predicts well or badly (15–18).

As noted in section 5d, the first is trivially true and the second misleading. The third is not so easily dimissed.

The problems that it raises are perhaps most easily seen within the context of a far-fetched example. Suppose that the Gross National Product of the United States is discovered to be closely correlated with the Peruvian anchovy catch of the previous year. To keep matters simple, assume that for every year since data were collected on both variables, this correlation is found to be almost perfect. Friedman is surely correct to insist that (a) if our *only* objective is to predict next year's American GNP, and (b) if *none* of the available alternative models predicts at all well, then we might use this year's anchovy catch to forecast next year's GNP. What Friedman fails to emphasize is that the economist's goals include both prediction and control. If we believed that the American economy was headed for an inflationary boom, for example, few would advocate offsetting that boom by paying Peruvian fishermen not to catch anchovies. The reason is obvious. Most economists when asked to assess the worth of any causal model of human behavior instinctively look for believable mechanisms relating the dispositions of the human actors to the stimuli and overt actions being considered. The anchovy case is unlikely to survive this test.[39]

This example is merely one way of illustrating a general point. The assessment of any causal hypothesis always proceeds in the first instance in terms of the consistency of *all* aspects of that hypothesis with *all* aspects of one's knowledge, experience, and beliefs deemed to be relevant. If the hypothesis predicts well on the basis of assumptions that seem to be wildly inconsistent with other evidence, we worry. If our only objective is to predict, and if we lack alternatives for prediction purposes, we may well use that hypothesis despite those worries. If instead our objective includes control, and the inconsistencies concern the absurdity of the dispositional mechanisms hypothesized, we would tend to reject the hypothesis in question and choose instead an alternative that

39. Here, too, by cleverly choosing his examples Friedman obscures a fundamental problem. If maximizing profits is a condition for business survival (at least in competitive situations), then one may be satisfied to postulate that businessmen behaved "as if" they were trying to maximize profits. The same point can be made about expert billiard players and the calculation of complex geometric patterns. As the anchovy example demonstrates, however, the search for appropriate dispositional postulates is seldom simplified by the knowledge that an ability to approximate the disposition postulated is a necessary condition for professional survival.

includes more believable mechanisms, however inferior its prediction record is compared with that of the rejected hypothesis.

In practice, of course, the choice is often not as simple as the anchovy case suggests. It is also not as simple as Friedman suggests. By focusing almost exclusively upon microeconomics and the goal of prediction, Friedman—or at least the simple Friedman—is in the strongest possible position to argue that the unrealism of assumptions is irrelevant. If the only priority is to predict aggregate pricing behavior and (as noted in section 5d) none of the alternatives to the neoclassical competitive model offers clear-cut predictions in most circumstances, then the triumph of the neoclassical model is assured whatever its assumptions may be.[40] By virtually ignoring macroeconomics, Friedman manages to avoid the prediction difficulties and problems of control outlined in section 6. Those difficulties, to review, are that none of the currently available models predicts exceptionally well, and several predict with about the same degree of imprecision. (In the light of arguments just cited, one should perhaps add that none can be dismissed out of hand on the grounds of incorporating absurd behavioral mechanisms.) In the face of such dilemmas, and with the priority of control, the policy maker does instinctively what Quine argues we always do: he makes all elements of any hypothesis confront the tribunal of all available evidence collectively. That such a confrontation will not always yield a definitive answer is evidenced by the present dispute as to which model—monetarist or Keynesian—should be used for purposes of national policy formulation.

The complex Friedman begins with a tautology. The validity of an hypothesis is defined as the ability of that hypothesis to predict. The only test of the validity of an hypothesis is therefore whether it predicts well.[41] The crucial issue is whether the assumptions of that hypothesis should or should not be subjected to an independent test. To argue the extreme position that they never can be so tested or never should be so

40. Even within microeconomics, Friedman focuses only upon the simplest of the objectives considered in section 5a. Predicting price and quantity responses to certain exogenous changes is far less ambitious than demonstrating that the marginal equivalences postulated by the competitive model are achieved, or achieved to a tolerable degree, within any given economy.

41. Friedman 1953:20, 8, 31 n. 22. Occasionally Friedman drops the word validity and writes that "a hypothesis can be tested only by the conformity of its implications or predictions with observable phenomena" (p. 40).

tested, one would have to argue that in the initial choice of assumptions no preliminary check is made with relevant evidence to establish consistency with that evidence. The complex Friedman never takes this position. Just what the specific nature of these checks should be is never made entirely clear, but repeatedly in his essay the argument is advanced that some screening process is desirable if not unavoidable. Thus, for example, one choice criterion advocated for assumptions is "intuitive plausiblity" (26), with the meaning of that term made more apparent in the discussion of the assumption "man seeks his own interest." Any hypothesis employing this assumption, Friedman argues, "then gains indirect plausibility from the success for other classes of phenomena of hypothesis that can also be said to make this assumption; at least, what is being done here is not completely unprecedented or unsuccessful in all other uses" (29). This surely constitutes an admission that some screening of assumptions is desirable and that the screening process consists of checking for consistency between the assumptions in question and the sum total of relevant knowledge, experience, and beliefs.

To summarize: all economists (including the complex Friedman) would regard as unacceptable the position of the simple Friedman—that the realism of assumptions can never be checked or should never be checked independent of the prediction capabilities of the hypothesis of which those assumptions are a part. The realism of assumptions is always a source of concern, although with only the priority of prediction and lacking alternatives, our tolerance for unrealism may be very high. The position of the complex Friedman is unassailable—that assumptions are subjected to a preliminary screening process, but that the only test of the validity of an hypothesis is its ability to predict, where validity is *defined* in terms of ability to predict.

Into the maelstrom precipitated by Friedman's essay Samuelson entered with a point that was, in his own wording, "so innocuous as to be platitudinous."[42] The point was the one noted above. When the assumptions of a theory are markedly at variance with available evidence, we always worry, although in certain circumstances we may still choose to use that theory.

Samuelson chose to make that point in a curious way. Assume (a) that

42. Samuelson 1964:736. This is the second of three related articles by Samuelson. The other two are 1963 and 1965a.

all phenomena can be organized into homogeneous sets, and (b) that the only relationship between sets is one of descriptive similarity; that is, a theory relates sets in this manner and not by referring to mechanisms at work in cause-and-effect generalizations. Now define

A = the minimal assumptions of theory B, and
C = the full consequences of theory B.

With the assumptions noted, and in the language of set theory, one can then conclude that

$$A \equiv B \equiv C;$$

or translated back into words, that the minimum assumptions of a theory are identical with that theory and with its full consequences.[43] Put in terms of the minimum assumptions of preference theory and the complete factual implications of that theory, the two "imply each other mutually" (1964:738).

This conclusion, in turn, implies that the unrealism of any part of a theory, such as its assumptions, does have bearing on the worth of the entire theory. Samuelson preferred to speak of this implication as a proof that the "F-Twist" was fallacious (1963:234), the F-Twist having been previously defined as "A theory is vindicable if (some of) its consequences are empirically valid to a useful degree of approximation; the (empirical) unrealism of the theory 'itself,' or of its 'assumptions,' is quite irrelevant to its validity and worth" (1963:232). More simply put, if assumptions, theory, and consequences are identical in the sense of mutually implying one another, one cannot maintain that the unrealism of one is not shared by the other two. [44]

By structuring his attack against Friedman in this way, Samuelson shifted the resulting methodological discussion away from the obvious point noted at the outset and toward two related questions, both of which Samuelson answered in the affirmative: (a) whether "a description (equation or otherwise) that works to describe well a wide range of observable reality is all the 'explanation' we can ever get (or need desire) here on earth" (1965a:1165), and (b) whether "the validity of the *full* consequences of a theory implies the validity of the theory and so of its

43. Although the distinction between A and C is sharply drawn by Samuelson, the distinction between A and B remains unclear.

44. "It is nonsense to think that C could be realistic and B unrealistic, and nonsense to think that the unrealism of B could then arise and be irrelevant" (1963:235).

minimal assumptions."[45] Critics of Samuelson's position who resisted one or both[46] were attacking, respectively, the second assumption noted above and the first conclusion implied by both assumptions.[47] What the critics seem to have missed is that if both assumptions are granted, then the conclusions about the equivalence of minimum assumptions and full consequences is unassailable. If reality can be organized into homogeneous sets and no known mechanism links those sets, then the appropriate way to formulate theories—and to reach methodological conclusions about theories—is with the language and logic of set theory. The peculiarities of Samelson's approach therefore lie not so much with the conclusions derived from the two assumptions noted as with the assumptions themselves.

What is peculiar about the position that "a description (equation or otherwise) that works to describe well a wide range of observable reality is all the 'explanation' we can ever get (or need desire) here on earth"[48]? The answer would seem to be that most people do desire more. With respect to the theories of the natural sciences, most individuals seem to include in their associated ideas of cause and effect the notions of both correlation and mechanism, with the latter often reflecting a belief in forces at work or the transmission of energy. The difficulties with this viewpoint, and the tentative justification for it, have both been discussed in Chapter I. With respect to theories of human behavior, most individuals seem to bring to causal explanations the same two ideas—correlation plus mechanism—although the nature of the mechanism remains unclear. Problems associated with this viewpoint have been considered in Chapter II. The clash between Samuelson and his critics is thus, at bottom, a clash over personal beliefs. From one perspective, theorizing about observable phenomena consists of subsuming facts under probabilistic generalizations that link quasi-homogeneous sets of causes and effects, the linkage itself often reflecting a belief in mechanisms at work ensuring that similar causes will indeed have similar effects. Another viewpoint—Samuelson's viewpoint—is to deny any belief in

45. Samuelson 1965a:1165. Samuelson initially made a slip in wording, referring in this context to the idea that "a theory ... is much wider than any of the consequences deduced." In a later article he corrected "any" to read "any and all" (1964:736; later corrected in 1965a:1165).
46. See especially Machlup 1964; Garb 1965; A. P. Lerner 1965; and Massey 1965.
47. See above, page 140.
48. Samuelson 1965a:1165.

mechanisms, especially those with connotations of force or the transmission of energy.[49] Theories therefore proceed in terms of inference
based upon classification, with the rules of inference being those of set
theory or the syllogism. Precisely because this clash is over personal
beliefs, no amount of argumentation is likely to convince adherents to
the first point of view that the second is superior, and vice versa. What
also seems assured—and is evidenced repeatedly in the attacks upon
Samuelson—is that those who subscribe to the more conventional
cause-and-effect viewpoint will have difficulty grasping what it is that
Samuelson is denying when he equates description with explanation.[50]

What of the assumption that observable phenomena can be classified
into homogeneous sets? The feasibility of inference by classification in
practice depends upon the ability to implement the law of the excluded
middle. That law asserts that everything is either p or not p. As repeatedly emphasized in Chapters I and II, classifying diverse phenomena
into quasi-homogeneous sets is an excruciating and ongoing problem
in all disciplines. Nowhere are those problems more evident than in
those disciplines bent upon analyzing human behavior. But even in the
natural sciences, as Quine reminds us, "All is tentative, all admits to
revision—right down . . . to the law of the excluded middle" (1957:17).
What critics of Samuelson may have in mind when they assert that a
theory "is much wider than any of the consequences deduced"[51] are
difficulties associated with deciding the appropriate limits of a theory
when applying that theory to observable phenomena. If by "the full
consequences of a theory" one means "all conceivable applications,"
then full consequences are unlikely to be known. If they cannot be
known, they are unlikely to be viewed as being identical with the theory
itself.[52]

49. Friedman never once uses the word cause, but he does write of "forces," of billiard
players "making" balls move and sunlight "contributing" to the growth of leaves (1953:20,
21, 24). Samuelson avoids any reference to force in his three related articles, but on one
occasion he refers to "causality statements like those of classical mechanics" (1965a:1165).
For a discussion of the ambiguity in Friedman's approach to mechanism ideas, see
Nagel 1963a:218.
50. See, for example, Garb 1965; A. P. Lerner 1965; and Wong 1973.
51. Machlup 1964:733.
52. Samuelson's willingness to gloss over the difficulties of relating theory to fact
in many of his methodological statements would seem to explain why he objects to
Marshall's assertion, "It is obvious that there is no room in economics for long trains of
deductive reasoning." It was obvious to Marshall precisely because of these difficulties.
See Samuelson 1952:57–58; and Marshall 1952:637, 644.

In sum, the crucial methodological confrontations raised by Samuelson relate to semantics and personal beliefs. Samuelson's beliefs may be atypical, but they cannot be stigmatized as incorrect. Each social scientist must judge for himself whether or not they are acceptable, but the appropriate domain for those judgments is no wider than the individual who makes them.

8.   Summary and Conclusions

As noted at the outset of this chapter, economics is an engine of analysis, an apparatus of the mind consisting primarily of generalizations that trace interrelationships that often are not intuitively obvious to those lacking this apparatus. The achievements of the profession since Marshall's day include considerable alterations in the nineteenth-century machinery. The discovery of game theory, the elaboration of the neoclassical model, the development of input-output analysis, growth theories, and Keynesian macroeconomic models—these are but a few of the products of creative tinkering, restructuring, and invention of the past seven decades. The purpose of the engine, also as noted at the outset, is to enable the economist to explain, predict, and control observable phenomena. Here, too, the profession is not without its triumphs. The empirical legitimacy of theories can now be explored more effectively with the aid of computers, econometrics, and improved data collection. To review only the achievements discussed in sections 5 and 6, microeconomics will often permit accurate forecasts of the directional impact on price and quantity of prospective changes in various economic and policy variables; macroeconomic theory can now so guide national policy that the worst ravages of the business cycle should be forever buried in the past. These are, in turn, but highlights from a list of achievements which by the standards of any other social science are impressive in the extreme.

This chapter began, however, with a different focus. The controlling question was whether economic theory could match the theory of mechanics in the accuracy of its associated generalizations. Within this frame of reference, its achievements appear singularly unimpressive. Likely tendencies linking causes and effects can often be predicted with a tolerable degree of accuracy, but about the precise magnitudes of these tendencies economic theory has almost no conclusions that will survive the acid test of repeated empirical testing. Almost a century ago

Marshall summarized the general problems that still confound attempts to make the discipline more precise: "The forces of which economics has to take account are more numerous, less definite, less well known, and more diverse in character than those of mechanics; while the material on which they act is more uncertain and less homogeneous" (1952:637). In terms of the framework developed in Chapter I, this statement emphasizes the difficulties in converting the flux of observable economic phenomena into homogeneous sets and in linking those sets in cause-and-effect relationships. At both stages—the formation of sets and the assembling of sets deemed relevant—the economist is ever conscious that his abstraction threatens to be excessive in the sense that the resulting generalization will predict tendencies only moderately well and exact magnitudes not at all well. One measure of the latter is the unsatisfactory record of large-scale econometric models. Another is the indeterminacy that surrounds the question of how closely a given economy approximates the marginal equivalences of the neoclassical competitive model. A third is the poverty in the extant literature concerning dynamic (vs. static) adjustment processes, despite the fact that such processes dominate most, if not all, observable economic phenomena.

Faced with empirical problems that, at best, admit only to approximate solutions, the economist who favors the elegance and precision of mathematics may drift ever further away from realism and ever more toward abstract theorizing. The general public is unlikely to welcome the results. Even in Cournot's day, that public evidenced impatience with "theories and systems" and called for a pragmatic political economy "such as will throw the light of experience on the important questions which are being agitated before the country" (1897:1). The signs are manifold that the profession is again drifting into irrelevancies. The charges of casual empiricism, of myopic specialization, of baroque mathematical refinements—these are but the tip of an iceberg of dissatisfaction well characterized by Kenneth Boulding as the suspicion that economics has been guilty, or is about to be guilty, of a "monumental misallocation of intellectual resources."[53] Perhaps most strident of all are the voices of radical economists who call for the resuscitation of those questions long since abandoned concerning the determinants

53. Boulding 1966a:12. For evidence of dissatisfaction in recent presidential addresses, see Galbraith 1973b; Leontief 1971; Hahn 1970:1–2; Phelps Brown 1972.

of social and political systems and their interaction with the production and distribution of economic goods. A sympathetic echo, softer in tone but similar in implication, can be heard from institutionalists who note the potential narrowness of focusing exclusively upon quantifiable variables and mathematical relationships. Surely, they argue, the great issues of the day cannot be broached unless the intellectual boundaries of the profession are extended beyond confines such as these.

The economic historian can hardly be a disinterested observer of such debates. A distinctive characteristic of the newer breed of economic historian is a willingness to apply economic theory as a tool for unraveling the causal forces of the past. The strengths and weaknesses of that tool are easily summarized from all that has gone before. Economic theory can often successfully reveal the directional tendencies of causal interactions. As a tool for discovering the precise numerical magnitudes of these interactions, however, its limitations are far more impressive than its accomplishments. And yet it is for the second purpose—the specification of precise magnitudes—that economic theory is frequently employed in newer approaches to historical problems. Can this engine of analysis achieve in historical studies what it so seldom achieves in contemporary work? And what criteria can be used to detect failure once the iron discipline of comparing forecasts with accomplished fact is irretrievably removed? Last but by no means least, how can one judge the validity of numerical conclusions generated by counterfactual speculation harnessed to precisely specified equations portraying economic relationships, when counterfactuals by their very nature concern developments in a world that never was? These are the controlling themes of Chapter V. Before they can be examined, the nature of that other tool of historical analysis—counterfactual speculation—must be explored in some detail. The latter is therefore the subject of Chapter IV.

IV Counterfactual Speculation in History, Economics, and the New Economic History

> An historian cannot do what a scientist might do, that is repeat the whole process after having abstracted one, or more, of the factors to see whether the result in such case would be the same. He cannot unscramble the eggs of history in order to make up his mind which of them spoiled the taste of the dish that had to be eaten.
>
> —G. Kitson Clark[1]

1. Introduction

Few aspects of the new economic history have produced such a storm of protest as its enthusiastic endorsement of counterfactual speculation. Most of its practitioners seem to argue that any causal statement implicitly or explicitly involves a counterfactual statement.[2] In asserting that C was the cause of E, surely one must mentally think of the difference that C made, and that is equivalent to comparing the situation with and without C. These economic historians are therefore not playing a different game from other historians who attempt causal explanations. They are merely being more honest about the rules. If correct, this argument could undermine much of historical explanation. Counterfactual speculation according to most historians is virtually impossible when one attempts to deal with the major causal forces of the past.[3] How can one know what Europe would have been like without the religious bigotry of the sixteenth century, or the political upheavals of the eighteenth century, or even without Napoleon's defeat at Waterloo? History, they argue, is a "seamless web," that metaphor presumably designed to indicate that its causal forces are intertwined

1. Clark 1967:22–23.
2. See, for example, Cochran 1969:1568; Davis 1971:110; Fogel 1967:285; Green 1968:111–112; North 1968a:470. For a notable exception to this view, see Gerschenkron 1968:51–53.
3. Conflicting views are not impossible to find. See, for example, H. S. Hughes 1960:29.

in complicated and often unknowable ways. One cannot therefore mentally remove one of them and speculate about the residual.

Both positions reflect a serious misunderstanding of the issues. Practitioners of the new economic history are wrong to assert that causal analysis necessarily involves counterfactual speculation. Nor do they appear to grasp, or grasp fully, the profound epistemological problems of such speculations. The historians' sins are of a different order. Frequently they condemn the use of counterfactuals and then proceed to use them. Those who both condemn and never use them do not usually understand one or more of the following crucial points: (a) when a list of causes is presented, historians generally insist upon some weighing of the relative importance of those causes; (b) efforts to weigh relative importance usually involve counterfactual speculation; (c) this is the main reason why such speculation is used in the new economic history; (d) finally—and most important of all—if weighing of relative importance is not derived by counterfactual speculation, it is *extremely* difficult to specify how such weighing can be derived. The purpose of this chapter is neither to endorse nor to condemn the use of counterfactuals. Its sole objective is to lay bare the nature of the problems associated with their use. The starting point may seem oblique: a consideration of the perspectives of the layman and the philosopher as they ponder the legitimacy of counterfactual speculation. The historian and the economist will be heard from later on.

2.   Counterfactual Conditionals: Some General Problems

Understanding what is implied by counterfactual speculation at first glance may seem to be comparatively easy. The thought process in question is suggested by the longer variant "contrary-to-fact conditional." Speculation is of the "if . . . then . . . " variety, with the "if" clause, or antecedent, made deliberately false, or contrary to fact. "If Hitler had successfully invaded England, then Churchill would have been executed" might be one example. We know that Hitler did not invade England. Had he done so successfully, the above argument suggests unfortunate consequences for Sir Winston. But how do we know that Churchill would not have escaped? Or have lost his life in the defense of his country? Or committed suicide? In general terms, since counterfactual speculation by its very nature is concerned with events that never took place, how can we decide if the results of that speculation are correct or incorrect, or at least persuasive as against not persuasive?[4]

Enter the philosopher. His basic concern is that the usual truth function logic does not seem to be sufficient for an analysis of counterfactual conditional statements. He often begins to explain his difficulties with generalizations such as "All coins in John's pocket at time t were pennies."[5] This generalization suggests the counterfactual: "If a nickel had been in John's pocket at time t, then it would have been a penny." The layman, as is so often the case, is not puzzled at all. He simply points out that this particular generalization is "purely statistical," with no binding causal mechanism implied about what would have happened to coins inserted into John's pocket at time t, or at any other time for that matter. He might even go on to note that when a layman does use generalizations in support of counterfactual speculation, that speculation is often a condensed argument with many of the causal mechanisms not made explicit. In the Hitler example noted above, he would not feel obliged to spell out why Nazis took a dim view of Sir Winston's continued existence. He would assume a common knowledge about the history of World War II and a common belief in how nasty fellows behave when they capture someone whom they genuinely dislike.

If this is too complicated, the layman might add, consider the case of a match lying unlit on the table. (The philosopher should perk up at the mention of one of his favorite examples.) Surely it is reasonable to assert "If I had struck that match, then it would have lit." The reasonableness of this assertion stems from the belief that when oxygen is present (C_1), and the match head is dry (C_2), and the match is struck (C_3), then it will light (E). In ordinary conversation, one just assumes that the conditions C_1 and C_2 are present, hence the condensed argu-

4. In more technical language, the basic verification problem is that "a counterfactual by its nature can never by subjected to any direct empirical test by realizing its antecedent" (Goodman 1947:114).

5. See Mackie 1962:72. Another favorite starting point concerns the ambiguity in the following example. If one begins by noting that Bizet was French and Verdi was Italian, and then attempts the counterfactual beginning "If Bizet and Verdi had been compatriots," the rules of logic give no way of choosing between completing the sentence with "then Bizet would have been Italian" as against "then Verdi would have been French" (Mackie 1962:75). As Rescher has summarized this general problem, "Belief-contravening suppositions outrun the possibility of logical resolution because of their contextual ambiguity, which can only be removed by further information not available from the supposition itself" (1961:189).

ment "If C_3, then E." The philosopher, however, is still puzzled. The example under consideration links four factual observations: oxygen is present (C_1), the match head is dry (C_2), the match is not struck (not-C_3), and the match is not lit (not-E). If one of these is negated, or (not-C_3) is reversed to C_3, why, he asks, is the obvious inference to negate (not-E), or reverse it to E? Why not say, "If the match had been struck (C_3), then oxygen would not have been present (not-C_1)"?[6] Again the answer seems obvious to the layman. His causal law "If ($C_1 + C_2 + C_3$), then E" does not link the act of striking matches to the presence of oxygen but rather to the lighting of the match. Knowing what to change if (not-C_3) is reversed is as simple as understanding the nature of the causal law in question. The philosopher might then ask the layman to explain what a causal law is. And that—as noted elsewhere[7]—is anything but a simple question, even for a layman.

3. The Role of *Ceteris Paribus* in Counterfactual Speculation

Counterfactuals enter into historical analysis and into everyday discourse in at least two quite different ways. The first concerns causal analysis of fact, where counterfactual statements are used to underscore the importance of a particular causal factor that actually was operative in the situation under consideration. To cite but two fashionable examples, if slavery had not existed in America, then the Civil War would not have been fought; or alternatively, if railroads had not existed in America, then Gross National Product in 1890 would have been 5 percent less than it actually was. In both examples, the historian begins with the causal facts of the case, mentally removes one of those operative causal factors, and speculates about the residual in order to assess the importance of the factor mentally removed. Of this, more in section 5. The second type of counterfactual speculation is difficult to summarize other than to say it is not associated with causal analysis of fact. A frequently used procedure is mentally to add (rather than subtract) a particular causal factor and speculate about the impact which that mentally added factor might have had. If Hitler had invaded England, if the Greeks had discovered gunpowder, if Grant had been given command of the Northern army in 1862—these are the type of speculations involved.

6. See, for example, Mackie 1962:76–77.
7. See Chapter I.

Subsequent analysis will be concerned almost exclusively with the first of these—with counterfactual speculation only as a complement to causal analysis of fact. To understand the special epistemological problems raised by this usage of counterfactuals, one must first understand the role played by *ceteris paribus* in such speculation. Two examples will be explored, the first concerned with causal analysis of a discrete event (the lighting of a match); the second with causal analysis of a change in an economic variable (the quantity of beef demanded).

The first begins with a review of points made previously. If a philosopher observes a smoldering match and asks, "Why did it light?" and I reply, "Because I struck it," he would point out that I have used a condensed argument. The particulars of the case are explained by subsuming them under the causal generalization

If a match is struck, then it will light, *ceteris paribus*,

with the Latin phrase appended to encompass the fulfilling of all other relevant sufficient conditions (the presence of oxygen, and so on).

I might also say, perhaps with equal conviction, "If I had not struck the match, then it would not have lit." The philosopher would then note that I should be more cautious. After all, many factors can substitute for my striking action, not the least of which is his striking action. What I should have said therefore is, "If I had not struck the match, then it would not have lit, *ceteris paribus*." The Latin phrase is now used to preclude substitutes for the causal factor being mentally removed—my striking action.

This simple example illustrates two contrasting uses of *ceteris paribus*. In causal analysis of fact, that phrase is appended to causal laws to encompass the fulfilling of all other relevant but unspecified sufficient conditions. In counterfactual speculation that accompanies causal analysis of fact, the same phrase may be used to preclude all other substitutes for the causal factor being mentally removed. The presence of oxygen is important if the task is to explain the lighting of a match, but its prospective absence is of no concern if the task is to make a counterfactual assertion that links the absence of striking to the absence of ignition.

From the standpoint of economics, however, the match example is too simple. Consider the problem of explaining why the quantity of beef produced and sold in America in a given year increased by a specified amount. The economist might approach this problem with a model that explains increased demand in terms of falling beef prices and rising incomes. The model itself would describe the numerical responsiveness of the effect variable (the quantity demanded) to each of the cause variables (falling prices and rising incomes). Here too the phrase *ceteris paribus* would be appended to the explanatory model to encompass the fulfilling of all other relevant sufficient conditions, such as the absence of anarchy and the presence of a market.

The same model could then be used to solve for X in the counterfactual "If the price of beef had not fallen last year, then the quantity demanded would have been X pounds less than it actually was." This counterfactual is possible if and only if the economist can calculate the response of his effect variable to a revised collection of causes. Those causes must include all of the sufficient conditions not explicitly removed by the counterfactual—that is, all of the conditions buried in the *ceteris paribus* of the initial causal analysis—*and* all of the relevant substitution processes that would have developed in the absence of a price decline. The model will specify some of those likely substitution processes, but not all of them. The phrase "*ceteris paribus*" is then appended for a second reason: to exclude all substitution processes except those explicitly incorporated into the model. The main contrast with the match-striking example would seem to be this: the ignition case requires only enough information to justify a counterfactual about the absence of ignition, whereas in the beef example, the counterfactual requires sufficient information to calculate the prospective modification in an economic variable. In the second instance, the phrase *ceteris paribus* therefore has a dual role: to include all other unspecified sufficient conditions and to exclude all substitution processes except those indicated by the model being used to make the counterfactual estimate.

The general point of importance for subsequent discussion is that *if* the counterfactual statement involves the mental removal of a causal factor actually observed to operate, then (a) to that counterfactual statement must be appended the phrase "*ceteris paribus*," and (b) that phrase always has the function of precluding the occurrence of all substitution processes except those explicitly considered in the counterfactual. This need to preclude substitutes, or more correctly, this need to know about the prospective development of substitutes in a world minus the causal factor being mentally removed, will be found to be one of the special epistemological problems raised by the use of counterfactuals in economic history.

4.   Does Every Causal Statement of Fact Imply a Counterfactual?

The answer to this question is implicit in the foregoing discussion. If the goal of causal analysis of fact is merely to cite those factors whose occurrence made the subsequent occurrence of the effect probable, counterfactual speculation is not required. Suppose (to take that now familiar case) an historian returns home to find a match smoldering in the ashtray of his study. To his query of why it was lit he receives the reply, "Because your five-year-old son struck it on the table." Just before delivering the traditional lecture about playing with fire, he notices that the afternoon sunlight, focused through his reading glasses left on the study desk, is causing the area recently vacated by the match in question to become very hot. Whether that match would have been lit without the intervention of his son is, he realizes, far from a clear-cut issue. But on the subject of what caused that particular match to ignite on this occasion he has no doubts whatsoever. Hence the lecture on playing with fire.

As this example suggests, a conviction about "what did it" may be accompanied by no conviction whatsoever about what would have happened if the factors that "did it" had not occurred. In more general terms, causal explanation of observed facts requires only the following: (a) knowledge of, or belief in, a general regularity of the form

$$\text{Probably, if } (C_1, \ldots, C_n), \text{ then } E,$$

and (b) the judgment that the particular event to be explained is of type E and that the actual antecedents to this event are of types $(C_1, \ldots, C_n)$. The would-be explainer of such events does *not* need to know whether, if a particular C_1-type of antecedent had not occurred, a substitute C_1-type of event would have developed in its stead. He does need to know that among the actual antecedent events that did occur, a particular one does fill the bill as a C_1-type.[8]

8. An awareness of these problems may or may not lie at the heart of Redlich's distinction between hypothesis and figment (1965, 1968). The meaning of the latter term is not entirely clear, figment being used as synonymous with counterfactual; as equivalent to any "as if construct"; and finally as the end product of "a heaping of assumptions on

5. When Must Counterfactual Speculation Accompany Causal Analysis of Fact?

a. The Problem of Weighing Relative Importance

The type of example considered in section 4 is unlikely to appeal to the economist. Instead of a list of causal factors judged to be "not without influence," he prefers an estimate of how much influence each causal factor had. In an explanation of (say) why American iron output expanded in 1843, he wants some indication of how much of that expansion can be attributed to C_1 (railroad demand for iron rails), to C_2 (changing iron technology), and so on. The latter approach might be viewed as the economist's desire to measure marginal productivity writ large.

Historians tend to have similar preferences, although they usually are much less self-conscious about their ambitions and the procedures used to realize those ambitions. Once again the issue turns upon the acceptability of simple enumeration as an approach to causal explanation. Historians rarely settle for a list of relevant factors. They generally want some assessment of the relative importance of at least some of the causal factors on the list. Examination candidates who confront the question, "What were the causes of World War I?" cannot expect a high honor grade if they present only a list, however long that list may be and however correct the items on it. What is required is some "weighing" of the factors cited. Similarly, the professional historian whose written work features causal analysis that does not proceed beyond simple enumeration of relevant causes can expect from his colleagues such demeaning phrases as superficial or second-rate.[9]

The crucial question is therefore how relative importance is to be estimated. The historian's answer appears to be largely in terms of a comparison of the world that actually was with the world as it would have been minus the cause whose importance is to be scrutinized. In

---

assumptions," even when the assumptions in question relate to facts, not to counterfacts (1965:484–487; 1968:99–100; and his letter to Conrad, quoted in Conrad 1968:53 n. 27). Figments are distrusted by Redlich primarily because they lead to models, and models lead to a "one-sided exaggeration," "a distortion of reality" that is not history at all, but "quasi history" (1965:484, 489–492). All historical explanation would seem to be threatened with this same demeaning phrase, insofar as all causal explanation necessarily involves abstraction, and therefore distortion. The relevant question for economic models would seem to be whether the abstractions in question capture the main causal forces at work. If they do, the result is surely not quasi history but the real thing.

9. See, for example Carr 1961:116–117; Elton 1970:124.

short, assessment of relative importance is based upon counterfactual speculation. In terms of the cooking metaphor of Kitson Clark, the historian who asserts that unscrambling the eggs of history is impossible often attempts in the next paragraph, chapter, or book to assess relative importance by mentally unscrambling the observed ingredients, one by one, in order to judge how each affected the taste of the dish that was served up by their combined effects. The problem for this section is to decide whether all attempts to assess relative importance invariably require some form of counterfactual speculation. Three approaches to assessing relative importance will be considered: the historian's assessment in terms of what is and is not a necessary condition, or alternatively, in terms of how each causal factor affected the probability of the effect occurring, and the economist's assessment in terms of the quantitative contribution of each causal factor to the observed change in an economic variable.

b. The Historian's Weights: Changing Probabilities

The historian who would assess the relative importance of various causal factors must obviously decide (a) what the measure of importance is to be, and (b) how that measure is to be estimated. The special problems of estimating necessary conditions will be considered in the next section. The more general case would seem to be the estimation of changing probabilities. A given event, such as the outbreak of the American Civil War, will, in the first instance, always be explained as the result of a collection of causes $(C_1, \ldots, C_n)$, such as John Brown's raid, Lincoln's election in 1860, the firing upon Fort Sumter, and so on. The problem then becomes one of deciding the relative importance of at least some of the factors in the list $(C_1, \ldots, C_n)$. Most historians would probably agree that the election of Lincoln was more important than John Brown's raid. What does "more important" mean in this context?

Recall that causal explanations consist of subsuming facts under generalizations of the form

$$\text{Probably, if } (C_1, \ldots, C_n), \text{ then } E.$$

One possible measure of importance is to ask how the probability of E was changed by each of the causal factors cited. To say that C_1 was "more important" than C_2 would then imply that when C_1 occurred, the probability of E increased by more than it did when C_2 occurred. Notice that if the only measure of importance desired is a grouping of causal factors under the two headings "major" and "minor," then only the roughest estimate is required of the difference that occurrence of the causal factor made to the probability of the effect occurring. In the same spirit, if factor C_1 is judged to be more important than factor C_2, which is in turn considered to be more important than factor C_3, the implied judgment is that the first increased the probability of E more than the second and the second more than the third.

Counterfactual speculation enters this type of analysis as one obvious way to assess changing probabilities. A slightly more elaborate case of the match-striking example will help to illustrate why. Suppose, to return to the circumstances accompanying the lecturing of the five-year-old about playing with fire, that the following can be clearly established:

(1) at 10:30 A.M. the boy's mother unlocked the study door (C_1),

(2) at 11:00 A.M. the family cat entered through an open window in the study, and in doing so moved the reading glasses into a position on the study desk (C_2),

(3) the boy entered the study at 2 P.M. and struck the match shortly thereafter (C_3), and finally

(4) if the boy had not ignited the match, the afternoon sunlight focused through the reading glasses would have caused the match to ignite at 2:15 P.M. (C_4).

How important was the act of unlocking the door to the subsequent ignition of the match?

One possible approach is to ask how the odds of ignition were changed by the unlocking. At first glance, two different assessments appear to be possible. One might attempt to ask, just before the unlocking, what the prospects were for ignition, assuming perfect foresight. Alternatively, one might ask after ignition, what would have occurred if the door had not been unlocked. Although the would-be assessor seems to be choosing between two different points in time to make an estimate, both estimates come to the same thing because the phrase "perfect foresight" is merely a device for adding into the first assessment all of the relevant events that occurred between the first point in time and the second. Put another way, there is a symmetry between asking (a) By how much did the probability of E increase when

C_1 occurred (assuming perfect foresight)? and (b) How much less likely would the occurrence of E have been if C_1 had not occurred? The symmetry results from the point just made: that the supply of co-operating causes is made identical in both cases by assuming perfect foresight when trying to answer the first question.[10]

The contrived example of match striking illustrates that two kinds of information are required to estimate, by the technique noted, the relative importance of a given causal factor C_1 in terms of how it changed the probability of E:

(1) A knowledge of what other factors in the collection of relevant causes $(C_2, \ldots, C_n)$ were themselves caused by C_1. (In our example, C_3 was only possible because of C_1.)

(2) A knowledge of what processes, if any, would have substituted for C_1 and its effects if C_1 had not occurred. (In our example, C_2 and C_4 would have substituted for C_1 and C_3.)

The example itself may seem to have a curious structure. The cat's action plus sunlight and reading glasses could have substituted for unlocking and the boy's striking action, and the first set of causal factors were in fact replaced by the second set. This suggests that no single factor was important—a conclusion that may be taken as symptomatic of a defect in the previous reasoning. The defect, however, is not in the reasoning but in the expectation that in any causal process, some factors must always be very important. In a world of readily available substitutes, no single factor should appear to be of overwhelming significance. That is, after all, what is implied by the word "substitute."[11]

An alternative approach is possible that does seem to avoid the use of counterfactuals altogether. The historian might simply try to estimate the changing probability of the effect occurring as causes actually

10. The economist might view this problem as analogous to measuring marginal productivity. Marginal product is always joint product, with the marginal productivity of a given factor influenced by the supply of cooperating factors. The point about perfect foresight might therefore be viewed as an attempt to keep the supply of cooperating factors constant as the marginal product of each factor is assessed by removal, here the supply in question being all factors in operation when the effect occurred and the constancy consisting of that same collection of factors minus whatever cause is being scrutinized.

11. The Marxist's discounting of the importance of great men in history is a variant of this appeal to the ready availability of substitutes. Thus Georgi Plekhanov writes that if Robespierre had been accidentally killed in 1793, "his place would ... have been taken by somebody else, and although this person might have been inferior to him in every respect, nevertheless, events would have taken *the same course* as they did when Robespierre was alive" (1940:46).

happened, each cause being added in according to actual temporal sequence. Recourse to a few symbols will help to contrast the resulting procedure with the counterfactual approach. Let causes occurring at a later point in time be indicated by higher subscripts; that is, C_5 occurs after C_4. Assume (a) that effect E occurs at time $(t + n)$, and (b) that it is viewed as being the product of a list of causes

$$(C_1, \ldots, C_t, C_{t+1}, \ldots, C_{t+n}).$$

What is the relative importance of causal factor C_{t+1}?

One answer is to estimate the difference in the probability of two causal assertions:

Probably, if $(C_1, \ldots, C_t)$, then E,

and

Probably, if $(C_1, \ldots, C_t, C_{t+1})$, then E.

The estimated difference is then the contribution of C_{t+1} to the likelihood of E occurring. The counterfactual approach is to estimate the difference between yet another pair of causal assertions:

Probably, if $(C_1, \ldots, C_t, C_{t+1}, \ldots, C_{t+n})$, then E,

and

Probably, if $([C_1, \ldots, C_t, C_{t+1}, \ldots, C_{t+n}] - C_{t+1})$, then E.

The first approach differs from the second only in the supply of co-operating causal factors included with the one factor whose importance is to be assessed. The counterfactual assessment includes all those factors that actually did affect E except for C_{t+1} (and its associated effects) independent of temporal sequence. The alternative under consideration excludes all relevant causes that occurred after the occurrence of C_{t+1}.

The attractiveness of the latter is that it seems to require no counterfactual speculation. All that is required is knowledge concerning (a) the facts of the case, (b) how those facts can be subsumed under a probabilistic generalization, and (c) how the probability of the effect changes as different causal factors are added. Recall Marc Bloch's characterization of the historian's assessment procedure quoted in Chapter II: "When the historian asks himself about the probability of a past event, he actually attempts to transport himself, by a bold exercise of the mind, to the time before the event itself, in order to gauge its chances, as they appeared upon the eve of its realization" (1953:125). The present approach requires two bold exercises of the mind, one gauging the probability of E just before C_{t+1} occurred (for example, the probability of civil war just before Lincoln's election), and the second gauging the probability of E just after C_{t+1} occurred. The difference between the two would then be the change in the probability of E (civil war) that a contemporary observer might reasonably assign to causal factor C_{t+1} (Lincoln's election). Thus, the counterfactual approach might be viewed as being that assessment of changing probability that a contemporary observer with perfect foresight would have made as causes occurred; the alternative approach, as being the assessment that would have been made by a contemporary observer with whatever knowledge the historian deems reasonable.

The wording just used suggests that the first approach is a better approximation to the "true" impact on the probability of the effect occurring than is the second. The latter really concerns perceived probability changes, those perceptions being conditioned by what has actually occurred and forecasts based upon that knowledge and generalizations linking that knowledge to the effect in question. Note also that importance as measured by the second approach will be enormously conditioned by temporal ordering, because that ordering will determine the supply of cooperating causal factors. (Compare, for example, how important the cat's action in moving the reading glasses into position would seem to be according to this second approach, and how unimportant that action is according to the counterfactual approach.) Finally, importance will also vary depending upon whether or not one adds in with causal factor C_{t+1} those subsequent effects of C_{t+1} that are in turn causes of effect E. (Thus, for example, the importance of unlocking the study door will vary depending upon whether one adds with it the later effects of that unlocking.) The more subsequent effects are added in, the more the second approach begins to approximate the first approach using counterfactuals.

Which of these two possibilities will be preferred is, in the last analysis, a matter of taste. The first will be found to be preferred by economists for reasons that should be apparent once the relationship between model building and counterfactual speculation is clarified.

c. The Historian's Weights: Necessary Conditions

The historian may be tempted to argue that all of the foregoing misses the point. The main type of weighting, he may insist, is a comparison of necessary causes with other causes. Necessary conditions are important because they are indispensable. All other causes are less important because they are not indispensable.

Abundant evidence can be found to substantiate the claim that explanations couched in these terms have enormous appeal. As one distinguished practitioner of the craft put it, "The most satisfactory type of causal explanation in history simply tries to locate the factor which, when removed, would make the decisive difference in a given sequence of events—that is, the factor which, if thought away, would render the events in question inconceivable."[12] As noted in Chapter I, the word "necessary" is used in causal analysis in two different senses. The present usage differs from both, but is clearly meant to be an instance of that usage referring to indispensability. To review the logic: a given effect E can be produced by various collections of sufficient conditions. If a single cause C_1 is common to all possible collections, then C_1 is an indispensable cause in the sense that E is never observed to occur unless C_1 occurs. If one cannot know all possible collections of sufficient conditions for a given effect—and surely one cannot—then one cannot know which causes are common to all possible collections. Historians would seem to circumvent this logical difficulty with an assumption: that in the particular case being studied, whatever the list of possible substitutes for causal factor C_1 might be, none would have developed in the absence of C_1. What is offered as a necessary condition therefore is not that cause common to all possible collections of sufficient conditions for a given type of effect, but rather that cause for which substitutes are judged to have been unavailable in a particular setting. In practice, of course, the historian cannot "know" this to be the case, but he can express in these terms his judgments about the likelihood of substitutes developing.

This assessment technique contrasts sharply with the counterfactual approach of the previous section on one particular count. The previous approach required a judgment concerning the magnitude of the change in the odds of E occurring if C_1 had not occurred. The current approach

12. H. S. Hughes 1960:29.

requires only a judgment about absolute level: that the probability of E occurring in a world minus C_1 would have been zero. This wording underscores the point that the second approach, like the first, does require counterfactual speculation. One cannot judge a cause to be indispensable without some thoughts about what the world have been like if the indispensable had been dispensed with. What is generally not recognized is that to assess the importance of a cause in this manner requires counterfactual speculation which, by most standards, is venturesome in the extreme. Why this is so will be considered in more detail in section 6.

d. The Economist's Weights: Numerical Contribution

Economic analysis, as noted in Chapter III, is generally concerned with numerical effects: the price of bread, the quantity of iron produced, the value of goods imported. Like all effects, these are explained as the result of a given list of causes. The economist often attempts to gauge the relative importance of each one of those causes in terms of the net contribution of a given cause to the observed numerical change in the effect variable. Once again, counterfactual speculation will be found to be unavoidable.

Suppose, to fabricate some numbers, that the following facts have been established: (a) United States iron output increased by 100,000 tons per annum in 1843, (b) American imports and exports of iron were negligible at this time, and finally (c) a surge in New England railroad building in 1843 required 90,000 tons of iron for rails. Both economist and historian would presumably concede that the railraod building (C_1) was "not without influence" as a cause of the observed change in iron production (E). The economist, however, prefers to assess that influence in terms of the net contribution of C_1 to the observed change in E.

At first glance, that contribution appears to be 90 percent of a total of 100,000 tons. With a training that emphasizes the substitution patterns of economic theory, the economist instinctively resists such measures. From microeconomics he has learned that if increased railroad demand raised the price of iron, then into his assessment procedure must be incorporated the responses of other would-be users of iron to higher iron prices.[13] Numerical contribution can, of course, only be estimated

13. The response of supply price to increased demand is only one of a number of causal processes suggested by economic theory. Another is that if supply and demand

if causal relationships are expressed in numerical terms. This expression is possible only with some variant of the general technique outlined in Chapter III. That technique, to review, required three different steps: (a) the specification of suspected causal tendencies which were then incorporated into a model, (b) the relating of the theoretical constructs of the model to observed data, and (c) the use of that data and statistical techniques to make more specific the general tendencies specified in step 1. With the resulting model in hand the economist can then ask his own special variant of the question considered in the previous two sections: What would the effect on E have been if C_1 had not occurred? The only difference is that the effect is now a variable (the quantity of iron produced) and the impact of C_1 is estimated in terms of its numerical contribution to the observed change in E.

A numerical estimate, for all its aura of precision, is obviously not synonymous with truth. Several problems are particularly worrisome. All of them are endemic to any attempt to partition or weigh the relative importance of various causal factors. To confront such issues candidly is to raise the question whether counterfactual speculation of this sort is ever justified.

6. When Does Counterfactual Speculation Require Knowledge of the Unknowable?

The quotation at the beginning of this chapter suggests that at least one historian would respond to the question just noted with the one-word answer: Always. The curiosity is that historians—or at least most of the historians who attempt causal explanation—fluctuate between condemning counterfactual speculation as impossible and using that speculation in their efforts to assess the relative importance of causal factors. At least one reason for this inconsistency is their failure to maintain a sharp sense of when they are using counterfactual analysis and what they must know to justify its use. An example illustrating this general problem can be found in the heated exchange between Donald Coleman and Gary Hawke on the merits of old and new methods in economic history.[14]

---

curves have a conventional shape and the supply curve has not shifted, other factors besides railroad building have also shifted the demand curve for iron to the right. Otherwise the observed increase in total iron output would be less than the amount of iron taken by the railroads.

14. Hawke 1971; and D. C. Coleman 1971.

Coleman begins by linking in convincing style three distinct historical events (1969): (a) the dominance of the new draperies in the southern Netherlands during the latter half of the sixteenth century, (b) the exodus of Protestants from that area because of religious bigotry and military violence, and (c) the diffusion of new draperies within England after the arrival of these migrating Protestants. The behavioral assertions seem eminently reasonable, and the hypotheses seem consistent with the historical evidence. Something of a red flag is then waved in the direction of the newer breed of economic historian: "Just how far and how rapidly the manufacture of the lighter fabrics would have become established had religious bigotry and military violence not led to the celebrated diaspora of Protestants from the southern Netherlands is one of the many 'counterfactual' questions to which econometric ingenuity is unlikely to provide any answer different from a guess" (1969:426).

A shortage of data on such variables as migration, output, and prices would indeed seem to make the task of estimating the parameters of an econometric model unfeasible. Coleman nevertheless seems to anchor much of his agnosticism on a different rock. A sixteenth- and seventeenth-century world without its major acts of religious intolerence he finds impossible to reconstruct mentally with any degree of precision (1971:260). Exit counterfactual speculation, or so one would think. And yet the author himself is prepared to assert that "without the disasters, diffusion would surely have been slower, though it would still have occurred" (1969:426). If a Europe minus religious bigotry is truly impossible to imagine, then the diffusion of new textiles within that Europe must also be impossible to imagine. One cannot rule out counterfactual speculation and then proceed to engage in precisely the kind of speculation declared off limits.

When should it be declared off limits? Recall that all of the foregoing relates to a special use of counterfactuals. Our major concern has been causal analysis of fact, and counterfactuals enter only because of the desire to assess the relative importance of different causal factors observed to operate in a given historical situation. The knowledge required for such an exercise has been outlined in section 5. To assess the contribution of a single factor C_1 (for example, the unlocking of the study door) by asking the question, "By how much would the probability of E have fallen if C_1 had not occurred?" one needs to know: (a) what other factors on the list of causes of E were themselves caused by C_1, and (b) what substitution processes, if any, would have developed if C_1 and its associated effects had not occurred.

As discussed in section 2, the general epistemological problem with contrary-to-fact conditionals is that by their very nature they cannot be verified by realizing their antecedent (the "if" clause). In the present usage, that antecedent concerns the removal of a causal factor that did in fact occur. (In section 2 the counterfactual was posed, "If Hitler had invaded England, then Churchill would have been executed." The current problems are analagous to asking what would have happened if Hitler had not invaded Russia.) As is true of all counterfactuals, causal generalizations are used to guide or control such speculation. The economist and historian use their knowledge of relevant causal processes to trace the likely results of removal. The difficulty with assessing the relative importance of many of the causal forces that did occur in history is that those causal processes often appear to be extremely complex. The would-be counterfactual speculator therefore remains uncertain as to what should be mentally removed in addition to the single causal factor whose importance is to be assessed, uncertain as to the impact of that removal upon the development of substitute causal factors, and uncertain as to the likely impact of those substitutes upon the effect being studied. In section 5b counterfactual assessment was characterized in terms of comparing the probabilities of two different statements:

Probably, if $(C_1, \ldots, C_t, C_{t+1}, \ldots, C_{t+n})$, then E,

and

Probably, if $([C_1, \ldots, C_t, C_{t+1}, \ldots, C_{t+n}] - C_{t+1})$, then E.

The present difficulties concern problems of knowing what to subtract along with C_{t+1}, how that subtracting affects the remaining causal variables in the set, and finally what probability one should use to signify the relationship between this amended set of causes and the effect E.

Notice how sharply this contrasts with the causal analysis of section 4. There is an *enormous* difference between (a) attempting to identify some of the causal factors that actually contributed to an observed effect, and (b) attempting to specify what the world would have been like minus one of the causes that actually did occur. The first requires only the ability to identify *some* of the relevant antecedents. The second requires an ability to specify the likely relationship between a changed set of antecedents and their consequent. To cite but one example, identifying slavery as a cause of the American Civil War is a different assignment from specifying what America would have been like if slavery had not existed.

Notice further that all such specifications are guided or controlled by causal generalizations that are *always* probabilistic in structure; that is, of the form

Probably, if . . . , then . . . .

This type of counterfactual speculation will therefore always have an amorphous aspect because the linkage between causal antecedents and their effect has an amorphous aspect indicated by the use of the word "Probably." J. D. Gould has therefore greatly *understated* the complexity of this thought process when he writes, "We cannot suppose a non-X past without also banishing from that past all W, where X is a necessary cause of W; all Y, where Y is a sufficient cause of X; and all Z, where Y is a sufficient cause of X and a necessary cause of Z. And our knowledge of how things were related in fact may be inadequate to enable us to identify all W, Y, and Z" (1969:201). Our knowledge of how things are related *never* allows us to identify sufficient conditions; that is, that cause or collection of causes that leads inexorably to a given effect.

Again the historian may argue that the foregoing discussion misrepresents the basic problem. Slavery is a necessary condition for the American Civil War, he may insist, because the phrase "the coming of the Civil War" refers to the exact events, in all their manifold detail, leading up to Fort Sumter. This is equivalent to saying that the five-year-old's striking action was a necessary condition for the lighting of the match because the effect to be explained includes such characteristics as the exact moment of ignition, and if the effect is defined in these narrow terms, sunlight focused through reading glasses would not have acted as a substitute. In more general terms, the more detail that is incorporated into the effect to be explained, the less likely will it be that substitutes would have been developed for an effect so defined. The problem of estimating substitutes is therefore resolved—at least to the satisfaction of the historian—not by estimating those substitutes, but merely by making any substitution process less likely through the proliferation of detail in the effect to be explained.

This approach encounters at least two major difficulties. One is that the more detail added—or the less detail abstracted out—the more difficult it becomes to subsume the effect under any generalization or collection of generalizations. And causal explanation is possible if and only if some subsumption is possible. The other difficulty is that proliferation of detail may convert every causal factor into a necessary condition—a consequence that most historians would seem to resist. If they entertain causal explanation at all, they evidence a marked preference for variability in the importance of associated causes. A typical assessment is the following: "Contrasted with the accidents—assassination at Sarajevo, Austrian ultimatum—which explain the exact moment when war began, are the underlying causes (domestic difficulties in the Austro-Hungarian Empire, German imperialism, French thirst for revenge, the Anglo-German rivalry) which account for the very possibility of a European war."[15] What characteristics are to be included if the effect to be explained is something called "the outbreak of World War I"? If those characteristics do *not* include the exact moment when war began, then the Sarajevo assassination is not likely to appear to the historian as a necessary condition in the sense that without it the effect to be explained could not possibly have occurred. If instead those characteristics are made extremely time specific, then the more specific they are made, the more likely is that assassination to appear as a cause for which substitutes would have been unlikely to have developed.

The approach just outlined is attractive for one obvious reason. When the weighing of relative importance requires counterfactual speculation, that speculation requires knowledge about likely substitution processes in the world minus a given cause, and specifying the nature of such a world may be judged to be next to impossible, if not blatantly impossible. These problems are circumvented—or more correctly, the illusion is created that they have been circumvented—if the effect is described in such detail that the issue of substitutes is made to appear irrelevant. The economist encounters similar problems, but his attempt at circumvention is different.

15. Aron 1961:21.

Consider again the railroad building/iron production example outlined in section 5d. One of the builders might have had a genius for improving iron production. If not building railroads, he might have devised a new technology for the iron industry which would also have caused a surge in iron production. If we cannot know for certain whether this would have occurred in a world minus railroad building—and surely we cannot—then how can we possibly assess the *net* contribution of railroad building to the observed expansion in iron production?

The common device for circumventing such problems is to append *ceteris paribus* to any counterfactual assessment based upon a model that ignores such possibilities. As noted in section 3, the function of the Latin phrase is to preclude all substitution processes except those explicitly incorporated into the model in question. As repeatedly stressed elsewhere, however, this particular Latin phrase more often than not is a convenient device for disguising our ignorance. Any counterfactual speculation employing *ceteris paribus* to assess relative importance is, on close inspection, merely asserting that the resulting measure of importance is the correct measure, unless other ignored factors make it the incorrect measure. The problem for the economist might therefore be expressed as a question. Under what circumstances is the appending of *ceteris paribus* to counterfactual speculation justified? Or, when is the economist justified in asserting that causal factors other than those incorporated into his model were of trivial importance?

Another way to approach the same issue is to note the inevitable difficulties in interpreting the results of econometric models of the sort described in Chapter III. These models are designed to give numerical estimates of the sensitivity of a given effect, E, to variations in a given cause, C_1. Their numerical estimates can then be used to trace how that effect would have been altered if variations that did occur in C_1 had not occurred. The resulting magnitude is then taken to be the measure of the contribution of the actual variation in C_1 to the actual variation in E. In the case of the railroad building example cited earlier, the effect is the observed increase in iron production (100,000 tons), the cause variable is the amount of iron used for railroad building in 1843 (90,000 tons), and the estimates of numerical sensitivities include (a) how the supply price of iron responded to the changing demand for iron, and (b) how the demand by other users of iron responded to rising iron prices. Counterfactual speculation can then be combined with such a model to trace the change in supply price and the associated change in demand for iron by other iron users if railroads had not been built in 1843. The difference between this hypothetical iron output and actual iron output of 1843 then measures the net contribution of railroad building to the observed increase in iron production.

The foregoing merely summarizes the mechanics of counterfactual speculation using an economic model. Assessment of the legitimacy of the technique centers upon how one can be sure that the numerical sensitivities indicated by a particular model are reasonably good estimates of the true sensitivities. Several points noted in Chapter III are worth repeating. All such estimates are appropriately viewed as falling within certain confidence intervals, however those estimates are derived. The confidence intervals thrown up by econometric techniques are no better than the assumptions used to calculate them. For reasons outlined in Chapter III, these assumptions are unlikely to be viewed by the practicing economist as anything but a rough approximation for the reality that he would explain. Consider, for example, the assumption that all systematic influences have been incorporated into the model. Even the most ardent advocate of model building is likely to concede that this is not strictly true. The best he can hope for is that omitted influences are trivial.

Two inferences follow. The first is that once a seemingly precise numerical estimate is converted into the range implied by its associated confidence interval, assessment of the relative importance of a given causal factor may be sharply modified. At best, one may end up with a list of "major" and "minor" causes. The second inference is that one can—and should—always ask a variant of the question noted previously: Are omitted variables likely to have been trivial? Or, in a more general context: When is the economist justified in asserting that his economic model is a useful approximation to reality?

No answer seems possible beyond a handful of trite generalizations. The more simple the causal process under study; the fewer causal forces of obvious relevance ignored; the shorter the time period; the smaller the changes considered; the more the analysis turns upon the specification of rough magnitudes rather than exact magnitudes—in every case, the more the resulting causal explanation and associated counterfactuals are likely to be judged reasonable by economists and historians alike. As innocuous as these rules of thumb may seem to be, debates concerning their possible violation are likely to be a characteristic of the profession for the foreseeable future. The economic historian is often concerned with the long run; the institutionalist, with complex causal mechanisms; the newer breed of economic historian, with establishing precise magnitudes. Their resulting models and associated counterfactuals are therefore destined frequently to strain (although not necessarily rupture) the bonds of credibility. Which brings us by a circuitous route to one of the central tasks of this book: the brief elaboration and assessment of some of the explanatory mechanisms now fashionable with practitioners of the new economic history.

V Causal Explanation and Model Building in the New Economic History*

> Of all varieties of history the economic is the most fundamental. Not the most important: foundations exist to carry better things. How a man lives with his family, his tribe or his fellow-citizens; the songs he sings; what he feels and thinks when he looks at the sunset; the prayers he raises—all these are more important than the nature of his tools, his trick of swapping things with his neighbours, the way he holds and tills his fields, his inventions and their consequences, his money—when he has learnt to use it—his savings and what he does with them.
>
> —John H. Clapham[1]

As the quotation from Sir John Clapham suggests, economic history is concerned with production and distribution through time.[2] These are the explananda: the phenomena to be explained. What techniques should be used in attempting that explanation has been a subject of lively debate within the profession for over a decade. A revolution is not so much under way as a *fait accompli*, comprised mainly of new devices for attacking old problems.[3] The first question to be examined is what is new in the "new economic history." The second concerns the extent to which novelty has been synonymous with progress. Two obvious caveats must preface such a discussion. No single work can hope to survey thoroughly a literature which is not only vast, but expanding at the speed of the printing press. It follows that generalizations about dominant trends, past and future, will always do violence

---

*A shorter version of this chapter appeared in the *American Behavioral Scientist* 16 (1972), 631–651, Copyright © 1973 by Sage Publications, Inc.

1. Clapham 1957:Introduction.

2. Defining economic history is as simple as defining economics and then adding a time subscript. For possible definitions, see Chapter III, section 1. The term "business history," first coined in the 1920's, has "to date . . . been primarily concerned with the written record of decision making by individuals seeking private profit through production of goods and services" (Hidy 1968:474). A more recent variant, "business in history," has been concerned with "understanding the economic, political, and social causes and results of the actions of businessmen and their organizations" (Baughman 1971:313).

3. For one of the few dissenting voices on the subject of whether a revolution has taken place, see G. R. Taylor 1970:36. More representative of the profession are the views expressed in Andreano 1965c:3; and North 1963:128.

to some of the major contributions in the field. The objective of this chapter is therefore quite modest: to outline, primarily for the benefit of the noneconomist, some of the new analytical devices now being employed by specialists in a social science which, whether dismal or not,[4] does show signs of becoming esoteric.

1. The Road Ahead and the Road Behind

Long and tortured though the road behind may seem to be, familiarity with the issues encountered there will be indispensable for understanding and assessing the techniques of the new economic history. On the road ahead will be found mainly causal explanations embedded in economic models, the models in turn often combined with counterfactual speculation to assess the relative importance of various causal forces observed to operate in a particular historical setting. All three phrases—causal explanation, model building, and counterfactual speculation—should alert the reader to issues raised in previous chapters. The controlling themes of this book have been, and will remain, the uncertainty of knowledge and the unity of method in the causal explanations of all disciplines. The techniques of the new economic history are merely cases in point, as are the problems encountered in attempting to implement those techniques. Some review would therefore seem in order under headings which, by now, should be predictable: causal explanation, model building, and counterfactual speculation.

Causal explanations in the twentieth century tend to focus upon efficient causation and thus are governed by its central tenet: similar cause, similar effect. The resulting explanations consist of subsuming specific facts under generalizations that link causes (C) to effects (E) in statements of the general form

$$\text{Probably, if } (C_1, \ldots, C_n), \text{ then } E.$$

4. Sir John Clapham, for one, would resist such epithets: "Economic activity, with its tools, fields, trade, inventions and investment, is the basement of man's house. Its judicious structure and use have, in course of ages, provided, first for a privileged few and then for more, chances to practice high arts, organize great states, design splendid temples, or think at leisure about the meaning of the world. . . . The economic basement may be dull, but need not be. A patch of earth dug level, a right stroke with a felling axe, a neat bit of welding, a locomotive brought smoothly to rest, even a tidy balance sheet or a quick calculation in forward exchange, all yield the craftsman's, not to say the artist's, satisfaction" (1957:Introduction).

Why the word "Probably" is invariably needed to characterize the relationship between antecedents and their consequent has been discussed at length in Chapters I, II, and III. Once that requirement is recognized, the reader is inexorably led to several insights vital to understanding all methodological discussions of causation. Causal explanations cannot be deductive in form; that is, with all generalizations prefaced with the word "Probably," they can never be characterized as explanations derived by deductive inference from universal causal generalizations known to be universal. (As discussed at length in Chapter I, universal generalizations, to be universal, must be prefaced with the word "Always" or the word "Necessarily".) The methodological writings of those who fail to grasp this point, such as Hempel and Scriven,[5] are likely to be confused and a source of further confusion. More important, once this point is grasped, a central aspect of causal explanation—and a central theme of this book—emerges with startling clarity: the uncertainty accompanying all such explanations.

All this concerns the first phrase noted previously: causal explanation. The nature of model building in economics has been explored in Chapter III. From a set of axioms the economist can derive, by deductive inference, conclusions that may well offer insights into the nature of empirical reality, but—and the qualifying clause is all-important—once his task is to explain observable phenomena, the point just made comes to bear with irresistible force. Those premises in his axiomatic system that are causal generalizations can no longer be universal in form, but must instead be converted into the probabilistic form cited in the previous paragraph. Although originating primarily from economic theory, the causal generalizations employed by the economic historian will also be conditioned by the more general considerations raised in Chapter II. Whenever the problem is to explain human behavior, an indispensable input in formulating dispositional hypotheses will be that collective tribunal that is the would-be explainer's knowledge, experience, and beliefs concerning human behavior, including the knowledge of introspection—perhaps especially the knowledge of introspection. Whenever the problem is to explain economic behavior, the economist may venture as a first approximation the type of dispositional hypotheses considered in Chapter III: that

5. See Chapter II, sections 6b and 6e.

decision makers have a "rational" preference structure and seek to maximize utility if they are consumers or profits if they are businessmen.

The models of the new economic history, like all economic models, are powerful explanatory devices; in part because of their internal consistency; in part because, combined with statistical techniques, they can assure consistency between available data and the causal assertions embedded in the model; in part because they may facilitate the derivation of conclusions not intuitively obvious from the outset. One model in particular will be found to be lurking in many of the explanations that lie ahead. Few inferences in economic history based upon observed price data are possible without assuming that at least some of the marginal equivalences implied by the neoclassical model have been achieved, or achieved to a tolerable degree, in the competitive situation being analyzed. As noted in Chapter III, this same assumption pervades much of applied economics. Its use in historical analysis is merely one instance of a more general tendency within the discipline.

One phrase remains: counterfactual speculation. The reasons for its use and the associated dangers have been outlined in Chapter IV. If a central objective is to assess the relative importance of different causal factors in terms of their net contribution to the observed change in an economic variable, such as a rise in GNP or an increase in iron output, then the economist turned historian has no alternative but to engage in counterfactual speculation. The relationship between all three phrases should now be clear. This type of counterfactual speculation requires the construction of an economic model. The model, in turn, is a particular type of causal explanation, comprised (like all causal explanations) of probabilistic generalizations linking causes and effects in a system which (perhaps unlike many causal explanations) is internally consistent in terms of the assertions made.

The dangers should by now also be clear. One of the striking features to emerge from previous chapters is that only a handful of caveats are important in these matters, but to ignore any of them is to imperil our ability to understand and assess any causal explanation, including those that lie ahead. First and foremost is the realization that the phrase *ceteris paribus* is generally a device for disguising our ignorance—for converting probabilistic generalizations into seemingly universal generalizations, for converting tentative counterfactuals into seemingly precise counterfactuals. Secondly, we must be ever conscious that the mathematical elegance and numerical magnitudes of any given economic model may bestow an aura of scientific precision upon what is, in fact, tentative and imprecise. Hard upon this second caveat comes a third: the importance of keeping ever to the fore the fundamental reasons for this tentativeness—the incompleteness in the list of relevant causes considered in the model, the imperfections in the data upon which the parameters of that model are based, and the confidence intervals that accompany those numerical parameters precisely because our knowledge is imperfect. This tentativeness in turn implies that efforts to weigh the relative importance of causal factors by harnessing counterfactual speculation to an economic model can never yield precise numerical estimates appropriately viewed as precise, but only estimates of relative importance that are accompanied by all the uncertainties and associated confidence intervals of the model from which they spring.

From these considerations a single question emerges to dominate our future thoughts. All economic models, like all causal explanations, are intrinsically imperfect. But how much imperfection is too much? In attempting to find answers, the reader again does well to recall precautionary notes from previous chapters. Criteria for adequacy are, in the last analysis, determined by personal preferences, not scientific debate. We may discuss what licenses a given inference, but we would be hard pressed to say what licenses the license. The hope for a definitive resolution of all debates concerning the adequacy of models about to be discussed is therefore an ideal that must be jettisoned from the start. But where to begin, and how to proceed? As repeatedly emphasized in previous chapters, the adequacy of any hypothesis turns upon consistency: not merely the internal consistency of the causal assertions being made, but equally important, consistency between all available evidence and the hypotheses being advanced. One obvious test for the second type of consistency is to compare the assumptions of the economic model employed by the historian with available historical evidence. This technique flies in the face of a methodological precept often associated with the name of Milton Friedman: that a model's assumptions cannot be tested, or should not tested, in this manner. That precept is, however, patently absurd for reasons developed at length in Chapter III. Casting it aside is crucial for the historian, given his incapacity to verify the adequacy of his explanatory models by comparing forecasts derived from those models with subsequent events.

Buried in this last point is perhaps the most agonizing question of all. Modern applied economics, as sketched in Chapter III, has achieved but limited success in developing explanatory models that will predict, with great precision, future economic events. The inadequacies of these models are readily apparent precisely because of their undistinguished prediction records. But what of economic model building designed to explain the past? If electronic computers make relatively easy the task of devising models that "fit" with great statistical precision a collection of economic data from a particular era, and if the acid test of comparing forecasts with subsequent events is irretrievably lost, what then can take its place? Perhaps the only possible answer is the one noted previously: to seek for consistency, or the best consistency possible, between hypothesis and all relevant evidence. What should be obvious, but is almost never made obvious, is that no criteria seem to be available to resolve the principal type of dispute that now rages between old and new practitioners of economic history. The latter, with ingenuity, economic theory, and computers, devise explanatory models which, by various statistical tests, fit well the data of historical experience. The former then note the "glaring inadequacies" of these models, by which they seem to mean their neglect of many relevant causes, or at least of many causes believed to be relevant. How can this question of adequacy be resolved? Upon the road ahead, this will be found to be among the most formidable of burdens because—for all its importance—it is not easily resolved and laid aside.

The structure of subsequent discussion follows the logic implicit in these introductory remarks. The question of what is new in the new economic history is examined in section 2, the principal contenders being the use of quantification, economic theory, and statistical techniques. Section 3 attempts to lay bare the key assumptions of some of the specific analytical tools of the new economic history. The adequacy of general tools—quantification, mathematics, and economic theory—are considered in section 4, and the issue of the correspondence between historical evidence and the assumptions sketched in section 3 is then taken up in section 5. Summary thoughts and conclusions are appended in section 6.

2.   What Is New in the New Economic History?

To begin: what is new? The very presence of dispute in American economic history is something of a novelty. In the 1920's and '30's the atmosphere was mundane, if not soporific. N. S. B. Gras repeatedly complained about the lack of distinguished treatises and the absence of controversy (1927:29; 1931:327). "The subject," he concluded, "has no intellectual resilience" (1927:29). *The Journal of Economic and Business History* which began in 1928 collapsed four years later for want of funds. A successor appeared in 1941 with the founding of the Economic History Association (*The Journal of Economic History*), but the milieu of the '40's was hardly more promising. Arthur Cole surveyed the state of current research and found it largely at a standstill;[6] Herbert Heaton berated his colleagues for failing to make their subject matter live (1942:742); and as late as 1947, Thomas Cochran repeated the now-familiar complaint, "No new schools of thought built around the work of any great American economic historians have as yet appeared" (1947:20).

This final challenge was answered almost immediately. In January of 1949 the first edition of *Explorations in Entrepreneurial History* was published, its title indicating the school of thought that would come to dominate the 1950's. Success and vitality were apparently at hand. By 1960 a former editor of *Explorations* could conclude that economic history had gained an enviable respect and prestige among the members of the historical profession.[7] With a note of regret he added that its linkage with economic theory remained tenuous, many economic historians knowing "little economic theory and [finding] no use for what they do know."[8]

How curious that latter statement appears today. *Explorations in Entrepreneurial History* (second series) is now entitled *Explorations in Economic History*. Schumpeterian entrepreneurs have all but vanished from its pages before an onslaught of equations, correlation coefficients, and partial derivatives. Similar recondite symbols dominate every other major periodical in the field. The founding fathers of this new wave are,

6. See Aitken 1965a:5, referring to Cole 1944.
7. Aitken 1960:88.
8. Aitken 1960:87. The linkage between economic theory and business history was (and still is) even more tenuous. For discussions of the limited ability of the latter either to generate or to apply generalizations, see Hidy 1968:478; and Galambos 1966:3.

first and foremost, professional economists. To their banners have rallied younger colleagues armed with matrix algebra, simulation techniques, and whatever other slings and arrows can be borrowed from the pure theoretician. The resulting cerebral blitzkrieg has been, for most historians, largely unintelligible and not a little disconcerting. Even older members of this new guard, as they survey their protégés at cliometrics gatherings, must occasionally be tempted to echo Wellington's sentiments on the eve of Waterloo: "I don't know what effect these troops will have on the enemy, but they frighten me."

The timing of the initial transformation remains obscure. It has been variously dated from seminal articles appearing in 1955, 1957, or 1958.[9] The accompanying debate is reminiscent of those attempts to date the inauguration of the clipper ship era from the launching of a single vessel. A major evolution in design takes time, although in retrospect the intellectual transformation was accomplished with startling rapidity. By the middle of the 1960's a mere handful of architects had restructured the craft of economic history and provocatively reclassified their blueprints "cliometrics."[10] This neologism presumably was meant to signify the marriage of Clio, the muse of history, with that modern deity, Measurement. Historians of more conventional bent were quick to suggest a relationship less flattering—and less voluntary—than a marriage.[11] The union, however, was here to stay.

In its wake have come the predictable spate of articles endeavoring to define, clarify, or denigrate its novel aspects, multiple changes being rung on three controlling themes: (a) the use of economic theory in general and model building in particular, (b) the reliance upon quantification to buttress those models with historical data, and (c) the use of statistical theory, econometrics, and the computer to combine models with data in a single consistent explanation. All three would seem to be integral parts of the cliometrician's methodology. But are they new?

The use of economic theory in historical analysis is at least as old

9. The principal contenders are Meyer 1955; Davis 1957; Lovell 1957; Meyer and Conrad 1957; and Conrad and Meyer 1958. The slavery article by Conrad and Meyer is by far the most popular for dating the inception of the new economic history, more it would seem because of its subject matter than because of its initiation of new methodological devices.

10. The term was apparently coined by S. Reiter, with authorship for the more modest phrase "new economic history" belonging to J. R. T. Hughes. (See Davis 1968:75; and J. R. T. Hughes 1965:154.)

11. Even less flattering perhaps was Scheiber's suggested modification of cliometrician to cliomagician (1967:383).

as Adam Smith's *Inquiry into the Nature and Causes of the Wealth of Nations*. What is too often ignored by those who would emphasize continuity with the past is that the extensive use of economic theory in historical analysis by a large body of competent theoreticians is very much a development of postwar years. Its previous neglect was not only fashionable, but supported by most of the great scholars of the day. William Ashley, for example, believed that economic history required little more than "plain common sense" (1893:127), with a seconding vote from no less an authority than Alfred Marshall: "not very much analysis is essential; and most of what is needed may be supplied for himself by a man of active and inquiring mind" (1952:639). Sir John Clapham went further. Economic theory, he argued, was not only unnecessary but irrelevant.[12] Its theoretical constructs were comprised mainly of "empty boxes" of little use in the analysis of observable phenomena. His scant reliance upon those constructs in his monumental *Economic History of Modern Britain* set the tone—or at least mirrored the sentiments—of a generation. Eli Heckscher's famous "Plea for Theory in Economic History" (1929) was therefore destined to fall, if not upon deaf ears, at least upon those hard of hearing. Small wonder that a distinguished economic theoretician from the same era would observe that prior to Keynes's *General Theory*, "there was almost no link between history and theory except the now discredited interpretation of price movements in terms of the supply of gold."[13]

If widespread use of theory is comparatively new, widespread efforts at quantification are not. The latter, however, is very much a development of the twentieth century. About the relevance of economic theory Clapham had his doubts, but concerning the usefulness of numbers he had no doubts whatsoever: "Every economic historian should . . . have acquired what might be called the statistical sense, the habit of asking in relation to any institution, policy, group or movement the questions: how large? how long? how often? how representative?" (1931:328). The methodological distinctiveness of his profession, he asserted, "hinges primarily upon its marked quantitative interests" (1931:327)—a judgment that was at once premature and unduly modest, insofar as his own work was, according to A. P. Usher, "the first attempt to apply

12. Clapham 1922a. For his subsequent debate with Pigou see Pigou 1922; and Clapham's rejoinder (1922b).
13. J. Robinson 1962:77. For an indication of its neglect on this side of the Atlantic, see C. W. Wright 1938:695.

quantitative methods systematically to economic history on a large scale" (1932:186). Heckscher's plea may have gone largely unheeded, but Clapham's proved infectious. It was addressed, as Heaton noted, "to a craft which was already more than half converted to the search for quantitative data" (1942:735). By 1942 it had become, according to the latter historian, "perhaps the outstanding characteristic" of his generation.[14]

One year previously that generation had been urged by Simon Kuznets to become more sophisticated in their search (1941). Data analysis and manipulation were, after all, processes that could be greatly strengthened by the systematic application of statistical theory. This suggestion would be largely ignored until the advent of cliometrics. The latter's claim to originality lies here: not in the extensive use of quantitative data per se, but rather in the application of statistical theory and electronic computers to the problems of analyzing that data. Perhaps most awesome of all is its fusion of all three—economic theory, data, and statistical theory—in the construction of econometric models.

3.   The Methods and Models of the New Economic History

a. Introduction

The cliometric tools to be examined include four models and one arithmetic device. The models are (a) input-output models, (b) supply and demand models, (c) growth models, and (d) the Davis-North model of institutional change. The arithmetic device is simply a means of solving for missing data by postulating certain constancies in the relationships between numerical series. The goal of the first three models is the same as that outlined in section 5 of Chapter IV: to partition the relative importance of different causal factors in terms of their net contribution to the observed change in an economic variable. The model of institutional change attempts to implement the general procedures sketched in section 4 of Chapter III: from a set of axioms a number of conclusions are derived by deductive inference which—at least ideally—should not be intuitively obvious from the outset and which can then be used to help explain observed changes in institutions.

Assessment of the arithmetic device and of the first three models will

14. Heaton 1942:735. See also Ashton 1946:82; and Cochran 1947:21.

proceed in two stages. The present section will attempt to lay bare those assumptions which, in each case, must be made to justify the application of the tool. Problems associated with the validity of those assumptions will be considered in section 5. Assessment of the model of institutional change presents a puzzle, the nature of which is best explored after the model has been outlined.

b. *Arithmetic Interpolation and Extrapolation*

The economic historian often finds himself in the uncomfortable position of requiring for his research project data that either have not been preserved or were never collected. An estimate of Gross National Product for America in 1840, for example, cannot be constructed directly from surviving numbers. To cite only one of a host of problems, the 1840 Census of Manufacturing collected from a variety of industries reports on the value of their total sales, but nothing on the value of intermediate goods purchased. The difference between the two (sales minus intermediate goods purchased) is defined as the "value added" of a given industry, and value added is the indispensable building block for an estimate of total GNP. This statistical hiatus can only be overcome by an assumption. The 1850 American Census of Manufacturing did collect data on both total sales and intermediate goods purchased. If the ratio of purchases to sales was the same in 1840 as in 1850 for each industry, then 1840 intermediate good purchases can be estimated from the census data of 1840 plus the relevant ratio from 1850.[15]

Frequently the cliometrician will resort to some variant of this simple technique to fill in missing numbers. Peter Temin provides a case in point in his exhaustive study of the American iron and steel industry in the nineteenth century (1964a). Available data on the annual output of steel ingots and castings are relatively complete. Those for rolled steel are relatively incomplete. Estimates of rolled steel output for missing years are therefore made from the observed output of steel ingots and castings during years when rolled steel output was not reported, plus the observed relationship between the two outputs when both numerical series are available (Appendix C, 258). A similar procedure is employed by Robert Fogel. Estimates of total American iron

---

15. This is the method actually used by Robert Gallman 1960:59. See Table A-7, n. a.

production during the 1840's and '50's are derived from a relatively complete annual series of Pennsylvania iron production during this period plus observations on the relationship between Pennsylvania and national production during the six years when national data were collected.[16]

The same method pervades counterfactual speculation based upon economic model building. To estimate the contribution of American railroads to economic growth, Fogel needs as one of his numerical inputs what 1890 canal costs per ton-mile would have been if no railroads had existed (1964a). Data are readily available on freight charges levied by canals in 1890. These observed prices are then made equivalent to the hypothetical cost data required by two assumptions: (a) that canal freight charges equaled the costs incurred by the canals in moving the goods in question and (b) that canal costs per unit would have remained unchanged in a world with the bulk of railroad freight rediverted to alternative water transportation.[17]

c. Input-Output Models

Suppose that all technical relationships in the production process were constant. To put the same issue as a question, what would the implied model be if a variant of the constancy assumption in the above examples were writ large? The answer is that seemingly complex weapon of central planners: the input-output table. Cliometricians have also used this device, although infrequently. The next task is therefore to outline its basic assumptions and internal mechanisms.

Economics has a long-standing tradition of illustrating complicated mechanisms by the use of oversimplified and somewhat absurd examples. Following in those footsteps, let us assume that on his first voyage to America, Columbus discovered the island community of Pinzonia with friendly natives, a monetary unit called the dollar, and exhaustive statistical records on production and distribution. Production within the country is found to be limited to three commodities: wheat, flour,

16. More correctly, national data were collected in 1840 and 1850, while the ratio of national to Pennsylvania production can be derived from the 1844 Home League survey and an American Iron and Steel Association survey for 1854, 1855, and 1856. "Taken as a group, the six ratios suggest that the changing position of Pennsylvania in the national market would be well described by a second degree equation. Such an equation was fitted to all six observations and used to estimate the desired ratios for years in which direct observations were not available" (Fogel 1964a:162–163).

17. See McClelland 1968.

and bread, each produced by only two factors of production: labor and land. (Foreign trade is nonexistent given an absence of local water craft and Columbus arriving empty-handed). During the twelve months ending December 31, 1492, the records of inputs and outputs of Pinzonia show the following:

(1) *The wheat sector:* $50 million worth of wheat was produced by paying out $10 million for labor and $40 million for land (the latter paid as rent, the former as wages). All wheat was sold directly to flour mills.

(2) *The flour milling sector:* $78 million worth of flour was produced by paying out $50 million for wheat, $20 million for labor, and $8 million for land. Flour output was sold either to bakeries or directly to consumers, the former taking $30 million of total output, the latter $48 million.

(3) *The bakery sector:* $59 million worth of bread was produced by paying out $30 million for flour, $25 million for labor, and $4 million for land. All bread was sold directly to final consumers.

These statistical facts can be neatly summarized in Table 1, the 1492 input-output table or transactions matrix for Pinzonia. Reading *across* a row labeled "Flour milling" on the extreme left indicates the output sold by that sector to each of the remaining sectors in the community, including direct sales to final consumers. Reading *down* a column labeled "Flour milling" at the top indicates the inputs purchased by that sector from all other sectors, including expenditure for wages and rental payments for land.[18] The sum of total payments for inputs ("Total gross outlays") must equal the value of total sales to all sectors ("Total gross output"). Restating the same points in the jargon of development literature, one can find all forward linkages for a given sector by reading across a given row, all backward linkages by reading down a given column.

As it stands, this table indicates nothing about the inner workings of the Pinzonian economy. It merely summarizes all available data on the value of inputs purchased and outputs sold by each sector or

18. All payments for "primary factors" would usually be lumped under a single entry labeled "Value Added." The value added of any sector, as noted above, is defined as total sales of that sector minus its expenditures for intermediate goods. In the case of our wheat sector, for example, intermediate good purchases are zero; in the case of the flour sector, value added is $28 million, or $78 million minus $50 million.

Table 1. Pinzonia input-output table for 1492 (in millions of dollars)

Using sector Producing sector	Bakeries	Flour milling	Wheat growing	Sales to consumers (Net final demand)	Total gross output
Bakeries	–	–	–	59	59
Flour milling	30	–	–	48	78
Wheat growing	–	50	–	–	50
Payments to primary factors					
Wages	25	20	10		
Land rent	4	8	40		
Total gross outlays	59	78	50		

industry in the economy. The original architect of this construct, Wassily Leontief, was not content merely to derive a statistical artifact.[19] His objective was "an empirical study of interrelations among the different parts of a national economy" (1941:3). Statistical artifact was therefore converted into analytical tool by the following assumptions:[20] (a) all goods must be produced under constant returns to scale; that is, if all inputs are doubled, output will double; and (b) each good can be produced by only one combination of inputs, or by one fixed "recipe" relating inputs and outputs.

These assumptions and the data of Table 1 imply that $5 worth of wheat will always require as inputs $4 worth of land and $1 worth of labor. If land can be rented for $4 per acre, labor costs $0.01 per hour, and wheat sells for $5 per bushel, these two assumptions plus the data of Table 1 imply that each bushel of wheat can *only* be produced by one combination of inputs: one acre of land plus one hundred man-hours of labor.[21] If

$$L = \text{man-hours},$$
$$A = \text{acres},$$
$$W = \text{bushels of wheat},$$

19. Leontief first developed his ideas in 1936 and 1941.

20. In addition to the assumptions noted, the simplest version of input-output analysis requires (a) that no process creates more than one output (i.e., no joint products), and (b) that temporal problems can be ignored, including those associated with capacity and capital formation. For further discussion of the technique and the assumptions, see Brady 1971; Christ 1955; and Dorfman 1954b.

21. The implicit assumption is that the time dimension for producing a bushel of wheat is 100 man-hours and land rental for that time period is $4 per acre. Much of the mathematics of input-output analysis concerns the transformation of dollar sales into input coefficients per unit of output. (See Brady 1971.)

then the above causal assertion might be expressed as[22]

$$100L + 1A \rightarrow 1W.$$

The above data plus assumptions now permit exact forecasts of how production will respond under a variety of hypothetical conditions. Triple the inputs of a given sector, and output will triple. (Assumption #1.) Add more men to wheat production without increasing the acreage used and output will remain the same. (Assumption #2.) The question most commonly harnessed to input-output analysis might be characterized as follows: if demand for products $(X_1 \cdots X_n)$ were to expand by $(\$K_1 \cdots \$K_n)$—or if dollar sales were to increase for each product by a specified amount—what impact would that change in demand have upon the industrial structure of the country?

William Whitney attempts to discover the answer for America of the late nineteenth century by first constructing an 1899 input-output table and then deriving how much of the observed structural shifts in production between 1879 and 1899 can be attributed to the changing composition of final demand during the same time period (1968). His final demand categories include domestic consumption, capital goods, and foreign trade; his output sectors are grouped under "Heavy Industry," "Light Industry," "Agriculture," "Mining," and "Services and Utilities." The conclusion reached is that the changing production structure— notably the declining importance of agriculture and the rise of industry—"can be traced primarily to domestic and foreign demand for various types of commodities" (1968:159), particularly foreign demand.

John Meyer uses the same analytical apparatus in a daring counterfactual exercise directed toward estimating how much of the retardation in British industrial growth during the last quarter of the nineteenth century could be attributed to lagging sales of exports (1955). He begins by estimating a hypothetical demand figure for 1907; namely, what British export sales would have been in 1907 if exports had maintained

---

22. The arrow in this formulation cannot be replaced with an equals sign, precisely because land and labor cannot be substituted for one another in the production process (assumption #2). In mathematical terms, this relationship could be expressed as

$$W = \text{minimum of} \left\{ \begin{array}{c} \dfrac{A}{1 \text{ acre}} \\ \dfrac{L}{100 \text{ man-hours}} \end{array} \right\}.$$

their growth rates of 1854 to 1872 between 1872 and 1907. This hypothetical demand figure is then added to other data on actual demand in
1907 to derive a column of revised "Net Final Demands" of the sort
appearing in the fourth column of Table 1. This combined total is then
applied to a British 1907 input-output table to estimate how large industrial output would have had to have been to satisfy this demand.[23] The
latter is then compared with actual 1907 industrial output to derive the
conclusion that "if exports had continued to grow in the last quarter of
the [nineteenth] century as in the third [quarter], English industrial
output would have more than maintained the rapid pace of the earlier
years."[24]

The great strength of input-output analysis is its ability to assess both
the direct and indirect effects of any given change in final demand upon
the industrial structure. Its great weakness—independent of the question of the validity of its assumptions—is its neglect of the determinants
of demand. To compensate for this deficiency, cliometricians usually
resort to an entirely different explanatory technique.

d. Supply and Demand Models: A First Approximation

The second type of model—one considering both supply and demand
factors—usually has as its objective the resolution of a puzzle which
might be characterized as follows. Historians assert that factors C_1, C_2,
and C_3 (for example, population growth, falling prices, and income
expansion) were instrumental in causing the change in a given variable
E from E_1 to E_2 (such as the increase in British textile production from
100,000 yards a year to 10 million yards). Can one partition the effects of
these three factors and designate how much of the change from E_1 to E_2
is attributable to each one? Understanding how this task is attempted
requires three different inputs: (a) a firm grasp of the causal assertions
implicit in ordinary supply and demand curves, (b) some familiarity
with elementary geometry and algebra, and (c) an awareness of the
relationship between counterfactual speculation and the goal of partitioning the relative importance of different causal factors.

---

23. The choice of 1907 was dictated by available data: this was the first year in which
the British took a comprehensive census of production in industry, agriculture, and
fishing.

24. Meyer 1955:12. Meyer's conclusion is predicated upon the further assumption
that increases in factor inputs would have been readily available to create the implied
expansion in output. For a criticism of this assumption, see McCloskey 1970:446–455.

Once again the technique can be easily explored by the use of an oversimplified (and somewhat fabricated) example, in this case from British economic history. Let us assume that: (a) all British cotton cloth produced between 1765 and 1800 was of a single quality; (b) demand for British cotton textiles at this time depended upon only three factors: the price of cotton cloth, the total population of Britain, and per capita income in Britain; and (c) the supply of British cotton textiles was determined by only two factors: the price of cotton cloth and the current state of technology. All of these assumptions could be modified to correspond more closely to historical reality. The only effect would be to complicate subsequent analysis without altering the basic method being applied.

If accurate data have survived, one can unequivocally establish the price charged and quantity sold in any given year. What can never be inferred directly from available data is which factors caused cotton textile prices to fall and output to expand. Information on prices charged and quantities sold during each of the thirty-six years 1765 to 1800 can be portrayed geometrically by the thirty-six dots appearing in Figure 1. (Output data would be annual totals; price data, averages for the year in question.) The cliometrician's task is to devise a system of equations which "fit" these data, in the sense that the data are *roughly* predicted by the equations. This in turn guarantees that surviving historical evidence—in this case, quantity and price information—is *roughly* consistent with the causal hypotheses embedded in the equations.

As noted in Chapter III, two different procedures are required in this kind of model building. The first is to specify the general form of equations that capture the causal interactions deemed relevant. The second is to give that general form specific values using econometric techniques. Only the first will be considered here. How and why it is attempted will perhaps be more readily apparent if Figure 1 is reduced to Figure 2a, with all but two of the thirty-six points removed from consideration. Point F in Figure 2a represents the price charged and output produced in 1765; point G, the price and output of 1800. The overriding problem initiating the search for equations is to assess how much of the movement from F to G can be attributed to each of the causal forces cited in the initial set of simplifying assumptions; that is, technological progress, responsiveness of suppliers and consumers to changing price, and increases in British income and population between 1765 and 1800.

Figure 1

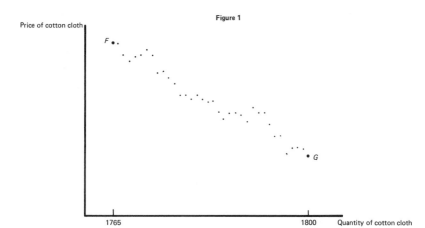

Figure 2a

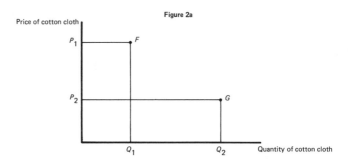

Figure 2b   **Figure 2c**

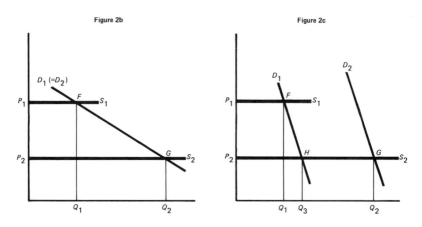

Suppose that historical reality can be represented accurately by the geometry of Figure 2b. The curve D_1 is the demand curve as of 1765. It indicates the quantity that would have been demanded in that year at different price levels *holding population and income constant at 1765 levels*. It is, in short, a magnificent counterfactual construct at every point except F, the actual point of observation. Assume for the moment that neither population nor income changed between 1765 and 1800. Then the demand curve for 1800, D_2, will be identical with D_1, the latter therefore having two points of observation: F and G.[25] On the supply side, S_1 indicates how much would have been supplied in 1765 at different price levels, *using the technology of 1765*. It too is a counterfactual construct at every point except F. Its horizontal shape (to be explained later) is derived from an assumption of constant costs. However much producers wish to supply can be supplied for the same cost per unit and consequently for the same price—in this case, the price P_1. The above wording about the sensitivity of suppliers to price variations must therefore be modified for curves of the S_1 type to this: below P_1 nothing will be offered for sale; at a price equal to (or higher than) P_1 an unlimited amount could be offered for sale. The revolutionary impact of Richard Arkwright, Samuel Crompton, and others upon supply conditions can then be portrayed as a fall in S_1 to S_2. The latter is the supply curve as of 1800, using the textile technology available in 1800.[26] It demonstrates geometrically that suppliers are willing to charge less in 1800 than in 1765 because their production costs have fallen in the interim.

One possible explanation of the data portrayed in Figure 2a is now embedded in Figure 2b. Technological progress lowered production costs; lower costs meant lower prices; and because of the extreme sensitivity of consumer demand to lower price (portrayed by the flatness of D_1 in Figure 2b), falling prices caused a sharp increase in output from Q_1 to Q_2. Of no importance whatsoever, at least according to Figure 2b, were changes in population and income.

This last assertion the historian knows to be highly suspect. Suppose that changes in population and income caused the aggregate demand

25. This amounts to assuming, among other things, a constancy in both consumer tastes and the prices of goods that compete with cloth in consumer budgets—both demand factors whisked aside as irrelevant in the initial set of simplifying assumptions.

26. The curve S_2 is also a counterfactual construct at every point except G. Because of the assumed identity of D_1 and D_2, the demand curve is a counterfactual construct at every point except F and G.

curve for British cloth to shift to the right, from D_1 to D_2, as portrayed in Figure 2c. This shift depicts the economic fact that *at any given price*, more cloth could have been sold in 1800 than in 1765 because of increased population and rising incomes. The curve D_2 depicts how, *if population and income remained constant at 1800 levels*, variations in price alone would have caused variations in the quantity demanded. It too is a counterfactual construct at every point except G.

The interpretation of the data in Figure 2a has now been radically altered. The supply side explanation is the same as before: technological change lowered costs and shifted the aggregate supply curve for cotton textiles from S_1 to S_2. The demand side explanation, however, is completely different in emphasis. The major reason that more cloth was sold as prices fell was not because consumers were sensitive to falling prices, but rather because population expansion and rising incomes caused consumers to demand more cloth at any given price. Recall that the impact of these latter forces is portrayed geometrically in Figure 2c by the shift in the demand curve from D_1 to D_2. Using this geometry and the *ceteris paribus* methodology of the counterfactual (that is, by assuming away all causal processes except those explicitly incorporated into the model), the historian can assert that if income and population had not changed between 1765 and 1800—or put geometrically, if D_1 had not shifted to D_2—*then* the output and price conditions of 1800 would have been Q_3 and P_2, rather than Q_2 and P_2.

At this point the cliometrician might exclaim "Eureka" or at least "Voilà." The puzzle noted at the outset has been solved. The importance of demand factors has been partitioned by the geometry of Figure 2c: the increase in output from Q_1 to Q_3 is explained by consumer sensitivity to lower prices; the increase in output from Q_3 to Q_2 is explained by population increase and rising incomes. (The problem of deciding the relative importance of population and income factors separately has yet to be broached.) Central to this partitioning process is the use of the counterfactual method outlined in Chapter IV. The output Q_3 can be derived *if and only if* one can extrapolate the demand curve of 1765 (the curve D_1) well beyond the point of observation (F), and the supply curve of 1800 (S_2) well beyond its point of observation (G), in both cases by impounding all nonprice factors that affected supply and demand in *ceteris paribus*. If this procedure is valid, the vague phrasing of historical analysis about the "probable importance" of various causal factors can be abandoned. One can now say precisely how important each factor was.

What assumptions are central to this bit of geometric dexterity, aside from those generally associated with the counterfactual method? Consider a subset of the larger problem just discussed: the determination of how important falling prices were as an explanation of increased consumer purchases of cloth. In terms of the geometry of Figures 2b and 2c, this problem can be solved only if one can draw through points F and G the supply and demand curves for 1765 and 1800; or as they have been labeled in Figure 2c, the curves S_1 and D_1, and S_2 and D_2. Suppose one knew positively that all supply and demand curves were linear, or straight lines. Available data could then be combined with the type of econometric technique discussed in Chapter III to estimate the slopes of these lines. If the slopes are known, then all necessary lines can be drawn in, and our problem is solved. One simply draws through points F and G those straight lines with the slope specified by econometric analysis. The relative importance of falling prices in stimulating demand and hence output is then indicated by the distance Q_1 to Q_3.

This is essentially the procedure followed by cliometricians, but with one slight modification. They do not "know" the actual shapes of supply and demand curves which must be included in their analysis. They can assume that these curves have a particular shape, and indeed one particular set of assumptions concerning the shapes of these curves tends to dominate most cliometric models concerned with supply and demand analysis. The following subsections give a brief sketch of those assumptions plus a brief description of the supply and demand functions implied by those assumptions. The question of their validity will be considered later.

e. The Log-Linear Demand Curve

To begin with demand curves: consider an even simpler variant of the cotton cloth example just cited. Assume that demand is influenced only by the price of cloth and total income in the country. Let

Q = the quantity demanded,
P = the price of cotton cloth, and
Y = total income.

The above causal relationship can then be translated into

$$Q = f(P, Y).$$

The equation merely asserts that "the quantity demanded is a function of price and income." If this functional relationship is known to be linear (that is, if it can be correctly represented by a straight line), then the very imprecise

$$Q = f(P, Y)$$

can be transformed into the more precise

$$Q = a + bP + cY,$$

using the general equation for a straight line learned by most high school students in introductory algebra. The remaining empirical problem would be to solve for the values of the small letters (or parameters) of the equation; viz., "a," "b," and "c," using available data and econometric techniques.

Linear demand relationships are the common assumption of cliometric models, but the linearity in question involves an equation in which the variables are expressed in logarithmic form. The above equation is therefore modified to

$$\log Q = \log a + b \log P + c \log Y.$$

Restating the same point, one can say that the nonlogarithmic demand function assumed by cliometricians to exist in the real world is

$$Q = aP^b Y^c.$$

The first equation is merely the logarithmic transformation of the second. Geometrically, this is equivalent to assuming that demand curves are linear as portrayed in Figure 2c, but with the axes now reading "logarithm of price" and "logarithm of quantity"; hence the name "log-linear demand curves."

The reason for the popularity of this curve in cliometric model building is easy to explain, but only after the economist's concept of elasticity has been defined. The slope of any curve is defined as "rise" over "run," or in terms of the geometry of Figure 2,

$$\frac{\Delta P}{\Delta Q}.$$

The Greek symbol delta (Δ) stands for "a small change" in price or quantity. The price-elasticity of a demand curve is defined as

$$\left(\frac{\Delta Q}{Q}\right) \div \left(\frac{\Delta P}{P}\right),$$

or the proportional change in quantity divided by the proportional change in price. It is not simply a numerical calculation. This particular measure, derived as it is from a specific demand curve, is meant to signify the precise causal linkage between a change in price and the resulting change in quantity demanded when other relevant causal factors are held constant.

Now back to the log-linear demand curve

$$\log Q = \log a + b \log P + c \log Y.$$

Recall that all straight lines have a constant slope. This logarithmic straight line asserts that "b" has a constant value,[27] and the value of b is the price-elasticity of demand.[28] Readers unfamiliar with calculus will have to take this assertion on faith; those with a knowledge of calculus can easily derive the requisite proof.[29]

27. For any equation of the form

$$Q = a + bY$$

the value of b is the slope of the straight line implied by the equation.

28. The value of c is the income-elasticity of demand, the latter being defined as

$$\left(\frac{\Delta Q}{Q}\right) \div \left(\frac{\Delta Y}{Y}\right),$$

or the proportional change in output resulting from a proportional change in income when other relevant variables are held constant.

29. Given the original form of the demand curve

$$Q = aP^b Y^c,$$

then

$$\frac{\partial Q}{\partial P} = abP^{b-1}Y^c. \qquad \ldots (1.1)$$

Given

$$aP^{b-1}Y^c = \frac{aP^b Y^c}{P} = \frac{Q}{P}, \qquad \ldots (1.2)$$

substituting (1.2) in equation (1.1) yields

$$\frac{\partial Q}{\partial P} = b\left(\frac{Q}{P}\right);$$

therefore

$$b = \left(\frac{\partial Q}{Q}\right) \div \left(\frac{\partial P}{P}\right).$$

To review: rather than postulating straight lines and solving for the slopes of those lines, cliometricians usually prefer to postulate log-linear demand curves and solve for the slopes of those curves, the latter being the elasticity of demand. Once price-elasticity has been determined, one can answer the question which is the *raison d'être* for the entire procedure: how much of the observed increase in quantity demanded can be explained by consumers' sensitivity to falling prices. A bit of algebra will show why.

Recall that

ΔP = the observed change in price (distance P_1P_2 in Figure 2a),[30]

P = the initial price level (P_1 in Figure 2a), and

Q = the initial quantity demanded (Q_1 in Figure 2a).

Our objective is to derive

ΔQ = the quantity change attributable to the fall in price (or distance Q_1Q_3 in Figure 2c).

If the assumption of log-linear demand curves implies a constant price-elasticity of demand, or in the above example, a constant value for

$$b = \left(\frac{\Delta Q}{Q}\right) \div \left(\frac{\Delta P}{P}\right);$$

and furthermore, if econometric techniques when applied to available data give an estimate of b, then one knows four of the five variables in the above equation:

$$b, Q, \Delta P, \text{ and } P,$$

and can solve for the fifth (ΔQ)—which is what one wanted to know.

Historians confused by (and possibly resentful of) the prevalence of technical terms can still acquire the necessary insight with nothing more than the geometry of Figure 2. The contribution of falling price to increased demand can be derived from the following: (a) data represented by points F and G, (b) the assumption that all demand curves are straight lines (that is, have constant slopes), (c) knowledge about the slope of those demand curves (acquired by applying econometric tech-

---

30. The assumption implicit in subsequent analysis is that all supply curves are horizontal straight lines. Geometrically, this guarantees that ΔP will not change when output is reduced from Q_2 and Q_3 in Figure 2c. The next section will discuss the reasons why such curves are common to cliometric models.

niques to available data), (d) knowledge about the specific shapes of supply curves (acquired in a manner described below), and (e) the assumption of *ceteris paribus* in nonprice factors, which validates the extension of D_1 beyond F and S_2 beyond G to derive point H, thereby determining Q_3: the quantity of output that would have been demanded if the price decline occasioned by technological progress had not been supplemented by other factors that also raised demand. The modus operandi with log-linear demand curves is exactly the same, requiring similar knowledge and similar assumptions about the linearity of logarithmic demand curves.

This method, as repeatedly emphasized, depends critically upon a single assumption about the general shape of all demand curves. If only demand curves could be specified, however, the above procedure would never solve anything. The other indispensable input is knowledge—and assumptions—about conditions of supply.

f. Supply Assumptions: Perfect Competition and Constant Costs

Two different but related sets of assumptions dominate cliometric models on the supply side. The first of these—by far the easier to grasp intuitively—postulates (a) market conditions of perfect competition and (b) production conditions characterized by constant costs. The second postulate asserts that as the total output of an industry expands, costs per unit of output do not rise (or do not rise in the long run).[31] Perfectly competitive markets are supposedly typical of the economic world of Adam Smith and the Kansas wheat farmer, but not typical of the world of John D. Rockefeller, General Motors, and the AFL. Each unit in the market, especially producers of goods and suppliers of labor, is assumed to be so small that his or her actions cannot directly affect observed market variables, especially price. The Kansas farmer, for example, acts on the assumption that world wheat prices will not be affected by variations in his output. He is a price taker, not a price maker. Perfect competition exists if, and only if (a) the product in question is perfectly standardized, (b) all participants in the market have perfect knowledge,

31. The postulates of constant returns to scale and constant costs are often used interchangeably. Constant returns to scale asserts that if all inputs are doubled, output will double. This is not equivalent to the assumption of constant costs unless, as the firms of a given industry vary their demand for inputs, the prices of those inputs remain unchanged. The latter situation might be viewed as a variant of the competitive assumption at the industry-wide level: no industry is large enough relative to the available supplies of factor inputs to affect input prices by variations in its total output.

and (c) as already indicated, the output of each producer is of negligible significance relative to total market supply. In short, perfect competition is not one assumption but three.

Notice how these assumptions simplify the geometry of Figures 2b and 2c. All supply curves become horizontal straight lines. Translated into words, these assert that output can increase without supply price rising because cost conditions in the industry remain constant per unit of output. (The existence of perfect competition rules out the possibility of some monopolist attempting to exploit demand increases by arbitrarily raising prices.) This in turn guarantees that supply conditions alone will always determine price—a conclusion which augurs well for our ultimate objective of partitioning causal forces. In Figure 2b, for example S_1 asserts that however much cloth might have been demanded in 1765, it could have been made available at the price P_1. Conditions of demand, as portrayed by D_1, will determine the actual quantity produced and sold, but demand variations can never cause prices to rise above P_1.[32]

Our first conclusion is that in a world of horizontal supply curves, supply conditions alone determine price and, by implication, all changes in price. But which supply conditions? The fall in price from P_1 to P_2 in Figure 2 was caused exclusively by technological progress, but only because this was the one causal factor allowed in our model on the supply side. The real world is often more complex. Over time, input prices can vary, combinations of inputs may be altered in response to these new prices, and what appears as technological change may simply be a shift to a different technique for the reasons just noted. The problem is again to partition causal forces and to decide how much of the observed fall in price (and change in output) can be attributed to different factors affecting supply.

g. Supply Assumptions: Perfect Competition and Cobb-Douglas Production Functions

Solving this puzzle requires the use of a basic analytical construct of economic theory: the production function. This "expresses the relation

---

32. If prices fell below P_1, supply would go to zero, but if *any* output is offered for sale, it will always be offered at the price P_1. The price-elasticity of supply, or

$$\left(\frac{\Delta Q}{Q}\right) \div \left(\frac{\Delta P}{P}\right)$$

is therefore infinite because the numerator is infinite.

between the maximum quantity of output and the inputs required to produce it, and the relation between the inputs themselves."[33] Notice that the technical maximization problem has been solved; that is, the production function describes only the maximum output that can be obtained from each combination of factor inputs.[34] Let us assume that the total output of a given industry is a function of available technology and three broad categories of inputs: labor, capital, and land or natural resources. In symbolic terms, let

O = total output,
L = labor inputs,
K = capital inputs,
R = land or natural resource inputs, and
A = an index of total factor productivity.

Then the causal assertion just noted can be expressed as

$$O = F(A, L, K, R).$$

As always, the crucial issue is to decide the general shape of the function. The cliometrician's usual choice is the curve already elaborated in demand analysis: the log-linear curve, or in this case, a log-linear production function. The above general equation is therefore converted into the more specific

$$\log O = \log A + x \log L + y \log K + z \log R.$$

This function usually appears in the literature in its nonlogarithmic form, or as

$$O = A \, L^x \, K^y \, R^z.$$

The first equation is simply the logarithmic transformation of the second. The meaning of A will perhaps be more apparent if the terms of the second equation are rearranged to give[35]

$$A = \frac{O}{L^x \, K^y \, R^z}.$$

33. Brown 1966:9.
34. Readers familiar with the geometry of economics textbooks can reinterpret this definition in terms of isoquants. A production function defines a set of isoquants (and vice-versa), each representing various combinations of inputs that produce a given output.
35. Economists will recognize that the implicit assumption is Solow's neutral technical change, where the marginal rate of substitution between factors is not affected by technical change. See Solow 1957:312.

The value of A expresses the relationship between factor inputs and output. If the latter doubles while the factor inputs remain the same, then the index A would double, indicating a doubling in productivity.[36] The equation itself is called a Cobb-Douglas production function after the two men (Charles Cobb, a mathematician, and Paul Douglas, an economist) who first advanced it as a possible description of economic reality.

If the production function of a given industry is Cobb-Douglas in shape, and if markets are perfectly competitive in the sense noted above (including an insensitivity of factor prices to variations in the industry's output), then supply conditions can once again be portrayed by the geometry of Figures 2b and 2c.[37] We are back in a world of horizontal supply curves, with all that such curves imply about the simplicity of partitioning causal forces, especially the conclusion that all price changes are caused exclusively by factors of supply. That particular conclusion, however, was reached without any recourse to such a complicated construct as an industry-wide production function. One needed only the dual assumptions of perfect competition and constant costs. The Cobb-Douglas production function is used to partition causal forces on the supply side; specifically, to determine how much of an observed decline in price or rise in output can be attributed to rising productivity and how much to changing factor inputs.

The industry-wide question can also be asked at the national level. Increases in Gross National Product are often viewed as the result of four causal factors: productivity gains plus increased supplies of land, labor, and capital. How much is caused by each factor? The cliometrician tends to attack both problems (industry-wide or nation-wide) with a Cobb-Douglas production function. The underlying assumptions are identical, but the method of attack may differ slightly, depending upon whether the unit of analysis is a specific industry or the entire economy.[38] For reasons that will become clear later on,

36. More precisely, "A is the ratio of an index of output to a geometric average of the inputs. Consequently A will rise whenever output increases more rapidly than the average increase in the inputs" (Fogel and Engerman 1971c:99).

37. This is true only of the long-run supply curve, which incorporates the effects of variations in capital inputs. See Fogel and Engerman 1971c:109. For an explanation of why supply curves are horizontal, see below, n. 42.

38. For an example of a direct duplication of the national method at the industry level, see McCloskey 1968. As outlined briefly by Fogel and Engerman (1971c:99),

subsequent discussion will focus exclusively on the second kind of problem: the partitioning of causal forces underlying an observed increase in national output.

Suppose that accurate data can be assembled from American records of 1840 on total output and total national inputs, or total supplies of land, labor, and capital actually used in 1840. (In terms of the symbols already used, this would give us national values for O, L, K, and R.) Assume further that comparable data are available for the year 1900. One can then easily calculate ΔL: the amount by which the labor inputs of 1900 exceeded those of 1840. Increases in capital and land inputs can be calculated in the same manner. One must be careful to distinguish between

ΔO = the total observed increase in output between 1840 and 1900, and

ΔO_L = the increase in output resulting exclusively from increases in labor inputs.[39]

The first is readily available from actual data. Our goal is to calculate the second.

The method of attack, not surprisingly, bears a marked resemblance to that applied with log-linear demand curves. The linearity of the Cobb-Douglas production function

$$\log O = \log A + x \log L + y \log K + z \log R \qquad \ldots (1)$$

implies a constant value for "x," "y," and "z." Each letter stands for an elasticity of output with respect to the factor input associated with that letter. That is, x is the elasticity of output with respect to labor

---

instead of using quantity data and the above formula, the economic historian can solve for the contribution of changing productivity using price data, the same assumptions, and a different formula. Examples of this approach may be found in North 1968b; and Walton 1967. (Walton suggests that his calculations pertain to a much simpler situation where all factor prices are constant. The constancy of shipbuilding costs, however, is far from clear [p. 67 n. 2], and Walton himself emphasizes the marked decline in interest rates [pp. 72–73] which lowered the cost of capital.)

39. In a similar fashion, previous demand analysis should have distinguished between

ΔQ = the observed increase in quantity, or distance $Q_1 Q_2$ in Figure 2, and
ΔQ_P = the increase in quantity demanded because prices fell.

This distinction was avoided to simplify the algebra. It becomes critical when analysis is expanded beyond the consideration of the causal significance of a single variable.

inputs, or in terms of the symbols already defined,

$$x = \left(\frac{\Delta O_L}{O}\right) \div \left(\frac{\Delta L}{L}\right). \qquad \ldots (2)$$

Recall that elasticity is not merely a number but a causal assertion. It measures in this case the proportional change in output that will result from a proportional change in labor inputs (other things being held constant, especially the state of technology).[40] Readers familiar with calculus can easily detect why a Cobb-Douglas production function implies constancy in the elasticity of output with respect to each input. Those without calculus must again take the assertion on faith.[41]

In the above formula for the elasticity of output with respect to labor inputs (equation 2), the value of three of the variables is readily available from aggregate data; namely,

$O = 1840$ GNP,
$L = 1840$ labor inputs, and
$\Delta L =$ the amount by which 1900 labor inputs exceeded those of 1840.

If only one knew the value of x, one could solve for ΔO_L by substituting the four known values in equation (2) and solving for the fifth. The quest for a device to partition the relative importance of changing labor inputs therefore reduces to an empirical problem: find a specific value for x.

40. Similarly y is the elasticity of output with respect to capital inputs, and z is the elasticity with respect to natural resource inputs.
41. Given

$$O = AL^x K^y R^z,$$

then

$$\frac{\partial O}{\partial L} = AxL^{x-1}K^y R^z. \qquad \ldots (2.1)$$

Since

$$AL^{x-1}K^y R^z = \frac{AL^x K^y R^z}{L} = \frac{O}{L}, \qquad \ldots (2.2)$$

then substitution (2.2) in (2.1) gives

$$\frac{\partial O}{\partial L} = x\left(\frac{O}{L}\right),$$

or

$$x = \left(\frac{\partial O}{O}\right) \div \left(\frac{\partial L}{L}\right)$$

$$= \left(\frac{\Delta O}{O}\right) \div \left(\frac{\Delta L}{L}\right).$$

At first glance this may appear to be a preposterous ambition. How can one possibly discover, for the entire economy, the relationship portraying the sensitivity of output to changing inputs of labor? Once more into the breach steps the economic theoretician armed with the supply side assumptions already noted. If the nation-wide relationship between total inputs and total output can be characterized by a Cobb-Douglas production function; and if the economy has highly competitive markets in the sense defined earlier; then it can be shown that the share of GNP paid to labor will always be constant, and—more dramatic for our purposes—that this share, expressed as a ratio to total GNP, will always give the missing value for x.

The proof of these assertions is somewhat complex and quite unnecessary for purposes of this discussion.[42] Our modest goal was simply to clarify assumptions used and procedures followed by cliometricians bent upon partitioning the relative importance of those forces judged to be the fundamental causes of observed increases in national output. These may now be summarized as follows:

(1) Total output is assumed to be a function of a few basic inputs— labor and capital; or these two plus land—and a residual causal factor labeled "productivity."

42. Given

$$O = AL^x K^y R^z,$$

then the marginal product of labor is given by

$$\frac{\partial O}{\partial L} = AxL^{x-1}K^y R^z = x\frac{AL^x K^y R^z}{L} = x\left(\frac{O}{L}\right).$$

If markets are perfectly competitive, the wage rate equals the marginal product of labor, and total wage payments are therefore

$$\frac{\partial O}{\partial L}(L) = x\left(\frac{O}{L}\right)(L) = x(O).$$

The share of total output received by labor is

$$\frac{x(O)}{O} = x,$$

which, as noted previously, is also the elasticity of output with respect to labor inputs. If all factors are paid their marginal product, thereby exhausting total output, then

$$x + y + z = 1,$$

which in turn implies that the Cobb-Douglas production function is subject to constant returns to scale. (For a more elegant treatment of the latter point, see Solow 1957:313.) At the industry-wide level, if variations in total output do not affect factor prices, then constant returns to scale implies a constant cost industry with horizontal supply curves (in the long run).

(2) Production functions are assumed to be Cobb-Douglas, or log-linear, in shape.

(3) This linearity assumption implies a constant value for the elasticity of output with respect to each of the several inputs.

(4) Assuming this production function and the existence of highly competitive markets, one can solve for the elasticity of output with respect to labor inputs merely by noting that fraction of total output, or GNP, paid to labor. The elasticities of other factors of production can be calculated in a similar fashion.

(5) The specific value of the elasticity of output with respect to labor (x) can be combined with observations on the initial level of output (O) and labor inputs (L) plus observations on how much labor inputs expanded (ΔL) to derive the increase in output directly attributable to that expansion in labor inputs (ΔO_L). (See above, equation 2.) In like manner, one can derive the increase in output attributable to the observed increase in other factor inputs.

(6) Of the total observed increase in output (ΔO), that portion which is as yet unexplained by increases in factor inputs is attributed to rising productivity.[43] This last item is therefore a catch-all phrase for a multiplicity of factors: technological progress, the exploitation of scale economies, improvements in organization, and (depending upon how factor inputs were measured in the first place) qualitative changes in

43. Let
$$\Delta O_A = \text{the residual increase in output.}$$
Given
$$x = \left(\frac{\Delta O_L}{O}\right) \div \left(\frac{\Delta L}{L}\right),$$
then
$$\Delta O_L = x(O)\left(\frac{\Delta L}{L}\right).$$
Therefore
$$\Delta O_A = \Delta O - [\Delta O_L + \Delta O_K + \Delta O_R]$$
$$= \Delta O - O\left[x\left(\frac{\Delta L}{L}\right) + y\left(\frac{\Delta K}{K}\right) + z\left(\frac{\Delta R}{R}\right)\right].$$
Notice further that the proportional gain in the productivity index is defined as
$$\frac{\Delta A}{A} = \frac{\Delta O_A}{O}.$$
Therefore
$$\frac{\Delta A}{A} = \frac{\Delta O}{O} - \left[x\left(\frac{\Delta L}{L}\right) + y\left(\frac{\Delta K}{K}\right) + z\left(\frac{\Delta R}{R}\right)\right].$$
This in turn explains the popularity of the type of formula appearing in Fogel and Engerman 1971c:99.

factor inputs, especially improvements in the quality of the labor force.[44]

The cliometrician's conception of the economic world is apparently dominated by the linear relationships implied by his analytical tools: log-linear demand curves, horizontal supply curves, and Cobb-Douglas production functions. With a handful of assumptions, surprisingly little data, and on occasion, econometric analysis of that data,[45] he can resolve extremely complicated puzzles concerning the relative importance of causal forces at work in the historical process. Without those assumptions, he is lost—or at least he loses his distinctive ability to analyze the problems of economic history. Should they, or should they not, be granted to him? And what criteria can one possibly use to decide whether a particular assumption is reasonable or unreasonable? Much of the remainder of this chapter will be devoted to illustrating how difficult both questions are to answer. Before the assumptions of cliometric models are assessed, however, two other models must be briefly sketched.

h. The Capital-Output Ratio: An Engine for Economic Growth

Economists of an earlier age—Smith, Malthus, Ricardo—viewed economic growth primarily as the consequence of the interaction of profits, investment, and capital accumulation. Curiously enough, new and rigorous models of economic growth almost disappeared from theoretical literature after the middle of the nineteenth century,[46] not to reappear—or not to reappear with a vengeance—until the decades following World War II.[47] These recent versions have been, in the main, variations on an old theme. Their central driving mechanism is still capital accumulation, on occasion supplemented by exogenous productivity gains.[48] Capital formation is usually linked to those variables affecting the community's willingness to save and to invest.

44. For a brief outline of how total labor inputs can be adjusted for qualitative improvements (thereby lowering the unexplained residual), see Engerman 1971:251–255.

45. Those familiar with the procedures of regression analysis will instantly recognize the convenience implied by the linearity assumptions noted above.

46. The notable exceptions which prove the rule were some of the writings of Karl Marx and Joseph Schumpeter.

47. At the headwaters of what is now a torrent can be found two articles by Harrod (1939) and Domar (1947).

48. For a survey of modern growth models, see Hahn and Matthews 1964; and Morgan 1969.

Advances in productivity, as the word exogenous implies, are viewed primarily as determined by unknown forces external to the model.

This long-term swing in the fashionability of economic growth with theoreticians found few responsive echoes within the profession of economic history. Practitioners of the latter, from Guy Callender to Robert Fogel, have almost universally agreed that the subject matter of economic history (in Callender's vigorous wording) "ought to be the wealth of nations in the literal sense of that word."[49] For generations they have awaited the formulation of theoretical models that would enable them to analyze more rigorously this central explanandum of their profession. Our problem is to decide whether this recent spate of growth models has facilitated the attainment of that objective.

One current and fashionable model of economic growth has already been sketched above. Demand factors are ignored, and changes in total output are explained in terms of (a) changing factor inputs, (b) the elasticity of output with respect to each input, and (c) an unexplained (exogenous) residual labeled "productivity." The end result is somewhat more sophisticated in conception and execution than another type of growth model which has dominated much of the theoretical literature during the postwar years. The main causal mechanism of the latter is embedded not in any elasticity coefficient, but rather in a single ratio: the marginal (or total) capital-output ratio. The task of this section is to outline how that ratio can determine economic growth.

Analysis of mechanisms must again be preceded by the definition of terms. The elasticity of output with respect to *capital* inputs in the above Cobb-Douglas model was given by

$$y = \left(\frac{\Delta O}{O}\right) \div \left(\frac{\Delta K}{K}\right).$$

Translated into words, it expresses the causal interaction between a proportional change in capital and the resulting proportional change in output (other relevant factors being held constant). A marginal capital-output ratio is defined as

$$\frac{\Delta K}{\Delta O}.$$

It indicates the causal linkage between an absolute increase in capital

<hr/>

49. Callender 1913:88. For more modern endorsements of Callender's viewpoint, see Cole 1968b:3; Fogel 1965:92; Gallman 1965:109–110; and Parker 1966:100.

inputs and the resulting change in total output. One notable difference between the two formulas is that the causal factor, capital, now appears in the numerator rather than the denominator. The substantive difference, however, is that a capital-output ratio postulates a constant relationship between absolute changes rather than between proportional changes.

How this mechanism works can perhaps be understood more readily when incorporated into a simple example. Suppose that a given country has only one form of capital: flour mills. More specifically, assume that each flour mill costs $100 to build, will last forever, and every year will add $50 to the total flour output of the country. The marginal capital-output ratio in this case is ($100 ÷ $50), or 2:1. For every $100 invested in new mills, total output will expand by $50 per year. (The assumption of an infinite life span could easily be modified. The only effect would be to complicate the arithmetic with an allowance for depreciation.)[50]

Additions to capital stock require an act of investment. Increments in capital stock at the nation-wide level might therefore be regarded as being identical with total (net) national investment. The "output" at this level of aggregation would, of course, be Gross National Product. A marginal capital-output ratio for the nation as a whole then indicates the causal relationship between investment—or increments in the capital stock—and GNP. Relying upon little more than this single mechanism, development economists such as Arthur Lewis and economic historians such as W. W. Rostow have attempted both to define an industrial revolution and to explain the growth in per capita income associated with industrial revolutions.[51]

50. If each mill lasted for 10 years and depreciated at a uniform rate of $10 per year, then the gross marginal capital-output ratio would still be as noted above; namely (2:1); but the net marginal capital-output ratio becomes [(100) ÷ (50 − 10)], or (2.5:1). The implication is that for every $100 invested, *net* output will be $40 higher in all subsequent years, with the remaining $10—also created in all subsequent years—reinvested to keep the capital stock intact.
51. "All the countries which are now relatively developed have at some time in the past gone through a period of rapid acceleration, in the course of which their rate of annual net investment has moved from 5 percent or less to 12 percent or more. This is what we mean by an Industrial Revolution. . . . The central problem in the theory of economic growth is to understand the process by which a community is converted from being a 5 percent to a 12 percent saver—with all the changes in attitudes, in institutions and in techniques which accompany this conversion" (Lewis 1955:208, 255). Rostow readily concedes that his own theory of investment behavior during his take-off stage is "pure Arthur Lewis" (1965:xiv). The take-off stage itself "is defined as an industrial revolution," and the central element in the definition of the take-off, as will be outlined below, is the change in the rate of investment (Rostow 1960:39, 57).

The implicit growth model (never made explicit by Rostow) is the essence of simplicity. Let

$$K = \text{total capital inputs,}$$
$$I = \text{annual (net) investment,}$$
$$GNP = \text{total national output.}$$

If annual increments in capital (ΔK) are equivalent to annual total net investment (I); and if one assumes, as Rostow does (1960:37 n., 141), that the marginal capital-output ratio for the nation as a whole is 3:1; then in terms of the above symbols,

$$\frac{\Delta K}{\Delta GNP} = \frac{I}{\Delta GNP} = \frac{3}{1}.$$

Suppose that total net investment is equivalent to 5 percent of GNP; or

$$\frac{I}{GNP} = 0.05.$$

These two equations can then be combined to yield a single relationship, insofar as

$$(\Delta GNP)\left(\frac{3}{1}\right) = I = (GNP)(0.05).$$

The implied growth rate in Gross National Product is then uniquely determined as

$$\frac{\Delta GNP}{GNP} = \frac{0.05}{3} = 1.67\%.$$

If total investment increases to 10 percent of GNP; or

$$\frac{I}{GNP} = 0.10;$$

then the implied growth rate in GNP can be derived from

$$(\Delta GNP)\left(\frac{3}{1}\right) = I = (GNP)(0.10);$$

or

$$\frac{\Delta GNP}{GNP} = \frac{0.10}{3} = 3.33\%.$$

If one also assumes that population growth rates in current under-developed countries will range between 1.7 percent per annum and 3.0 percent,[52] two dramatic conclusions follow:

(1) Nations which invest 5 percent or less of total GNP will experience a decline in per capita income because the population growth rate will exceed the growth rate in total GNP.

(2) Nations which invest 10 percent or more of GNP are sure to achieve a sustained rise in real per capita income because the resulting GNP growth rate will invariably outstrip that of the population.

This explains why the one operational criterion at the heart of Rostow's concept of the take-off is a doubling in the rate of national investment.

Get the investment-rate up to the point where the increase in output outstrips the rate of population increase—to, say, a rate of investment over 10% of national income—and the job is done. The difference between a traditional and a modern society is merely a question of whether its investment-rate is low relative to population increase—let us say under 5% of national income; or, whether it has risen up to 10% or over. With a capital/output ratio of about 3, a 10% investment-rate will outstrip any likely population growth; and there you are, with a regular increase in output per head (1960:20).

The historian will no doubt be impressed if not awestruck by the poverty of the explanatory mechanism. The point to be emphasized is that poverty notwithstanding, should one key assumption be granted, the model will give a coherent explanation of sustained rises in real GNP per capita. The now-familiar dilemma is again upon us: how to judge the legitimacy of assumptions; in this case, the legitimacy of assuming that every $3 invested will always produce an annual increment in total output of $1, whatever might be the size and composition of the capital stock, the form of the investment, the availability of other factors of production, and so on. If one chooses instead the more sophisticated growth model outlined previously, the same question is redirected to the assumptions of perfectly competitive markets and an aggregate Cobb-Douglas production function. These complex issues

52. Rostow 1960:141. Rostow appears to be somewhat confused about the relationship of population change to his overall model. If "historically, population rates of increase during the take-off decades were generally under 1.5 percent per annum" (p. 141), then a shift in the investment rate would have been unnecessary for the achievement of sustained growth in per capita income. A marginal capital-output ratio of three to one, as noted above, guarantees that total income will grow at 1.67 percent per year when only 5 percent of GNP is invested, and that will surely outstrip a population growth rate of "under 1.5 percent per annum."

will be the subject of section 5. The final task for this section is to outline the one remaining type of explanatory model that has gained a place of prominence in the literature of the new economic history.

i. A Model of Institutional Change

The two growth models outlined above share one glaring defect: they ignore both the determinants and consequences of institutional change. For short-run analysis of small variations, impounding the entire institutional framework in *ceteris paribus* may well be defensible. If the assignment is to analyze long-term development, a similar impounding would in effect banish from consideration a central aspect of the growth process. Unfortunately, few if any tools for analyzing institutional change can be borrowed directly from economic theory. Given the cliometrician's concern with applying those tools to the historical process, one might reasonably expect him to abandon the study of long-term change, at least in the short-term future. The alternative is to devise a new set of tools for himself. The latter option, while a demanding task of the first magnitude, has been chosen by several of the more courageous members of the profession.

Even as John Higham was announcing in 1970 that "cliometricians and institutionalists have parted company" (1970:462), Lance Davis and Douglass North were attempting to effect a reconciliation.[53] From that massive canvas labeled institutional change—a phrase distressingly vague as evidenced by the difficulties in defining the subject matter of an institutional school in either history or economic thought[54]—they deliberately chose a narrow focus: the study of those arrangements "between economic units that govern the ways in which these units can cooperate and/or compete."[55] Their ultimate goal is nothing less than a theory of institutional change. As a first step, they directed their

53. The main theoretical work is Davis and North 1971, briefly summarized by both authors in 1970, and even more briefly summarized by North in 1971. For attempts to apply the theory, other than those included in the above works, see North and Thomas 1970, 1971, and 1973. Although quite independent of the Davis-North effort, see also Domar 1970.

54. See, for example, Gruchy 1968.

55. Davis and North 1971:7. "The arrangement may be either a formal or informal one, and it may be temporary or long-lived. It must, however, be designed to accomplish *at least one* of the following goals: to provide a structure within which its members can cooperate to obtain some added income that is not available outside that structure; or to provide a mechanism that can effect a change in laws or property rights designed to alter the permissible ways that individuals (or groups) can legally compete" (*ibid.*).

energies toward devising a theory or model that would be able to predict two kinds of things:

(1) Given any established set of institutions and some disequilibrating force, the model ought to predict whether the newly emerging institutions will be purely individual (i.e. involve only a single decision maker), depend upon some form of voluntary cooperation, or rely on the coercive power of government.
(2) It should provide some estimate of the period of time that is likely to elapse between the initiating disequilibrium and the establishment of the new (or mutated) institutions. [1971:5]

Within the conventional taxonomy of behavioral sciences—stimuli, disposition, and response—the authors begin with the response (the spectrum of observed institutional changes), postulate the disposition (profit maximization), and seek to infer from that postulate which stimuli tend to produce which type of response; that is, which "level" of institutional change: individual, voluntary group, or group action harnessed to government intervention. From microeconomics they borrow both the dispositional postulate noted and the methodology of deducing from given postulates logical conclusions which should not be intuitively obvious from the outset.

Investment theory offers a precise and readily accessible framework in which to attempt those deductions. Would-be innovators of institutional change are viewed as duplicating the decision-making process of would-be investors. The decision rule is simple: always choose that innovation which promises the highest net receipts—or, more correctly, which promises the largest "present value" when all prospective receipts and costs are discounted back to the present. The list of relevant variables influencing this choice can also be borrowed directly from investment theory (1971:51–54). Expected net gain from a given institutional change will be higher: (a) the larger and more certain are its expected receipts, (b) the smaller and more uncertain are its expected costs, and (c) the smaller is the rate at which expected net benefits are discounted back to the present.

The authors provide an algebraic formulation for these general causal assertions which can be roughly summarized as follows. Let

R_t = total receipts in year t,
p_t = the probability of receiving R_t,
C_t = total costs in year t,

q_t = the probability of incurring C_t,

n = the number of years for which receipts and costs (flowing to or incurred by the decision-making unit) are generated by the proposed change, and finally,

r = the rate of discount (assumed by Davis and North (1971:53) to equal the interest rate available to the decision-making unit).[56]

Then

PV = the present value of all future net receipts associated with a given project,

$$= (p_0 R_0 - q_0 C_0) + \frac{(p_1 R_1 - q_1 C_1)}{(1 + r)}$$
$$+ \frac{(p_2 R_2 - q_2 C_2)}{(1 + r)^2} + \cdots + \frac{(p_n R_n - q_n C_n)}{(1 + r)^n}$$
$$= \sum_{t=0}^{n} \frac{(p_t R_t - q_t C_t)}{(1 + r)^t}.$$

(The subscript zero indicates initial receipts and costs; the subscripts $1, 2, \ldots n$ indicate the receipts and costs incurred during the first, second $\ldots$ and n^{th} years.) Present value will vary directly with p and R, and inversely with q, C, and r. The decision rule, to repeat, is to choose that institutional change—and by implication, that "level" of institutional change—with the largest expected present value.

The adjective "expected" suggests one minor defect in the formulation as it stands. A smaller expected gain may actually be preferred to a larger one if the former is quite certain and the latter is quite uncertain. In more technical language, most decision makers are risk-averse. Davis and North concede the pervasiveness of this bias (1971:19), but make no attempt to adjust their formula for its inclusion. (The adjustment would take the form of reducing all prospective net receipts to "certainty equivalents" before discounting those receipts, certainty equivalents being defined as the sum of money that one would be prepared to

56. For a discussion of difficulties inherent in assuming this equality, see Dasgupta, Sen, and Marglin 1972:Chapter 13.

accept as a certain income in exchange for the chance of making a larger and more uncertain income.)

The model's exclusive reliance upon profit maximization is also a tenuous oversimplification, as the authors readily concede. To elevate economic incentive to *primus inter pares* in the fabric of human motivation may well be justified if the actions under study have obvious economic consequences for the decision makers. Somewhat less defensible is its further elevation from mainspring to the only spring of relevance. Once diversity of motivation is conceded, specifying the perceptions and motivation of each decision maker becomes of crucial importance. William Cannon has found, for example, that the same organization problem within early American railroad companies evoked markedly different responses, depending upon whether the would-be problem solver was an entrepreneur-financier or an engineer-administrator (1972).

These two shortcomings—the ignoring of risk aversion and the exclusive focus on profit maximization—are merely refinements to be considered in subsequent research. The main defect is the theoretical poverty of the model itself. From the postulate of profit maximization and the mechanisms of investment theory Davis and North deduce the following conclusions (1971:54–56):

(1) The higher the discount rate, the more sharply will future net receipts and costs be discounted; therefore the less attractive will be those proposed changes with delayed payoffs and immediate costs; the more attractive will be those changes with immediate payoffs and delayed costs.

(2) The sharper the fall in the prospective interest rate that would accompany government intervention, and the more such intervention would enable *any* prospective costs to be passed on to others outside the initial decision-making unit, the more that unit will prefer to choose a level of institutional change featuring government participation.

Given the enormous uncertainty that would be likely to accompany the gauging of prospective benefits and costs for various proposed institutional changes, variations in the interest rate (at least within that range typical of interest rate variations) would seem unlikely to affect significantly the decision-making process. Investment theory in this case tends to underscore the importance of a variable which in actual practice is likely to have little or no influence upon the choice procedure.[57] This reduces the above list of conclusions to emphasizing the attractiveness of government participation if such participation lowers prospective costs to those who would effect institutional change. The conclusion has much to recommend it. The Davis-North methodology, however, should involve the derivation from a limited set of postulates logical conclusions that are both valid for the historical process and not intuitively obvious from the outset. Judged by the latter criterion, one cannot give full marks, or possibly any marks at all, to their theory of the determinants of the level of institutional change.

The method employed by these authors in pursuit of their second objective is somewhat obscure. For this reason their own views on the subject must be quoted in some detail:

It is to the theory of technological change and to modern political science that we turn for an explanation of the lag between the recognition of profits external to the existing institutional arrangement and the innovation of an arrangement capable of effecting their internalization. Unfortunately, neither the theory of technological change nor the modern work in political science is as closely specified as investment theory. As a result, we have been unable to 'squeeze out' of the analysis the predictive (or explanatory) implications that we managed in the case of 'level' decisions. Instead we view our work on lags as largely theory suggestive. We have drawn a number of *a priori* constraints from politics and technology and to a large degree have used history to test their usefulness rather than using the theory to explain the history (1971:56).

These a priori constraints, as suggested, are designed to indicate how certain factors will affect the lag in the implementation of institutional change. The authors' principal conclusions are that the lag will be shorter (a) the greater are the expected profits from change, (b) the smaller is the decision-making unit, (c) the greater is the degree of unanimity within that decision-making unit, and (d) the more obvious is the optimal choice among a spectrum of possible choices (1971:57–61). All of these are useful premises to explore behavioral tendencies whenever institutional change is contemplated. None of them would

57. Concerning a variant of this problem in the modern corporation, Richard Nelson writes, "A major objective of research and development policy is profit. But the tremendous uncertainties involved in predicting costs and returns seem to have precluded the systematic use of formal decision rules" (1959:121–122).

seem to require for their derivation any special knowledge of political science or the theory of technological change.

As noted at the outset, the writings of Davis and North constitute a timely and courageous effort to solve one of the more obvious deficiences in the cliometrician's analysis of long-term economic growth. Their book includes a vast array of case studies in American institutional change—by itself a feature that should make it required reading for economic historians, old and new. Their theory of institutional change, however, is not so much a consistent body of premises and conclusions as a handful of behavioral tendencies that should help to unravel some of the changes some of the time. Subsequent discussion will therefore not attempt a further assessment of the validity of their theory because judged strictly as a theory it appears to be comparatively empty.[58]

What should it assess? The above survey has indicated that cliometrics is distinguished by its use of quantification, economic theory, and statistical techniques. The particular tools that it would apply to causal analysis of the past include input-output tables, log-linear demand curves, Cobb-Douglas production functions, and nation-wide capital-output ratios. Section 4 attempts a general assessment of the general tools: quantification, mathematics, and economic theory. The merits of specific devices will be considered in section 5.

4. General Tools Assessed: Quantification, Mathematics, and Economic Theory

a. Quantification

Boswell: "Sir Alexander Dick tells me that he remembers having a thousand people in a year to dine at his house."
Johnson: "That, Sir, is about three a day."
Boswell: "How your statement lessens the idea."

---

58. The one other recent and comprehensive effort to develop a theory of institutional change—curiously ignored by Davis and North—is Hicks 1969. His objective is "to classify . . . economic states of society . . . [and] to look for intelligible reasons for which one such state should give way to another" (p. 6). Breathtaking in scope and rich with analytical insights, the book also fails to approximate its larger goal. Reviewers have been rather harsh, citing in particular the absence of historical documentation, the almost total lack of clarity in the specification of stages and mechanisms propelling society from one state to the next, and finally, the considerable violence done to historical fact by those generalizations which are clearly specified. See, for example, Bauer 1971; and Gerschenkron 1971.

Johnson: "That, Sir, is the good of counting. It brings every thing to a certainty, which before floated in the mind indefinitely."[59]

Quantification may not bring everything to a certainty, but it can give to many historical debates a perspective that would otherwise be completely lacking. How difficult it would be, for example, to discuss trading patterns in colonial America without the export and import data assembled by James Shepherd and Gary Walton, or industrialization in nineteenth-century America without Robert Gallman's estimates of the changing composition of Gross National Product.[60] Mere enumeration will seldom provide definitive answers to the great debates in economic history. It remains the indispensable starting point for framing many of the questions. Much of the raw material of economic reality is intrinsically quantifiable. Population, output, prices, income, exports, imports, capital stock—the list is almost endless and has no counterpart in any other social science. The economic historian is therefore particularly burdened (perhaps overburdened) by G. Kitson Clark's exhortation: "Do not guess, try to count, and if you cannot count, admit that you are guessing."[61]

Following such advice can be a full-time job. Cliometricians and historians alike are indebted to those who have devoted much of their lives to fashioning the building blocks for generations to come: for example, Gallman's GNP estimates for the nineteenth century (1966); Stanley Lebergott's exhaustive detailing of labor force statistics (1960 and 1966); and North's research on changing productivity and prices in ocean freighting (1958 and 1968b). Their masonry may not dazzle or excite, but without such foundations most of the hypotheses of American economic history would remain, in Johnson's phrase, "floating in the mind indefinitely."

That is the good news. The bad news is that quantification, like any other tool, can be misused. For Prometheus numbering may have seemed "pre-eminent among subtle devices,"[62] but most historians are continually impressed by its limitations. The human experience, they argue, is the product of a multitude of forces, few of which admit to

59. Hill, ed. 1887:204.
60. See, for example, Shepherd 1970; Shepherd and Walton 1969; Gallman 1960 and 1966.
61. Quoted in Aydelotte 1966:806.
62. Grene, ed. 1959:I, 327.

numerical representation. Some of the phenomena of economic history encounter the same difficulty. The expansion of trade in medieval Europe, for example, multiplied the variety of goods available "with all the widening of life that that entails. This is a gain which 'quantitative economic history' which works with index-numbers of real income, is ill-fitted to measure, or even to describe."[63] When a subset of relevant variables can be quantified, the ever-present danger is to focus upon the subset to the exclusion of the whole. Thus growth theory emphasizes such variables as investment and foreign trade earnings while virtually ignoring the role of attitudes, entrepreneurship, and power politics.

Even if all relevant variables can be quantified, and quantified easily, the unwary historian may still fall prey to the numerologist's sleight of hand. If he does, he has usually forgotten to ask those age-old questions of his profession: how good are the sources? and how representative is the evidence? Curiously enough, the human mind will often grant to numbers an aura of precision that it seldom if ever concedes to other forms of historical evidence. How superfluous Comte's warning seems to be that "A very absurd proposition may be very precise; as if we should say . . . that the sum of the angles of a triangle is equal to three right angles"[64] The issue of triangles may be self-evident, but for at least one of Comte's contemporaries, the fear of deception remained: "The mind is easily imposed upon by the affectation of exactitude which marks even the misstatements of statistics; and it adopts with confidence the errors which are appareled in the forms of mathematical

63. Hicks 1969:56. Similar reservations have been voiced by another distinguished theoretician: "The construction of long-run statistical series which are supposed to represent a quantitative description of the development of National Income, to measure the growing Productivity of Labour and so on, is now considered to constitute a practically indispensable preliminary stage of every serious analysis of economic change. Although, in many instances, such figures give a good description of prevailing general trends, the methodological position according to which numerical comparison constitutes the very basis of all empirical inquiry does not seem to be justified either in terms of the internal logic of the quantitative method in general, or its application to the study of economic change in particular. When an historical time series shows that the Gross National Product of some particular country is four times as large as it was sixty years ago, or that the productivity of the transportation industry has increased by 300 per cent from 1860 to 1960, the difference between the horse-drawn carriage, the railroad of 1860, the car and the aeroplane of 1960 seems to be neglected; and when we are told that in the preliminary calculation each type of vehicle has been given its proper weight before being included in the corresponding aggregate, this only means that these long-time series do not describe directly the observed facts, but rather represent results of more or less arbitrary numerical manipulations" (Leontief 1963:5).

64. Comte 1853:I, 30.

truth."[65] A similar sense of vulnerability before the onslaught of cliometrics would seem to pervade much of the historical profession today.

Data, like other fragments of surviving historical evidence, are shot through with biases, mistaken judgments, and errors. Exports often include a high component of guessing by the appropriate port official. Import fluctuations may reflect the vicissitudes of customs enforcement as much as the vicissitudes of trade. Women repeatedly understate their age to census enumerators; military chroniclers repeatedly overstate the size of opposing forces. (The Greek count of Persians at Thermopylae suggests an army far in excess of the dimensions of the actual battlefield even without the addition of the Greeks.)[66]

The agonizing, delicate question is *not* whether surviving numerical evidence is dead accurate, but whether it is likely to be correct enough for the purposes at hand. The classical tests of statistics offer no help in this regard. Each riddle must be solved by the historian using knowledge and intuition as best he can. Occasionally the answer is self-evident. A study seeking an upper-bound measure of the cost to America of British imperial policy can use with confidence the data supplied by dissatisfied Virginia planters concerning the "excessive charges" caused by the enumeration of tobacco.[67] The planters are unlikely to have understated their case, and exaggerated costs merely reinforce the upper-bound nature of the final measure. Sometimes a belief in the regularity of the underlying universe will prompt the most daring of extrapolations, such as Adolphe Quetelet's conclusion that the bodily proportions of Indians were roughly comparable to those of Europeans. (His sample was limited to twelve Indians visiting Brussels.[68]) The common experience of the economic historian, however, is to be bedeviled by uncertainties concerning both the accuracy of the sample data and the relationship between the sample and the larger universe of which it is a part. When the underlying universe is highly irregular and the surviving data scarce, the testing of hypotheses that require precise measures may simply not be possible.

65. Alexis de Tocqueville, quoted in Bruchey 1965:6.
66. Morgenstern 1963b:23.
67. McClelland 1969a:377–380.
68. See Ohlin 1966:68.

Conrad and Meyer's study of the profitability of slavery provides a dramatic case in point (1958). Their objective was to measure the rate of return from owning and operating an American cotton plantation based upon slave labor. The calculation actually made was the profit rate per unit of "slave-capital," the latter including both the cost of a prime field hand and the costs of all cooperating factors needed by the slave, such as land and agricultural implements. To these data must be added information on the value of cotton produced (per unit of slave-capital) and maintenance costs per field hand. Even readers unfamiliar with the topic will be impressed by the range of quantitative information required. The critical question is whether enough has survived to permit an educated guess concerning the average return on the average plantation.

One of many problems is the interaction of land values with cotton yields. The higher the yield (other things being equal), the higher the land price should have been. Various scholars have attempted to refine the original cotton yield estimates of Conrad and Meyer, but most have failed to scrutinize closely the merits of their associated land values.[69] These were apparently derived by Conrad and Meyer from two sources:[70] (a) Lewis Gray's estimate of $35 per acre for a large plantation devoted to upland cotton "say, in the Mississippi alluvium"[71] and (b) the report of a single farmer in Barbour County, Alabama, to *The Southern Cultivator* in 1846 concerning his operating costs during the previous two years, the relevant entry reading, "Say, 360 acres poor pine land at $6 per acre."[72] Taking these figures ($6 and

69. In particular Saraydar 1964; Sutch 1965; Foust and Swan 1970; and Fogel and Engerman 1971a. Saraydar apparently relies for his land prices upon the same sources as Conrad and Meyer, with Sutch, Foust, and Swan all following Saraydar's lead.

70. Conrad and Meyer do not cite specific sources for each number, but merely preface their data with the statement, "Estimates of plantation expenses have been taken primarily from three excellent, exhaustive records of the available material: J. L. Watkins' *The Cost of Cotton Production*, Lewis C. Gray's *History of Agriculture in the Southern United States to 1860*, and Kenneth Stampp's *The Peculiar Institution*" (p. 104). Saraydar was the first to point out that their actual sources for land prices were two observations in Gray's book (p. 326).

71. Gray 1958:I, 542. Gray notes in an accompanying footnote that this figure and other associated data "are based on various statements of the capital accounts of cotton plantations. The figures represent a composite modified according to the judgment of the present writer so as to be as nearly typical as possible."

72. *The Southern Cultivator* (Athens, Atlanta) 1846:IV, 11. The $6 figure, with accompanying source, is cited by Gray 1958:I, 542.

$35) as representative of the end points of a distribution assumed to be
uniform in structure, Conrad and Meyer calculated the average land
price as midway between the two.

Notice that the price of land will bulk large in the total cost of the
unit of slave-capital (about one-third in this study), and this cost in
turn will critically affect the implied rate of return to the plantation
owner. As a rough approximation, the above procedure has much
to recommend it. But is a rough approximation good enough? The
hypothesis being tested is not whether rough-hewn measures indicate
some positive financial return to the plantation owner. The issue at
stake is whether the actual return exceeded, equaled, or fell short of
the alternative return available to southerners at this time—a return
estimated by Conrad and Meyer at 6 to 8 percent (1958:101–103).
Finding their own estimated profit rate in the same range, the authors
concluded that slavery was profitable—that the private return from
slaveowning was approximately equal to returns available in other
forms of investment. What makes this conclusion suspect is not that
the underlying data are less than perfect. All historical data have their
tenuous aspects. The problem is that the final measure—the rate of
profit—must be accurate *within a very narrow range* to justify inferences
based upon a comparison of that profit rate with other investment
yields. This brings us back to the nature of the underlying universe.
The universe of land prices tends to be highly irregular. To use a handful
of observations to compute an average for the entire ante-bellum South
is therefore venturesome in the extreme. Even less defensible is the use
of that average in a calculation that must be accurate within a very
narrow range if one hopes to answer the question noted at the outset:
Was slavery profitable?[73]

Two other data problems should be mentioned. The first concerns
the divergence between the constructs of economic theory and the
actual numbers used as proxies for those constructs. Investment is
influenced by expectations of future profits, and those expectations in
turn are usually conditioned by profits earned in the immediate past.
Given a shortage of information on expectations, the latter is often
used in econometric models as a proxy for the former. The numerical

73. For a discussion of similar problems related to the measurement of social rates
of return on American railroads, see McClelland 1972b.

precision of the proxy then tends to mask the imprecision in the actual investment decision-making process. Another common difficulty is illustrated by the search for capital-output ratios made famous by models of economic growth. These postulate a cause-and-effect relationship between aggregate capital formation, or investment, and subsequent increases in output, or GNP. The difficulty is that the ratio of observed changes in investment divided by observed changes in GNP will not do as a proxy for the theoretical mechanism. Recorded growth in GNP is a function of a multitude of factors, only one of which is the capital stock. If the observed ratio is assumed to be identical to the theoretical construct, the result can be a five-year plan with much investment and very little growth because other contributing (and neglected) factors failed to keep pace with the expansion of the capital stock.

Finally, there is the matter of judgment. Facts seldom speak for themselves, and the same is true of numerical magnitudes. The historian remains indispensable in the weaving of a persuasive tale from surviving evidence, including data. What is perhaps less obvious is that part of the weaving process—and the judgment—have entered into the assembling of the data themselves. A veritable cornerstone of nineteenth-century research—Gallman's estimate of manufacturing output in 1839—has only 52 percent of its final total constructed directly from census information.[74] The remaining 48 percent has been estimated by a variety of ingenious procedures, all of which reflect a learned guess (but nevertheless a guess) concerning the nature of the manufacturing sector at that time. This is inevitable. Relevant theoretical constructs are often complex. Surviving data are seldom complete. A high component of personal judgment must therefore enter into "the attempt to pass from the scattered, incomplete primary data, affected by all the peculiarities of both the country's economy and its data gathering institutions, to measures that reflect as clearly as possible the rigorously defined concepts of economic analysis."[75] For that matter, a high component of personal judgment enters into all historical writing. What is too easily forgotten is that the more complicated numerical constructs of economic history do not represent objective truth. The worth of these measures, like the worth of any historical interpretation, will

74. Gallman 1960. On this point, see the comments following Gallman's work by Neal Potter (p. 68).
75. Kuznets 1957:553.

reflect the strengths and weaknesses of their architect—and nothing more.

At the turn of the present century Alfred Marshall accused his professional colleagues of failing to grapple at close quarters with the difficulties of quantitative analysis (1925a:309–310). The same charge would seem justified in certain historical circle today. Carl Bridenbaugh's injunction against worshipping "at the shrine of that Bitch-goddess Quantification" (1963:326); Arthur Schlesinger, Jr.'s much-quoted conviction that "almost all important questions are important precisely because they are *not* susceptible to quantitative answers" (1962:770)— these are symptomatic of a widespread resistance to quantification which is not without its dogmatic and irrational aspects. Some of the pitfalls of the method have been noted above. Like the Colt 45 of frontier fame, the instrument is no better than the man who uses it. The excesses of recent years—the academic bushwhackings and wild exchanges in the learned journals—would seem to reflect the frailties of humanity, not the intrinsic defects of the weapon. The intellectual pioneer cannot rely upon it to solve all of his problems. On occasion, however, he will find well-directed firepower advisable if not indispensable. And like the hand gun, quantification would seem here to stay.

b. Mathematics

So is mathematics, although for over a century the issue was touch-and-go. Cournot's pioneering study of 1838, *Researches into the Mathematical Principles of the Theory of Wealth*, anticipated the stumbling block for generations to come: "With one accord [theorists of repute] have set themselves against the use of mathematical forms, and it will doubtless be difficult to overcome . . . a prejudice which thinkers like [Adam] Smith and other . . . writers have contributed to strengthen."[76] By the close of the nineteenth century, the American economist Irving Fisher could find only about fifty books and articles in the entire world on mathematical economics worthy of inclusion in the bibliography of his doctoral dissertation.[77] Even as late as 1952, one hundred and

---

76. Cournot 1897:2. Another nineteenth-century pioneer in mathematical economics felt compelled to address the prejudice directly: "I am well aware that the notations used will at first appear somewhat cumbersome but I beg the reader not to be discouraged by this complexity, for it is inherent in the subject" (Walras 1954:35).

77. See I. Fisher 1892.

fourteen years after Cournot's work first appeared, mathematical analysis in economics had, according to Paul A. Samuelson, "no more than a foot in the doorway" (1952:63). Immediately thereafter, under the impetus of such theoreticians as Tjalling Koopmans, Leontief, and above all Samuelson, the unwelcome guest not only barged in but became master of the house. So comprehensive has the transformation been that today calculus and matrix algebra are indispensable tools for the young economist who would understand and contribute to the current journal literature. In the discreet wording of an older contributor, "Except in a few obstinate pockets of resistance, the use of mathematics in the social sciences is now generally accepted."[78] Also accepted is a progressive sophistication in the mathematics used. The modern era with its emphasis upon complexity and exquisite refinements in technique might even be judged to be more baroque than classical in style. Aesthetics, however, is not the issue. What matters to the economic historian is the usefulness of the tool.

The ultimate goal of economics—or at least one of its ultimate goals—is to find the underlying regularities in the interaction of economic variables and, wherever possible, to formulate those regularities in the language of mathematics. The two obvious questions are therefore (a) do such regularities exist, and (b) if they do exist, can they be adequately represented by mathematical devices. An affirmative answer in both cases would permit economists to reap all of the widely recognized benefits of mathematical logic. Assumptions become more clearly defined and readily apparent. Inconsistencies in assumptions become easier to detect. Perhaps most important of all is the facility with which mathematics enables the social scientist to handle the interaction of a large number of variables and to extract conclusions about those interactions which are not intuitively obvious.[79] Despite these advantages, it does not follow that "mathematics is the lantern by which what before was dimly visible now looms up in firm bold outlines."[80] Quantification, for all its advantages, does not always bring everything to a certainty which before floated in the mind indefinitely. The overriding issue is

78. Stone 1966:1.
79. A frequently overlooked benefit is that "there are some things which can be said in mathematics which cannot be paraphrased with tolerable accuracy in ordinary English. Consider, for example, that old stumbling block: is marginal cost the cost of the last unit produced or the first one not produced" (Dorfman 1954a:375).
80. I. Fisher 1892:119.

whether the bold outlines thrown up by mathematical analysis portray well or badly the reality which they presume to portray.

Much of the discussion of the limitations of mathematics as a tool of analysis in economic history is more appropriately included under the previous heading. The mathematics that the cliometrician tends to use requires the quantification of cause and effect variables. If variables cannot be quantified, the usefulness of mathematics is seriously impaired. The associated difficulties are perhaps more easily seen in the context of a simple example.

Suppose one believes (as most economists do) that economic growth is influenced by cultural milieu and the supply of entrepreneurs. Defining these three variables (growth, milieu, and entrepreneurs) as G, M, and N, respectively, one might express this belief as

$$G = f(M, N).$$

Why is it so difficult to duplicate the procedures outlined in section 6 of Chapter III—remove the brackets by postulating a general algebraic form for that function and then solve for the parameters of the function using available data and econometric techniques?

Both economic growth and the supply of entrepreneurs would seem to be intrinsically quantifiable (although correction for quality differences in the latter could be vexing). Furthermore, the directional relationship between "more" entrepreneurs and resulting economic growth seems to be relatively unambiguous: the more of the first, the more of the second.[81] The difficulty is that there is no obvious way to link the theoretical construct—the supply of entrepreneurship—to available data. Testing by econometrics or any other technique for the actual relationship between two variables therefore becomes impossible. The situation is analogous to Newton believing that mass influenced the force with which bodies attracted each other, but not having any observable data to represent the quantity of mass present in any given situation. In such cases, a strategic retreat from mathematics to the conventional verbage of historians becomes necessary:

81. Exceptions to this tendency are not impossible to imagine, as for example an increase in the supply of risk-loving entrepreneurs who divert capital resources from industrial pursuits to foreign exchange speculation. As a general tendency, however, few economists would challenge the assertion that an increase in the supply of entrepreneurs will benefit economic growth.

the supply of entrepreneurs influences, affects, or helps to generate economic growth. More than this we cannot say.

What about cultural milieu? As is so often true in historical analysis, what appears as a compact set of words is in fact a catch-all phrase for an entire constellation of factors. Some may foster economic growth, some may be neutral, and some may be detrimental. Most (if not all) factors in the set cannot be linked to available data, thereby relegating to obscurity the exact nature of their interaction with economic growth. How then can one sum a combination of effects, some positive, some negative, and few if any having a precise numerical magnitude associated with their effect? If a summation is not possible, then the universe of cultural milieus cannot be organized into categories labeled "more" and "less" beneficial to economic growth. The importance of a given cultural milieu can only be explored by the historian in terms of the specifics of each case, judging as best he can the impact of each relevant factor embraced by the more general term. The same point might be made with respect to religious fervor and the rise of capitalism, or to frontier environments and the rise of democratic institutions. One may sense or suspect that the two are related, but with no way of regularizing that relationship, these particular aspects of human experience tend to lie beyond the scope of mathematical treatment.[82]

The practical problems of using mathematics to analyze economic phenomena run much deeper than the previous discussion might suggest. Crucial to progress in the natural sciences has been acceptance of the belief that the natural world is subject to mathematical laws knowable by mankind. When Cournot therefore prefaces his economic

82. The reader may consider this point to be so obvious as hardly to warrant explicit consideration. Examples can nevertheless be found that suggest it is often overlooked. To cite but one instance from sociology, Stuart C. Dodd began by defining

$$T^{-2} = \text{acceleration in change}, I = \text{the change},$$
$$P = \text{the population changed, and } F = \text{societal force}.$$

Obviously hoping to borrow from Newtonian methodology, he then derived the formula

$$F = T^{-2}(I)(P).$$

"This redefinition of a societal force opens up a large field of sociologically significant data to exact measurement, insofar as indices can be devised to measure the societal changes involved" (Dodd 1939:622). To quote from one of Dodd's harsher critics, "However impressive this simplified transcription of physical concepts and their symbols looks, in application to 'societal' time, duration, change, acceleration, and force, these definitions are empty and useless. For they do not give any real unit for the measurement of societal change or of its acceleration, velocity or force" (Sorokin 1956:41).

study with the statement, "I have put aside questions to which mathematical analysis cannot apply" (1897:5), what determines how much he must put aside? A definitive answer cannot be given, in part, because new mathematics might always be devised to solve hitherto unsolvable problems. Within the limited framework considered in Chapter III, however, several issues are appropriately viewed as unresolved problems severely constraining the current use of mathematics as a tool of analysis in applied economics.

At the micro level—the level of analysis concerned with the behavior of individual decision makers—economics to date has achieved only limited success in modeling the ignorance and objectives of those decision makers. Applying to such problems the mathematics of maximization subject to constraints requires a range of assumptions which, as noted in Chapter III, are widely at variance with much of economic reality. The resulting model, like all models, is only designed as a rough approximation for that reality. That the approximation tends to be extremely rough is readily apparent in the insistence of those who advocate its use that the model in question is *not* designed to describe or explain individual behavior, but only group tendencies.

This is turn raises the question of the regularities evidenced by group behavior in economic matters. In thermodynamics and quantum mechanics, the indeterminacy at the individual level has not prevented the application of mathematics to describe and predict aggregate behavior. The empirical question is whether aggregate economic behavior does or does not show signs of marked regularities, including strong central tendencies. That question can only be answered on an ad hoc basis depending upon the type of behavior being studied. What is readily apparent in the current attempts to devise aggregate models of the sort described in section 6 of Chapter III—and is repeatedly reflected in other areas of contemporary economic research—is the limited success in discovering very precise central tendencies. This neither proves the absence of those tendencies nor demonstrates the inherent limitations of mathematics in economics. It does highlight the uncertainty accompanying the question noted at the outset: To what extent is the underlying reality that economists would explain subject to regularities that can be discovered and portrayed in mathematical terms? First approximations there may be in profusion, but close approximations remain, to date, comparatively scarce.

c. Economic Theory

The historian who would answer the question "Why?" has no alternative but to theorize. Werner Sombart's "no theory—no history" (1929:3) overstates the case, but whenever causal analysis is attempted, that analysis *must* be predicated upon generalizations of the sort discussed above. The only question for the historian is whether to make that theorizing explicit.

The great strength of economic theory is that it provides for this purpose a check list of possible causal interactions which (contrary to Marshall's suggestion noted earlier[83]) a man of active and inquiring mind is most unlikely to acquire on his own. Economic theory can also help to lay bare the assumptions implicit in the unconscious theorizing of others. The traditional linkage of Jackson's Bank War to subsequent financial chaos in the 1830's, for example, is defensible only if commercial banks initiated an unsound credit expansion in response to Jacksonian policies. In fact, commercial banks did no such thing, thereby exonerating Old Hickory from at least one charge: that of being a prime mover in the Panic of 1837.[84]

Two difficulties arise, however, both touched upon in Chapter III. As noted there, although the core of economics is fairly well defined, the margin remains obscure. The historian concerned with the causes and consequences of institutional charge, with the interaction of the economy with political, social, and cultural factors, is drawn irresistibly toward that margin and away from the main body of economic theory. Put another way, the usefulness of economic theory is crucially dependent upon the questions asked, and many of the questions asked by the historian with a broad focus cannot be readily answered by using the type of causal generalizations that are the core of contemporary economic theory.

Even when those questions do concern the type of behavior clearly falling within the purview of modern economic theory, this engine of analysis is not without its limitations as a guide to likely answers. Marshall's summary of the major difficulties, quoted earlier, bears repeating: "The forces of which economics has to take account are more numerous, less definite, less well known, and more diverse than

83. See above, p. 177.
84. See Temin 1969, especially Chapter 1.

those of mechanics; while the material on which they act is more uncertain and less homogeneous" (1952:637). A certain tension—a certain sense of precariousness—invariably accompanies much of the historical analysis of cliometricians. As evidenced by the devices considered in section 4, they tend to be preoccupied with precision: precision in measuring relevant numbers, in estimating numbers not immediately available, and in measuring the net contribution of different causal factors to observed changes in economic variables through counterfactual speculation harnessed to economic models. The major problems they encounter are the conventional problems of causal explanation cited by Marshall: the challenges to precision stemming from the nonhomogeneity of the events being analyzed and the complexity of forces acting upon those events. Both problems are solved by the cliometrician in the conventional way. Through abstraction, nonhomogeneous events are made homogeneous and diverse and complex forces are reduced to a handful of explicit forces. What is left in the explanatory model—the bare bones in terms of a limited set of interactions among a limited number of variables—is not usually advanced as a complete explanation of reality. It *is* advanced as a close approximation to the processes at work in the historical phenomena being studied. Again the question arises: How close is close enough?

One possible approach, as noted at the outset of this chapter, is to compare the assumptions of a given model with other evidence from the historical experience to which the model is applied. Two issues must be considered in this context, one perfectly straightforward, the other complex and ultimately enigmatic. Assumptions which directly contradict the known facts of history obviously will not do. A theory linking the rise of commercial institutions to Puritan theology, whatever its intrinsic merits, is of no relevance in explaining developments in a society which remains Buddhist to a man. As obvious as this point may seem, the literature of the new economic history is honeycombed with examples of explanations in terms of theoretical mechanisms which in turn are predicated upon assumptions that directly contradict accepted historical fact: the cost to colonial America of British imperial policy is estimated by Joseph Reid using a model that is valid only if American price inflation exceeded that of Amsterdam (the evidence suggests that American inflation was considerably less than Amsterdam inflation during the period in question);[85] the diffusion of the reaper is explained by a threshold model which depends crucially upon the assumption that each farmer owned his own reaper (abundant evidence can be found of cooperative purchase rather than individual ownership);[86] conclusions about relative factor scarcities in Britain and America during the nineteenth century are derived from a model which validates those conclusions only if production technologies in the two countries were identical and no natural resources or agricultural products were used in the manufacturing sector.[87]

The dubious worth of models which assume the opposite of the truth would seem to be self-evident. Anything but self-evident is the nature of the deficiencies in models which neglect in their explanatory mechanisms factors suspected of being important, but whose importance remains an unknown quantity. Consider again the problems raised by entrepreneurship. Development economists generally agree that "per capita income growth requires shifts from less productive to more productive techniques per worker, [and] the creation or adoption of new commodities, new materials, new markets [and] new organizational forms"[88]—all tasks critically dependent for their implementation upon the supply of entrepreneurship. Evidence can also be assembled to demonstrate (not surprisingly) that at any point in time a large percentage of business firms perform well below their maximum output, again partly because of a shortage of entrepreneurial ability.[89] Empirical growth models that exclude from consideration the role of entrepreneurs are therefore incomplete.[90] How incomplete they are, however,

85. Reid 1970; for criticism, see McClelland 1970.
86. David 1966; for criticism, see Davis 1968:87–88.
87. Temin 1966b; for criticism, see Fogel 1967:298–308. In fairness to Temin, it should be emphasized that his main objective was to demonstrate that the models implicit in Rothbarth's and Habakkuk's writings, when made explicit, do not justify the conclusions of the authors in question. Temin, however, does go on to speculate, "It is possible ... that the United States was not a labor-scarce, but a capital-scarce economy," citing as supporting evidence the higher interest rates in America compared with those of Britain and "the widely noted flimsiness of American machines" (p. 291).
88. Leibenstein 1968:77.
89. See Leibenstein 1966a.
90. Not all economic historians have been impressed with the importance of entrepreneurs. Chester Wright, for example, took the extreme position: "You find no counterpart of an Alexander, a Caesar or a Napoleon in economic history; a Fugger, a Rothschild or a Morgan does not appreciably alter its general course, even for a brief time" (1938:698–699). The more conventional viewpoint emphasizing the importance of entrepreneurs can be found in such writings as Leibenstein 1968; Baumol 1968; and Cochran 1965. For a discussion of the difficulties in defining entrepreneurship, see Harris 1970:347–348.

is impossible to gauge. Factors are neglected precisely because their contribution cannot be assessed. Only if they could be assessed would one know the extent of the imperfection in the incomplete growth model. If that could be known, presumably the contribution of the neglected factors would have been included in the growth model in the first place. This is a central difficulty of explanatory models employed by the cliometrician. Their deficiencies are readily apparent to the historian in terms of relevant factors ignored. What is not apparent, either to the historian or to the cliometrician, is how imperfect the resulting explanation is.

To sum up: all cliometric devices for unraveling the past, including those about to be considered, must face the general difficulties sketched above: the imperfections in surviving data; the needling question (usually unresolved) of how well the sample of surviving evidence delineates the larger universe from which it comes; the uncertain importance of relevant, nonoperational causal factors; the unknown degree of imperfection in any theoretical model resulting from its neglect of nonoperational factors and its use of assumptions which distort reality—an unknown which remains immutable for want of an operational way of testing how much that neglect and distortion affects the ultimate explanatory power of the model.

5. Specific Cliometric Tools Assessed

The cliometric tools to be examined include three models and one arithmetic device. The models are (a) input-output models, (b) supply and demand models, and (c) growth models. The arithmetic device merely postulates certain constancies in order to solve for missing data.

a. Arithmetic Interpolation and Extrapolation

The simplest of these, the arithmetic device, as its name implies, involves no economics whatsoever. The arithmetic procedures may consist of straight-line interpolation, the extrapolation of ratios from one period to another, or econometric curve fitting. In all cases, the objective is to use the relationship between two or more variables when all of them can be observed to estimate missing data when only some of them can be observed. The legitimacy of any given procedure can only be judged on an ad hoc basis. The postulate of no major changes over a ten-year period in the ratio of raw material purchases to final sales for ante-bellum American industry would seem eminently reasonable, especially when applied to industries that have experienced little technological progress in the interim.[91] The extrapolation of interregional trade patterns of the 1880's to America of the 1850's is considerably less credible.[92] The key question is always whether other historical evidence indicates that too many relevant variables have changed too much between the period of missing data and the period of observed data. The larger the change, the greater is the probable distortion from assuming whatever constancy is implied in the arithmetic procedure. Similarly, observed market data indicate, at best, only the structure of economic relationships at the margin. The further beyond the margin these relationships are extrapolated in counterfactual speculation, the more tenuous the results of that speculation become.

b. Input-Output Models

Evaluating the worth of cliometric models also requires some attempt to determine the legitimacy of assumptions embedded in each model. The procedure once again is to scrutinize the correspondence between assumptions and historical reality—or, more correctly, between assumptions and other evidence concerning the historical process under study. Because all assumptions necessarily involve abstraction, exact correspondence is unlikely to be observed. Judgment is therefore inevitably introduced in much the same way as it was introduced into the assessment of arithmetic devices. The issue is how much divergence is too much, and that will depend critically upon the extent to which observed divergences imperil the model's ability to explain what it purports to explain.

The key assumptions of input-output analysis, as noted in section 3, are really two in number: (a) all goods are produced under constant returns to scale; that is, if all inputs are doubled, output will double, and (b) each good can be produced by only one combination of inputs, or one fixed recipe relating inputs and output.

For analyzing the probable impact of small changes in demand upon a complex industrial structure over a short time period, the tool

91. See Gallman 1960:59, Table A-7.
92. See Fogel 1964b:381–382; for criticism of Fogel's procedure, see Fishlow 1965:209–210.

is without a serious competitor. The larger the proposed change and the longer the time period, the more uneasy one becomes about the rigidity implied by the assumptions. A counterfactual postulating a radical shift in demand raises immediately the question of whether available factor supplies could have met that demand. (Input-output analysis per se indicates nothing about the probable answer.[93]) If the counterfactual harnessed to input-output analysis concerns both a radical shift and a prolonged time period, further doubts enter concerning the assumed inflexibility in production coefficients. Abundant factors of production can and do replace scarce factors over time, and technological progress frequently reduces the use of both.

Even if all of its assumptions are deemed acceptable for the problem under study, input-output analysis is singularly unhelpful in (a) explaining why demand changed (demand changes are taken as exogenously given), (b) analyzing the determinants of basic factors of production (these too are determined by forces outside the model), and (c) analyzing the causes and effects of technical change (the fixed coefficients of production imply an absence of technical change). Add to these reservations the fact that constructing an input-output table is a horrendous statistical undertaking, and one is not surprised to find that the tool is seldom used by practitioners of the new economic history. The discussion must therefore turn—as the cliometrician frequently turns—to models that incorporate both supply and demand factors in a single consistent explanation of a range of historical phenomena.

c. Log-Linear Demand Curves

The assumption that the demand curves of economic reality are log-linear in shape is common to most cliometric models that include demand factors in their explanatory variables.[94] The assumption itself is seldom justified explicitly, and such infrequent justifications as are offered emphasize "goodness of fit" in the sense that the estimated log-linear equation closely approximates the observations which the equation is designed to explain.[95] Occasional reference is also made

93. This is McCloskey's main criticism of Meyer's use of input-output analysis for late nineteenth-century Britain. See above, n. 24.

94. See, for example, Fogel and Engerman 1971b:150–153; Passell and Schmundt 1971:41; Pope 1972:401 n. 53; Temin 1967:467; G. Wright 1971b:112.

95. Fogel and Engerman 1971b:153.

to the "goodness of fit" achieved by similar equations employed in recent studies of twentieth-century consumption data. The charm of the equation itself, as enunciated by one of the pioneers in its use, is mainly "goodness of fit, ease of estimation, and immediacy of interpretation."[96] Doubts about its theoretical properties have been voiced by econometricians, inasmuch as a complete set of log-linear demand equations would imply rather strange consumer behavior; specifically, that if incomes rose and prices remained unchanged, the proportional expenditure on each good would have to remain the same. (In more technical language, the log-linear demand system implies that the income elasticity of demand for all goods must be equal to one.[97]) The rebuttal is pragmatic: for short-run studies of small changes, a log-linear system may give a close (if not an exact) approximation to economic reality.

Historians may have other misgivings. To them the equation may seem to be nothing more than a figment of the cliometrician's imagination, bearing no apparent relationship to the real world. The reply in this case is to ask what evidence would indicate a relationship with the real world. The historian's own methodology consists of nothing more than advancing hypotheses and then demonstrating that surviving evidence is consistent with those hypotheses. Surely the same procedure is being followed here. The equation *is* the hypothesis, and goodness of fit is equivalent to demonstrating the consistency of surviving *numerical* evidence with that hypothesis. The historian must, of course, decide whether the general causal assertions of the equation are believable. Once he concedes the relevance of the causal factors in the equation—once he agrees that demand is influenced by those variables listed on the right-hand side of the equation—then the determination of how those variables influenced demand can only be settled by postulating a specific form for the equation and observing how well that form fits the data. The real dilemma occurs when two or more different equations fit the data about equally well. This is analogous to that conventional dilemma of historical analysis: how to choose between two competing hypotheses when surviving historical evidence is consistent with both.

96. Houthakker 1965:278.
97. See, for example, Yoshihara 1969:261–262.

Current research by econometricians (as distinct from cliometricians) is now focusing upon alternative equation forms that fit contemporary consumption data as well as, or better than, the log-linear demand system.[98] The relevance of these alternative forms for historical analysis has yet to be explored by practitioners of the new economic history. The one serious attempt to test alternative equation systems on nineteenth-century American data led to discouraging results. In 1875 the Massachusetts census collected information on the incomes and expenditures of 397 families in the state. Jeffrey Williamson tested these data against three different demand equations, each of which implied "quite different things about household behavior" (1967:113). His main conclusion was: "In terms of goodness of fit, it is difficult to discriminate among the three functional forms except that for food, and one of its components, groceries, the constant elasticity function is definitely inferior" (115). Despite these reservations, Williamson chose the constant elasticity or log-linear equation for his later analysis, essentially because of its convenient properties (115).

To review: the goodness of fit of log-linear demand equations used to date in cliometric models indicates only a consistency of numerical evidence with the hypotheses embedded in the specific equations. The better the fit, the more consistent is the evidence. What remains unknown is whether alternative equations would fit the data even better, and whether those alternatives would be more consistent with other nonnumerical evidence.[99]

d. Supply Conditions of Perfect Competition and Constant Costs

As noted in section 3 two different sets of assumptions dominate the supply-side analysis of cliometric models. The simpler of the two— the combination of perfect competition with constant costs—is evoked when the only problem is to specify the general shape of the supply function. If the assignment is to partition the relative importance of causal forces operating on the supply side, the usual assumptions are

98. See Yoshihara 1969; and Parks 1969. A survey of this literature is given in Bridge 1971:Chapter 3.

99. An alternative system of equations would also seem preferable for studies of long-term changes of large magnitudes, given the peculiar theoretical properties of log-linear demand equations noted earlier. The evidence does not support the hypothesis that the income-elasticity of demand is unity for such goods as food and consumer durables. See, for example, Kuznets 1966:98–99.

perfect competition plus a Cobb-Douglas production function (the latter specifying a particular relationship between inputs and output).

To begin with the first set. The assumption of constant costs, although frequently made, is seldom defended. When it is, reference is usually made to the ready availability of factor supplies—a circumstance that should minimize variation in input prices as the output of the industry expands and contracts.[100] In their study of the ante-bellum iron industry, Fogel and Engerman also cite the observed constancy in the average size of firm and the absence of evidence suggesting that larger firms were more likely to survive—both observations consistent with an absence of economies of scale and therefore an absence of decreasing costs (as opposed to constant costs).[101]

The assumption of perfect competition, also frequently made, is infrequently defended by reference to the number of firms in the industry under study as being "large." Additional support can on occasion be marshaled by reference to prevailing foreign competition in those markets in which the industry is attempting to sell its products.[102] As noted earlier, perfect competition is not one assumption but three: knowledge is perfect, the product is standardized, and no participant in the market is large enough to affect market variables directly. These conditions are seldom if ever met. The assumption of perfect competition may nevertheless provide a useful explanation of market behavior:

If there are a "reasonable" number of alternative buyers and sellers

If the effect on the market of the entry or withdrawal of a few of them is not "appreciable"

If buyers are "reasonably" well informed about quality differences.[103]

The problem once again is to decide how much divergence is too much, and that decision will hinge—as always—upon what the model purports to explain.

The assumption of perfect competition is used by Peter Temin in his analysis of the ante-bellum iron industry of western Pennsylvania to

100. Fogel and Engerman 1971b:156–157; Temin 1964a:32.
101. Fogel and Engerman 1971b:156.
102. Fogel and Engerman 1971b:156; McCloskey 1968:285.
103. Eckaus 1972:72.

infer (a) that prices closely approximated real costs of production, and therefore (b) that observed movements in price could be considered indicative of changing supply conditions (1964b). The same assumption of an identity between price and costs becomes considerably more suspect when applied to the steel industry of the late nineteenth century or to the American railroad sector of 1890.[104] How much competition diverged from perfect and how much prices diverged from costs is, of course, the central question in both cases. The tradition of science—and presumably of a social science—is that he who asserts must offer proof of those assertions. When the price-cost relationship of perfect competition is used to analyze an industry featuring the likes of Andrew Carnegie or J. J. Hill, the cliometrician would seem under some obligation to offer evidence demonstrating that the apparent marked divergence of his assumptions from reality does not affect his ultimate conclusions. Without that evidence, the merits of both the model and its conclusions remain obscure.

The same caveat applies to the assumption of constant costs. The image of the ante-bellum iron industry expanding and contracting its output without seriously affecting the price of factor inputs is not likely to be contested by most historians of the period.[105] The image of 79.2 billion ton-miles of railroad freight being rediverted to alternative carriers in 1890 without affecting the per-unit costs of those alternative carriers has considerably less appeal.[106] Here, too, the cliometrician who asserts what is not intuitively obvious has an obligation to marshal evidence demonstrating that any probable divergence of his assumptions from reality is unlikely to affect significantly his final conclusions.

e. Supply Conditions of Perfect Competition and Cobb-Douglas Production Functions

What of the second pair of assumptions common to supply side analysis? The combination of perfect competition with the assumption of an industry-wide or nation-wide Cobb-Douglas production function

104. The assumption is used for analysis of the steel industry in Temin 1963 and criticized in Smolensky 1963. The same assumption is used by Fogel in his calculation of social saving attributable to the railroads in 1890 (1964a) and criticized in McClelland 1968.
105. Fogel and Engerman 1971b:156; Temin 1964a and 1964b.
106. See Fogel 1964a:28; for criticism of the assumption, see McClelland 1968.

raises a complicated assessment problem. It begins with yet another construct of economic theory, the elasticity of substitution, which measures how easily factors of production can be substituted for one other. (The equation defining the elasticity of substitution is somewhat complex and need not be elaborated for purposes of this discussion.[107]) In a world characterized by the constant production coefficients of input-output analysis, output can be created by only one fixed combination or recipe of inputs. Factors cannot be substituted for each other, and the elasticity of substitution is therefore zero. In a world characterized by Cobb-Douglas production functions, the substitution of one factor for another in the production process is much easier. The elasticity of substitution in this case happens to be unity, and it is this characteristic which constitutes the most distinctive feature of the Cobb-Douglas production function. Why this is so need not concern us here.[108] One might note in passing that the ease with which factors can be substituted for each other is the reason why the share of each factor in total output should be observed to remain constant over time (and that constant share was the critical ingredient in the partitioning of causal forces described elsewhere). To cite an example: the national

107. "The elasticity of substitution ... tells us how rapidly diminishing returns set in to one factor of production when its price falls relative to another factor price. For two factors of production, labour (N) and capital (C), it is represented symbolically by

$$\sigma = \left[\frac{d\left(\frac{N}{C}\right)}{\left(\frac{N}{C}\right)}\right] \div \left[\frac{d\left(\frac{fC}{fN}\right)}{\left(\frac{fC}{fN}\right)}\right],$$

where fN is the marginal product of labour, and fC is the marginal product of capital. The ratio of the marginal product of capital to the marginal product of labour is the marginal rate of substitution of labour for capital. ... Hence the elasticity of substitution as defined in the formula relates the proportional change in the relative factor inputs to a proportional change in the marginal rate of substitution between labour and capital. ... Intuitively, it can be thought of as a measure of the ease of substitution of labour for capital" (Brown 1966:18). The nature of the above formula is perhaps more clear if one defines

$$u = \frac{N}{C} \text{ and } R = \left(\frac{\partial x}{\partial C}\right) \div \left(\frac{\partial x}{\partial N}\right)$$

where (x) represents output. The elasticity of substitution is then

$$\sigma = \left(\frac{du}{u}\right) \div \left(\frac{dR}{R}\right).$$

(See Brown 1966:35.)
108. See Brown 1966:35–36.

labor supply might increase, thereby lowering the relative price of labor. All producers would then try to use more of this cheaper input. In a Cobb-Douglas world, so readily can labor be substituted for other inputs that any increase in its supply will never precipitate a sharp decline in its price. More specifically, the decline in labor's price will be offset by the increased quantity used in such a way that labor's share of total output will remain virtually unchanged.

The historian thoroughly confused by the prevalence of jargon and unspecified theoretical inferences need only focus upon two points (or accept on faith two assertions). *If* the production process is Cobb-Douglas in structure, *then* one ought to observe that the elasticity of substitution (however it is defined) is not significantly different from unity when available data are subjected to econometric testing. If the production process is Cobb-Douglas in structure *and* markets are highly competitive, then one ought to observe a constancy over time in the share paid to each factor of production. These constitute two independent tests of whether the world is Cobb-Douglas in structure and one test of whether it is both Cobb-Douglas and highly competitive.

What is the evidence? Cliometric studies of nineteenth-century data on occasion do refer to the constancy of the share paid to each factor of production over time.[109] Somewhat less frequently evidence is cited from modern studies of postwar American manufacturing that indicates an elasticity of substitution not significantly different from unity when cross-section data are subjected to econometric testing. (Whether or not time series data support the same conclusion is still a subject of debate.[110]) If the manufacturing production processes in nineteenth-century America resembled those of the modern era, then the modern data—and recent studies of that data—do lend tenuous support to the representation of industry-wide production conditions by an industry-wide Cobb-Douglas production function.

109. For their study of the ante-bellum iron industry, Fogel and Engerman cite the constancy of factor shares between 1860 and 1870 (1971b:156); for his aggregate study of the British economy, McCloskey cites the constancy of factor shares between 1870 and 1914 (1970:450 n. 1); for his aggregate study of the American economy, Gallman cites the constancy of factor shares in the nineteenth century (1972:37)—an empirical assertion questioned below. In their study of ante-bellum agriculture, Fogel and Engerman merely note that various studies "for the post-bellum years between 1870 and 1960 [give] ... the labor share [ranging] from about 0.33 to 0.70. ... The value of 0.60 was chosen rather arbitrarily as a plausible value for a labor share about the middle of the nineteenth century" (1971d:358).

110. For a survey of this literature, see Jorgenson 1972; and Bridge 1971:Chapter 6.

The case for applying the same function to nation-wide analysis is much less convincing. The ignoring of all demand factors—and perforce the ignoring of all Keynesian problems—can be justified only by assuming that in the long run supply will create its own demand. For nineteenth-century America, with its flexible price structure and highly competitive environment, that assumption does not appear to be unreasonable. Doubts begin to arise, however, when one notes that nineteenth-century American data do not indicate that the share of total output paid to labor was relatively constant over time, either for the economy as a whole or for broad subsectors such as agriculture and industry.[111] Equally damaging is Lebergott's contention that such constancy as can be observed may well be a fabrication of the collection procedure. "We find that these data . . . were originally estimated with so many constancies stipulated in the estimation procedure that we can safely conclude nothing from them about the constancy of labor's share" (1964:54). As for the share of other factors of production, "We conclude that the conceptual problem of disentangling capital from labor returns to entrepreneurs makes useless a discussion of labor's share in total national income—as well as in any industry dominated by entrepreneurial activity, such as agriculture, construction, and trade and service."[112]

The challenge does not end here. A key theoretical difficulty is that if an aggregate production function is to exist at all—if national supplies of a few basic inputs are to be viewed as combining, within the context of a specific production function, to create national output—then one must also assume that production conditions within all firms in the economy are *very* similar with respect to capital used, labor proportions employed, and output created. An exploration of the precise assumptions required would lead the discussion unnecessarily into one of the more thorny paths of economic theory.[113] What is significant for our purposes is that the theoretician who first elaborated those assumptions

111. See Budd 1960:373.
112. Lebergott 1964:54. See also Denison 1964; Scitovsky 1964:20; and Solow 1958.
113. "For the existence of an aggregate capital stock . . . what is required is that the production functions of individual firms differ at most by capital-augmenting technical differences . . . [for] the existence of labor and output aggregates [what is required is that] every firm must hire the same proportions of each type of labor and produce the same market basket of outputs" (F. M. Fisher 1971a:305). For attempts to modify the stringent assumption of disembodied technical change—the assumption that capital formation is not a vehicle for carrying technical change into effect—see Solow 1960; and Thurow and Taylor 1966.

also noted that for a diverse economy they "are far too stringent to be believable."[114] The same author did concede that *if* the observed share paid to each factor of production remains relatively constant over time, then a nation-wide Cobb-Douglas production function—although an artificial construct—will still predict certain macroeconomic variables fairly well.[115] This justification for reinstating an aggregate Cobb-Douglas production function into the analysis of long-term growth is unacceptable in the American case for the simplest of reasons: the requisite constancy in factor shares is not supported by available data on those shares.[116]

The implications are rather far-reaching. To cite but one example, Fogel and Engerman's pathbreaking work *Time on the Cross* (1974) contains two novel assertions upon which much of that book is built: (a) southern agriculture was more efficient than northern agriculture in ante-bellum America, and (b) black slave labor was more efficient than free labor. As their reviewers have pointed out,[117] the second is derived from the first. Fogel and Engerman demonstrate to their satisfaction that southern agriculture was more efficient, rule out other explanations for that efficiency, and then infer (rather than demonstrate) that the cause must have been the superior productivity of slave labor. The key economic question therefore concerns the validity of the estimation procedures used to derive their conclusions about southern agriculture. To calculate relative regional efficiency Fogel and Engerman use an aggregate Cobb-Douglas production function for all of northern and southern agriculture. Many of the numerical inputs can be shown to be highly suspect.[118] Even more suspect is the legitimacy of using an aggregate Cobb-Douglas production function for all of the reasons cited above. To accept these criticisms is, in effect, to dash into ruins a central pillar—really *the* central pillar—of *Time on the Cross*, leaving in a state of confusion and uncertainty all of the associated inferences.

114. F. M. Fisher 1971a:305. The initial article specifying the assumptions was F. M. Fisher 1969.
115. F. M. Fisher 1971a:306–307.
116. "It is obvious that, since a Cobb-Douglas production function implies the constancy of labor's share, such a function cannot be expected to explain wages well in an economy in which that share is not constant" (F. M. Fisher 1971a:306). For a brief survey of other problems, see Nadiri 1970:1144–1146.
117. See, for example, David and Temin 1974:744, 764–767.
118. For example, see above, n. 109; also David and Temin 1974:767–778.

To review: for manufacturing studies of nineteenth-century America the assumptions of perfect competition and an industry-wide Cobb-Douglas production function can be given at least tenuous support by observations on the multiplicity of firms and the constancy of factor shares in total output and by twentieth-century studies of American manufacturing which suggest that (at least for the twentieth-century industries examined) the elasticity of substitution of factors of production does not appear to have been significantly different from unity. The same assumptions applied to the nation as a whole will not do. Factor shares do not appear to have been constant over time, and what constancy can be observed is highly suspect given the manner in which the data were initially assembled. Last but by no means least, the assumptions that one must make to guarantee the existence of *any* aggregate production function are so stringent that these aggregate production functions cannot be regarded even as good approximate descriptions of the manner in which output is generated within a diverse economy. The student of American economic history may therefore be tempted to conclude what at least one econometrician has concluded within a broader framework: that "any attempt to use production functions for long-run purposes seems bound to fail."[119]

f. Capital-Output Ratios, Growth Models, and Technological Progress

More believable alternatives appear to be distressingly scarce. Growth models of the Rostow/Lewis type, relying primarily or exclusively upon the driving force of capital accumulation harnessed to a fixed capital-output ratio, can be dismissed as blatantly inadequate. The historical record contradicts their main empirical assertion: the rate of investment did not rise from 5 percent or less to 10 percent or more of GNP during the formative years of industrialization in the now-developed countries.[120] Recent studies of twentieth-century data show, at best, a poor correlation between income and investment, at worst, a negative correlation between economic growth and the marginal capital-output ratio (at least in the short run).[121] Again the evidence contradicts the theory: in this case, the postulate of constancy in a nation-wide marginal capital-output ratio. This is hardly surprising.

---

119. Bridge 1971:397.
120. See Kuznets 1965.
121. Leibenstein 1966b; also for a brief survey, see Morgan 1969:397–399.

To cite only one of a host of problems, what production conditions would allow the expansion in output to be tied so rigorously to variations in capital inputs? One theoretical possibility would be an economy that was heavily endowed with surplus labor; with all production functions featuring fixed technological coefficients of the input-output variety; and with all output created by only two inputs: labor and capital. The example merely helps to illustrate the absurdity of assuming a constancy in a nation-wide marginal capital-output ratio. As for the overall importance of this particular input to the growth process, the prevailing opinion among development economists is that capital accumulation per se explains very little of the observed long-term growth in per capita income achieved by developed countries, nor is the pattern expected to change in the near future.[122]

The driving force usually regarded as the prime contributor to advances in per capita income is technological progress,[123] and about the origins of this variable economists know distressingly little. A. W. Whitehead's judgment that "the greatest invention of the nineteenth century was the method of invention"[124] may seem more rightly applied to the twentieth century, but however systematized this method has become since the days of Matthew Boulton and James Watt, the forces determining how it will be administered, to what problems, and with what results are still largely an unsolved mystery. The difficulty of predicting future inventions or even of judging the worth of the current stock is suggested by the London *Times* forecast in 1906 that "all attempts at artificial aviation . . . are . . . foredoomed to failure," and four years later the announcement by the British secretary of state for

122. Estimates have been made that no more than 10 to 30 percent of the observed rise in per capita income for a variety of countries over a variety of time periods can be attributed to increases in the stock of capital "with the lower part of the range more probable" (Morgan 1969:397). For American estimates, see Davis *et al.* 1972:39; and Denison 1962. For generalizations concerning the evidence of many nations, see Leibenstein 1966b:20; and Kuznets 1966:80–81. The main difficulty with accepting this evidence as conclusive proof of the relative unimportance of capital accumulation is that these estimates are often based upon growth models incorporating aggregate Cobb-Douglas production functions—a procedure highly suspect in the American case for reasons already noted.

123. See, for example, Hahn and Matthews 1964:832; and Kennedy and Thirlwall 1972:62. The phrase "technical progress," as previously noted, is a catch-all for such developments as improved organization and changes in the quality of inputs, as well as for the adoption of new machines and new techniques of production.

124. Quoted in Jewkes, Sawers, and Stillerman 1958:32.

war that "we do not consider that aeroplanes will be of any possible use for war purposes."[125]

The contours of this process are not entirely shrouded in darkness. Current evidence suggests that profit incentives have some influence on the actions of would-be inventors.[126] Jacob Schmookler has demonstrated that patent activity is positively correlated with changes in the demand for the product which the patented inventions are designed to improve.[127] The inventive process itself, however, is still regarded by most historians as being largely random and capricious—particularly so in those primeval days before the advent of the modern corporation, research and development departments, and the systematic harnessing of science to problems of technology.[128] If correct, this view would effectively preclude the formulation of a rigorous and widely applicable theory of the inventive process. That in turn would effectively limit the chances of devising a comprehensive theory of economic growth.[129]

To sum up: cliometric models incorporating Cobb-Douglas production functions and log-linear demand curves can yield a set of equations that incorporate a number of the foremost causal mechanisms of economic theory. When applied at the industry-wide level, these equations sometimes fit quite well much of the data which they are designed to explain. Growth models based upon aggregate Cobb-Douglas production functions or upon nation-wide marginal capital-output ratios may also be found, on occasion, to fit quite well the principal macroeconomic data of a given society. In the latter case, however, neither model would seem to be consistent with much of available evidence, and both require, to be valid representations of the growth process, assumptions that appear far too stringent to be considered as reasonable first approximations for a diverse economy. Finally, our

125. Quoted in *ibid*, pp. 230–231.
126. See Nordhaus 1969a:16–28; Nelson 1959.
127. Schmookler 1966. His results appear in condensed form in Schmookler 1962.
128. See, for example, Jewkes, Sawers, and Stillerman 1958:226; Nelson 1959:121–122. Even Schmookler conceded that "technological change is the *terra incognita* of modern economics" (1966:3).
129. Perhaps one of the most promising suggestions for the direction of future research has been made by a cliometrician. "It is not an economic history, but a piece of intellectual history, that is needed—a history that will show ideas developing from ideas and transmitted from one group to another, responding sometimes to local factor proportions, but exhibiting the continuous assault, at ever deeper levels of penetration, of the mind of man upon external nature" (Parker 1966:102–103).

knowledge about the determinants of that one factor considered central to the growth process—technical change—is nothing short of abysmal. The implied conclusion is both obvious and exasperating. The development economist and the economic historian would both welcome new theoretical constructs to facilitate their analysis of long-term change. At least to date, both wait in vain.[130]

Significant progress has been made, but only in achieving better solutions for problems of a lesser scope, or more cautiously, better approximate solutions. For the analysis of short-run patterns of undramatic changes, without unduly straining the credibility of most readers, the cliometrician can often use those assumptions and tools that are the stock in trade of the economic theoretician: profit-maximizing behavior by operators of small-scale firms producing in highly competitive markets; relatively constant costs for limited variations in output; relative constancy in other production relationships to facilitate the search for missing data. Across much of the time and space that is the history of Western market economies, these often appear to constitute reasonable first approximations to reality. More tenuous but perhaps still useful within the same arena—the analysis of short-run patterns of undramatic changes—are such tools as log-linear demand curves and industry-wide Cobb-Douglas production functions for partitioning the relative importance of those causal forces underlying short-run economic change. The larger goal of partitioning the impact of causal forces underlying long-term economic change—for many, the most exciting goal of economic history—would seem as yet beyond our grasp.

6. Causal Explanation and Model Building in the New Economic History: Prospect and Retrospect

I always say the chief end of man is to form general propositions—adding that no general proposition is worth a damn. [Oliver Wendell Holmes][131]

Every year, if not every day, we have to wager our salvation upon some prophecy based upon imperfect knowledge. [Oliver Wendell Holmes][132]

130. For skepticism concerning the worth of available growth theories as guides for advisors to less developed nations, see Ackley 1970:91; Foley, Shell, and Sidrauski 1969:698; Hahn and Matthews 1964:890; Leontief 1968:73–74; Morgan 1969:403.
131. Howe, ed. 1961:II, 13.
132. Abrams v. United States, 250 U.S. 616, 630 (1919).

The first of these quotations was also cited at the beginning of this book. Its purpose, then and now, is to underscore the uncertainty that accompanies every causal generalization. Implicit in the second quotation is the strongest argument against the first. For all their imperfections, causal generalizations have been, and will remain, an invaluable guide for human action. We mortals are, as Max Born noted, invariably committed to "playing dice for our little purposes of prognosis."[133] Those players who rely upon available generalizations do better in the long run than those who do not—or so we believe, and much in our personal experience supports that belief.

The historian plays a different game. His problem, insofar as it concerns the use of causal generalizations, is to explain the past, not predict the future. And yet the point just made applies with equal force. The key to success—or to the best possible success—is reliance upon the best possible generalizations. The cliometrician merely tries to follow this prescription in a self-conscious way. To the task of explaining economic history he brings the special tools of quantification, economic theory, and statistical techniques. His strengths reflect the strengths of his tools: the clarification of dimensions given by quantification; the mass of causal generalizations, often subtle and complex, offered by economic theory; the particular kind of consistency between hypothesis and available data provided by statistical techniques. The cliometrician's weaknesses, as one would expect, reflect the limitations of these selfsame tools. In his attempt to unravel the economic history of the past, he often finds that not every relevant variable can be quantified, and those that can are subject to the inevitable imperfections in historical data; not all of the needed causal generalizations can be borrowed from economic theory, and those that can inevitably ignore some relevant causal factors; not all of the numerical sensitivities linking causes and effects can be estimated by statistical techniques, and those that can are subject to all of the uncertainties and the confidence intervals of the model from which they spring.

However constraining such limitations may be, one cannot accept, or even condone, the type of accusation typified by Gunnar Myrdal's claim that growth theories focusing only upon economic variables are "doomed to be unrealistic, and thus irrelevant" (1958:235). All

133. Quoted in Schilpp, ed. 1949:176.

causal explanations consist of subsuming facts under generalizations; all generalizations are formulated by abstraction; all resulting abstractions are imperfect; and because of the associated imperfections, all generalizations linking causes and effects must be prefaced with the word "Probably." In short, all causal explanations are unrealistic. The relevant issue, as repeatedly stressed in previous discussions, is how much unrealism is too much, and that (also as repeatedly stressed elsewhere) depends upon the uses to which these causal generalizations are put. There is therefore a unity of method in all causal explanations and a unity in the kinds of problems that arise in attempting to formulate such explanations. The cliometrician's techniques and the problems that he encounters in implementing them are appropriately viewed as case studies within this more general framework.

For all these unexceptional qualities, the cliometrician's procedures—or many of those procedures—have about them a special sense of the precarious. As noted in Chapter III, contemporary economic theory is often useful to predict tendencies, but has a relatively undistinguished record in forecasting exact magnitudes. The cliometrician would use this same theory in economic models to derive, by counterfactual speculation, the relative importance of various causal factors observed to operate in a given historical setting. The end result may seem to be precise and must often be accurate within comparatively narrow bounds to justify the kinds of inferences subsequently made. The more precise the end result must be to justify the inferences, the more daring and tenuous this form of intellectual speculation becomes; because despite the human craving for certainty and precision, in science, in the social sciences, and in this particular application of a social science to problems of historical analysis—that now familiar phrase—all is tentative, all admits to revision.

In a survey of extant growth theories in 1959, Nobel laureate Simon Kuznets decried the narrow formalism of economic models, but castigated with equal vigor the amorphous, broad-gauged, nonoperational hypothesis that emphasized the role of social, political, and cultural factors in the growth process: "The outcome is either withdrawal into the refuge of mathematical models operating with a few variables, or amateurish cogitations on a vast theme. One has the advantage of formal elegance, and the other, that of at least calling attention to the wider array of factors that have to be taken into account; but neither outcome is satisfactory" (1959:15).

The same dichotomy in options would seem to typify the current state of economic history. Two warring camps confront each other with distrust, occasional hostility, and a minimum of communication. On the one side is a small band of competent economists: rigorous in their methods, preoccupied with generalization, and accused of battering the subtle fabric of history into the Procrustean bed dictated by their theoretical models, available data, and statistical techniques. On the other side is ranged the vast majority of historians, their preferences and scholarship reflecting the antiquarian's instinct for the unique and the humanist's distrust of universal propositions. Their faults—or so the other side maintains—include a propensity to condemn cliometrics with little understanding of its methods, substituting instead under the guise of subtlety what is in fact confused, nonoperational, and, on occasion, inconsistent causal analysis of the historical process. The challenge for the present generation might therefore be condensed into a single question: Is there no middle ground?

Bibliographic Note

The simplest objective for a bibliography to achieve is the duplication of references cited in the body of the work. The purpose is to allow the reader who has forgotten a citation, or who encounters a later and abbreviated citation, to track down the complete version without backtracking through footnotes. A second objective is to list relevant works for the topics covered. If that list becomes inordinately long, a third priority is to preface such a list with a critical bibliography offering some evaluation of the more important books and articles. Achieving the first is a trivial accomplishment. Achieving the second and third to any tolerable degree of perfection in a work such as this is impossible. What follows therefore is a list of works which, for various reasons of varying importance, were found to be useful in the writing of this book. The list is prefaced with a commentary that is not comprehensive, but merely attempts to suggest to the novice some points of departure that may prove helpful in pursuing the issues raised in each chapter.

Chapter I

One of the best introductions to problems of methodology, epistemology, and explanation is a book by Ernest Nagel (1961), with the misleading title *The Structure of Science*. Brief and readable introductions to the general problems of causal explanation may be found in articles by Herbert Feigl (1953), J. R. Lucas (1962), Daniel Lerner (1965b), and Bertrand Russell (1953). Hume's views on the subject in summary form can be found in C. J. Ducasse (1966). For a closer look at the scientist's perspective on such problems, the reader might skim Volume I of A. D'Abro (1952), or consult two articles by Nagel (1953a, 1965) on various types of scientific explanation. A classic on the changing metaphysical foundations of natural science is Edwin Burtt (1951).

An introduction to the various concepts of probability from the perspective of a philosopher may be found in Max Black's article (1967) in the *Encyclopedia of Philosophy*, and from the perspective of a social scientist in Bruno de Finetti's article (1968) in the *International Encyclopedia of the Social Sciences*. Also useful although somewhat technical is Harold Jeffreys' survey (1955). As a preliminary to reading Rudolf Carnap, the reader might find it useful to consult Paul Meehl's brief discussion (1958) of the two concepts of probability. A summary of Carnap's position by Carnap is provided in Carnap (1945). Brief summaries of that position by others include the articles by John Lenz (1956) and Wesley Salmon (1967). A compact attempt to relate the concepts of probability and causation is available in Hans Reichenbach (1953). For those with a grounding in the relevant mathematics, a recent and exceptional survey of the different types of probability is available in Terrence Fine (1973).

Chapter II

The phrase "philosophy of history" has two quite different meanings, only one of which has as its main concern problems of epistemology and methodology. A concise survey of both meanings is provided in William Dray's article (1967) in the *Encyclopedia of Philosophy*. For a more comprehensive introduction to the problems of historical explanation, the reader might consult either Patrick Gardiner's book (1952) or Isaiah Berlin's article (1960). Useful guides to the many and often conflicting points of view on this subject are the collections of readings compiled by Patrick Gardiner (1959) and Fritz Stern (1956).

Historians seldom attempt to write explicitly about the methodological problems of their profession. Among the notable exceptions are books by Marc Bloch (1953), G. Kitson Clark (1967), G. R. Elton (1970), and J. H. Hexter (1971). Also by an historian, but somewhat more controversial, is David Fischer's survey (1970) of some of the defective practices in his profession. Other useful sources for historians' views of their own craft are the articles in Sidney Hook's *Symposium* (1963), especially those contributed by Bernard Bailyn, Carl Degler, Leo Gershoy, and Leonard Krieger.

The main ideas of Collingwood appear in his *Idea of History* (1946); those of Dilthey have been translated by H. A. Hodges (1952). Summaries and criticisms of their views may be found in a variety of sources, including Leon Goldstein (1970), Louis Mink (1968), and William Walsh (1960). A survey of the origins and possible meanings of the word *verstehen* is available in Theodore Abel (1948).

Carl Hempel's seminal article was Hempel (1942). His original position was later modified in Hempel and Oppenheim (1948) and further elaborated in Hempel (1962, 1963, and 1964). These views, in their original or modified form, have been repeatedly summarized and/or attacked by other writers. Among the more concise attempts are the articles by Alan Donagan (1959), Maurice Mandelbaum (1961), and Michael Scriven (1962).

William Dray provides an outline of his own position in Sidney Hook's *Symposium* (1963) and a more extended version in his book (1970). His views have also been repeatedly summarized and/or attacked by other writers, including James Leach (1966) and Maurice Mandelbaum (1961). The latter contrasts the views of Dray with those of Hempel.

By comparison with the previous authors, Michael Scriven's contribution to this debate has drawn relatively little commentary. That contribution is outlined in two principal sources, Scriven (1959b) and (1963).

Chapter III

An introduction to economics from a conventional point of view can be acquired from such conventional textbooks as Paul Samuelson (1973) or Richard Eckaus (1972). An indication of how the same subject matter is viewed from a modern and left-of-center perspective is available in John Kenneth Galbraith (1973a) or Joan Robinson and John Eatwell (1973). An older classic that still wears well is Alfred Marshall (1952). Recently compiled and useful for the beginning student are the survey articles in Nancy Ruggles (1970), especially those by James Tobin and Robert Solow on macroeconomics and microeconomics, respectively. More advanced surveys of specialized fields can be found in the back issues of the *Economic*

Journal, the *Journal of Economic Literature*, and the *American Economic Review*.
Textbooks on econometrics vary from the extremely elementary (and for that reason, not very helpful), such as V. O. Key, Jr. (1954); to the more rigorous but still introductory, such as Ralph Beals (1972) or Edward Kane (1968); through such middle-level books as Wonnacott and Wonnacott (1970); to such staples of graduate courses as J. Johnson (1963). Problems of defining econometrics are discussed in Gerhard Tintner (1953). General articles surveying the state of the art or the limits of the tool include J. K. Gifford (1968), J. Johnson (1967), Dale Jorgenson (1970), Edwin Kuh (1965), Gerhard Tintner (1966), and William White (1967).
Distinguished works by economists on the methodology of their discipline are comparatively rare. The older classics include John Cairnes (1888) and John Neville Keynes (1891). More recent writings on the topic include Frank Knight (1951 and 1956), T. C. Koopmans (1957), Oskar Lange (1945/46) and the collection of articles in Sherman Krupp (1966a). Milton Friedman's principal contribution is the lead essay in Friedman (1953). The three articles by Paul Samuelson that sparked the most controversy are Samuelson (1963, 1964, and 1965a). His other contributions include Samuelson (1952, 1955, and 1965b).
Friedman's position has been repeatedly examined in methodological articles, generally by those hostile to his position. Notable exceptions include the writings of Fritz Machlup, especially Machlup (1955 and 1966). Friedman's views are compared with those of Machlup in Jack Melitz (1965). The more unfriendly reviews of Friedman's position include D. V. T. Bear and Daniel Orr (1967), Richard Cyert and E. Grunberg (1963), Ernest Nagel (1963a), Eugene Rotwein (1959), Stanley Wong (1973), and the three articles cited previously by Samuelson (1963, 1964, and 1965a). By comparison with Friedman, Samuelson's statements on methodology have provoked far less comment. Criticisms may be found in Gerald Garb (1965), Abba Lerner (1965), Fritz Machlup (1964), G. J. Massey (1965), and Stanley Wong (1970).
The literature by and for economists does include a number of other methodological debates, but by the standards of the philosopher, none of these is particularly distinguished. Among the best known are the exchanges between G. C. Archibald and the "Chicago School" [Archibald (1961 and 1963), Friedman (1963), and George Stigler (1963)]; T. W. Hutchison's debate with Kurt Klappholz and J. Agassi on the testability of propositions [Hutchison (1960) and Klappholz and Agassi (1959 and 1960)]; Hutchison's debate with Machlup on the possibility of verifying assumptions [Hutchison (1956) and Machlup (1956)]; Hutchison's debate with Frank Knight on whether economics is a science [Hutchison (1941) and Knight (1940 and 1941)]; and T. C. Koopmans' dispute with Rutledge Vining "on the choice of variables to be studied" [Koopmans (1947 and 1949b) and Vining (1949a and 1949b)].

Chapter IV

A compact survey of most of the major philosophical problems associated with contrary-to-fact conditionals is available in R. S. Walters' article (1967) in the *Encyclopedia of Philosophy*. Also useful as introductions to the subject are J. L. Mackie (1962), Nicholas Rescher (1961), and William Sellars (1958). Less intelligible to the layman but among the older classics are Roderick Chisholm (1946) and Nelson Goodman (1947). The writings of economists and historians on this topic (again by the standards of the philosopher) have been comparatively undistinguished. One of the best efforts is J. D. Gould (1969).

Chapter V

Most of the major economic historians of previous generations have written articles surveying the methods, accomplishments, and prospects of their discipline. Some of the best surveys include Thomas Cochran (1947), Arthur Cole (1968a), N. S. B. Gras (1927), and Herbert Heaton (1942). More concerned with problems of defining the discipline and evaluating its methods are W. J. Ashley (1893), T. S. Ashton (1946), Guy Callender (1913), J. H. Clapham (1931), Edwin Gay (1941), John U. Nef (1944), and Chester Wright (1938). Most of the more accomplished and comprehensive surveys of the methods and achievements of the new economic history have been written by cliometricians. These include Lance Davis (1968), Davis, Hughes, and Reiter (1960), Albert Fishlow and Robert Fogel (1971), Fogel (1964b, 1965, 1966), Alexander Gershenkron (1967), Douglass North (1965), and Peter Temin (1971a). The date of the article is indicative of how much of the period since the mid-1950's has been surveyed, with the more recent articles—predictably—offering the most comprehensive surveys. A number of methodological papers on economic history have been assembled in Ralph Andreano (1970). An extensive and recent survey of both business history and economic history is available in James Baughman (1971).

Most of the principal articles of the new economic history can be found in the *Journal of Economic History* and *Explorations in Economic History* (formerly *Explorations in Entrepreneurial History*, second series), although in recent years a number have begun to appear in the British publication *Economic History Review*. Less frequently, major articles have appeared in periodicals not primarily devoted to economic history, such as *American Economic Review, Review of Economics and Statistics, Journal of Political Economy*, and *Quarterly Journal of Economics*. Among the more successful attempts to assemble important articles are those by Ralph Andreano (1965c) and Fogel and Engerman (1971c), although most of the contents of the latter is likely to be intelligible only to the expert economist. One of the best introductory textbooks to American economic history—perhaps the best in terms of data assembled, hypotheses discussed, and evidence considered—is Lance Davis *et al.* (1972).

The same source is one of two obvious starting points for those in search of numerical series of special importance to American economic history. The other is U.S. Bureau of the Census (1960). Many of the pioneering efforts to compile comprehensive data series may be found in Volumes 24 and 30 of the National Bureau of Economic Research *Studies in Income and Wealth*, such as those of Robert Gallman (1960 and 1966) and Stanley Lebergott (1960 and 1966). For data on international comparisons, the indispensable starting point are two books by Simon Kuznets (1966 and 1971).

Innumerable articles and a few books have been written on the merits and demerits of using quantification in historical analysis. Writings by historians include William Aydelotte (1966 and 1971), Lee Benson (1957), Charles Dollar and Richard Jensen (1971), J. H. Hexter (1966), and S. Thernstrom (1967). Among the older classics on this topic written by economic historians are J. H. Clapham (1931), Eli Heckscher (1939), and A. P. Usher (1932). More recent pleas for quantification by cliometricians can be found in the survey articles cited previously. Two first-rate studies devoted specifically to the pitfalls in historical statistics are Oskar Morgenstern (1963) and Goran Ohlin (1966).

Older pleas by economic historians for the use of economic theory in their discipline are comparatively rare. The outstanding exception is Heckscher (1929). Recent pleas by cliometricians can be found in their survey articles noted above.

Two pioneering articles on the use of statistical theory in economic history are Simon Kuznets (1941) and John Meyer and Alfred Conrad (1957). The literature giving close scrutiny to the uses and limitations of econometrics in economic history is surprisingly limited. Perhaps the most distinguished is Gavin Wright (1971a), although R. L. Basmann (1965) and G. N. von Tunzelmann (1968) may be more helpful to those without special expertise in the subject.

On the complex issue of the uses and limitations of mathematics in applied economics (including its use in economic history), most of the writings by economists appear, yet again, to be comparatively undistinguished by the standards of the philosopher. Articles on the subject include Kenneth Arrow (1951), William Baumol (1966), Robert Dorfman (1954a), James Duesenberry (1954), Oskar Morgenstern (1963a), Paul Samuelson (1952), and George Stigler (1950).

No effort will be made to summarize the principal articles and books written by cliometricians. A list of accomplishments can be found in any of the recent surveys noted above. Writings that bear upon the specific issues raised in Chapter V are noted in the footnotes of that chapter, although the coverage in those footnotes must be regarded, at best, as being representative of work being done. One omission from the institutional section that should be corrected here concerns two forthcoming books by John Hughes, *Social Control in the Colonial Economy* and *Social Control in the American Economy*. Both promise to be scholarly contributions of the first importance.

Bibliography

Abel, Theodore. 1948. "The Operation Called *Verstehen.*" *American Journal of Sociology*, LIV (Nov.), 211–218.

Abelson, Raziel. 1963. "Cause and Reason in History," in Sidney Hook (ed.), *Philosophy and History*. New York: New York University Press. Pp. 167–173.

Achinstein, Peter. 1965. "Theoretical Models." *British Journal for the Philosophy of Science*, XVI (Aug.), 102–120.

Ackley, Gardner. 1970. "Economic Stabilization and Growth," in Nancy D. Ruggles (ed.), *Economics*. Englewood Cliffs, N.J.: Prentice-Hall. Pp. 89–100.

Aitken, Hugh G. J. 1971. "The Entrepreneurial Approach to Economic History," in George Rogers Taylor and Lucius F. Ellsworth (eds.), *Approaches to American Economic History*. Charlottesville: University Press of Virginia. Pp. 1–16.

——. 1965a. "Entrepreneurial Research: The History of an Intellectual Innovation," in his *Explorations in Enterprise*. Cambridge, Mass.: Harvard University Press. Pp. 3–19.

—— (ed.). 1965b. *Explorations in Enterprise*. Cambridge, Mass.: Harvard University Press.

——. 1963. "The Future of Entrepreneurial Research." *Explorations in Entrepreneurial History*, 2d ser., I (Fall), 3–9.

——. 1960. "On the Present State of Economic History." *Canadian Journal of Economics and Political Science*, XXVI (Feb.), 87–95.

Alchian, Armen A. 1950. "Uncertainty, Evolution, and Economic Theory." *Journal of Political Economy*, LVIII (June), 211–221.

Alexander, Alex. 1967. "The Supply of Industrial Entrepreneurship." *Explorations in Entrepreneurial History*, 2d ser., IV (Winter), 29–44.

Allen, R. D. G. 1960. "The Structure of Macro-Economic Models." *Economic Journal*, LXX (March), 38–56.

Allport, Gordon W. 1962. "The General and the Unique in Psychological Science." *Journal of Personality*, XXX (Sept.), 405–422.

Anderson, John. 1952. "Hypotheticals." *Australasian Journal of Philosophy*, XXX (May), 1–16.

Anderson, Leonall C. 1973. "The State of the Monetarist Debate." Federal Reserve Bank of St. Louis, *Review*, LV (Sept.), 2–8.

Ando, Albert, Franklin M. Fisher, and Herbert A. Simon. 1963. *Essays on the Structure of Social Science Models*. Cambridge, Mass.: M.I.T. Press.

Andreano, Ralph L. 1965a. "Alfred Marshall's *Industry and Trade*: A Neglected Classic in Economic History," in his *New Views on American Economic Development*. Cambridge, Mass.: Shenkman. Pp. 317–329.

——. 1965b. "Four Recent Studies in American Economic History: Some Conceptual Implications," in his *New Views on American Economic Development*. Cambridge, Mass.: Shenkman. Pp. 13–26.

—— (ed.). 1970. *The New Economic History: Recent Papers on Methodology*. New York: Wiley.

—— (ed.). 1965c. *New Views on American Economic Development*. Cambridge, Mass.: Shenkman.

Archibald, G. C. 1961. "Chamberlin versus Chicago." *Review of Economic Studies*, XXIX (Oct.), 2–28.

——. 1967. "Refutation or Comparison." *British Journal for the Philosophy of Science*, XVII (Feb.), 279–296.

——. 1963. "Reply to Chicago." *Review of Economic Studies*, XXX (Feb.), 68–71.

——. 1959. "The State of Economic Science: A Review Article." *British Journal for the Philosophy of Science*, X (May), 58–69.

Aristotle. 1908. *The Works of Aristotle*. Translated and edited by John A. Smith and William D. Ross. *Metaphysica*, vol. VIII. Oxford: Clarendon Press.

Aron, Raymond. 1961. *Introduction to the Philosophy of History*. Translated by George J. Irwin. Boston: Beacon Press.

Arrow, Kenneth J. 1951. "Mathematical Models in the Social Sciences," in Daniel Lerner and Harold D. Lasswell (eds.), *The Policy Sciences: Recent Developments in Scope and Method*. Stanford: Stanford University Press. Pp. 129–154.

Arthur, C. J. 1968. "On the Historical Understanding." *History and Theory*, VII, No. 2, 203–216.

Ashley, W. J. 1893. "On the Study of Economic History." *Quarterly Journal of Economics*, VII (Jan.), 115–136.

——. 1927. "The Place of Economic History in University Studies." *Economic History Review*, I (Jan.), 1–11.

Ashton, T. S. 1946. "The Relation of Economic History to Economic Theory." *Economica*, XIII (May), 81–96.

Aydelotte, William O. 1966. "Quantification in History." *American Historical Review*, LXXI (April), 803–825.

——. 1971. *Quantification in History*. Reading, Mass.: Addison-Wesley.

Bailyn, Bernard. 1963. "The Problems of the Working Historian: A Comment," in Sidney Hook (ed.), *Philosophy and History*. New York: New York University Press. Pp. 92–101.

Barker, Evelyn. 1963. "Rational Explanations in History," in Sidney Hook (ed.), *Philosophy and History*. New York: New York University Press. Pp. 174–184.

Basmann, R. L. 1965. "The Role of the Economic Historian in Predictive Testing of Proffered 'Economic Laws.'" *Explorations in Entrepreneurial History*, 2d ser., II (Spring/Summer), 159–186.

Bauer, P. T. 1971. "Economic History as Theory." *Economica*, XXXVIII (May), 163–179.

Baughman, James P. 1971. "New Directions in American Economic and Business History," in George A. Billias and Gerald N. Grob (eds.), *American Economic History: Retrospect and Prospect*. New York: Free Press. Pp. 271–314.

Baumol, William J. 1966. "Economic Models and Mathematics," in Sherman R. Krupp (ed.), *The Structure of Economic Science*. Englewood Cliffs, N.J.: Prentice-Hall. Pp. 88–101.

——. 1968. "Entrepreneurship in Economic Theory." *American Economic Review*, LVIII (May), 64–71.

——. 1967. "Methodology," in his *Business Behavior, Value and Growth*. New York: Harcourt, Brace and World. Pp. 1–9.

——. 1963. "Toward the Construction of More Useful Models," in Alfred R. Oxenfeldt (ed.), *Models of Markets*. New York: Columbia University Press. Pp. 172–188.

Beals, Ralph E. 1972. *Statistics for Economists: An Introduction*. Chicago: Rand McNally.

Bear, D. V. T., and Daniel Orr. 1967. "Logic and Expediency in Economic Theorizing." *Journal of Political Economy*, LXXV (April), 188–196.

Becker, Gary S. 1962. "Irrational Behavior and Economic Theory." *Journal of Political Economy*, LXX (Feb.), 1–13.

Beer, Samuel H. 1963. "Causal Explanation and Imaginative Re-enactment." *History and Theory*, III, No. 1, 6–29.

Bell, Peter F. 1967. "The Direction of Entrepreneurial Explorations: A Review Article." *Explorations in Entrepreneurial History*, 2d ser., V (Fall), 3–11.

Bellman, Richard. 1961. *Adaptive Control Processes*. Princeton, N.J.: Princeton University Press.

Benson, Lee. 1957. "Research Problems in American Political Historiography," in Mirra Komarovsky (ed.), *Common Frontiers of the Social Sciences*. Glencoe, Ill.: Free Press. Pp. 113–183.

Berlin, Isaiah. 1954. *Historical Inevitability*. London: Oxford University Press.

——. 1960. "History and Theory: The Concept of Scientific History." *History and Theory*, I, No. 1, 1–31.

Bitter, Francis. 1963. *Mathematical Aspects of Physics*. Garden City, N.Y.: Anchor Books.

Black, Max. 1967. "Probability," in Paul Edwards (ed.), *Encyclopedia of Philosophy*, vol. VI. New York: Macmillan. Pp. 464–479.

Blalock, Herbert M. 1968. "The Measurement Problem: A Gap between the Language of Theory and Research," in Herbert and Ann Blalock (eds.), *Methodology in Social Research*. New York: McGraw-Hill. Pp. 5–27.

——, and Ann Blalock. 1968. *Methodology in Social Research*. New York: McGraw-Hill.

Bloch, Marc. 1953. *The Historian's Craft*. New York: Alfred A. Knopf.

Bogue, Allan G. 1968. "U.S.A.: The 'New' Political History." *Journal of Contemporary History*, III (Jan.), 5–27.

—— (ed.). 1973. *Emerging Theoretical Models in Social and Political History*. Beverly Hills: Sage.

——, and Margaret Bogue. 1957. "'Profits' and the Frontier Land Speculator." *Journal of Economic History*, XVII (March), 1–24.

Boring, Edwin G. 1963. *History, Psychology and Science: Selected Papers*. Edited by Robert I. Watson and Donald T. Campbell. New York: Wiley.

Born, Max. 1949. *Natural Philosophy of Cause and Chance*. Oxford: Clarendon Press.

Boulding, Kenneth E. 1966a. "The Economics of Knowledge and the Knowledge of Economics." *American Economic Review*, LVI (May), 1–13.

——. 1952. "Implications for General Economics of More Realistic Theories of the Firm." *American Economic Review*, XLII (May), 35–44.

——. 1963. "The Uses of Price Theory," in Alfred R. Oxenfeldt (ed.), *Models of Markets*. New York: Columbia University Press. Pp. 146–162.

——. 1966b. "The Verifiability of Economic Images," in Sherman R. Krupp (ed.),

The Structure of Economic Science. Englewood Cliffs, N.J.: Prentice-Hall. Pp. 129–141.

Bowers, Raymond V. 1964. "Sampling," in Julius Gould and William L. Kolb (eds.), *A Dictionary of the Social Sciences.* New York: Free Press of Glencoe. Pp. 614–615.

Brady, Dorothy S. 1966. "Introduction," in National Bureau of Economic Research, *Output, Employment and Productivity in the United States After 1800.* Studies in Income and Wealth, vol. XXX. New York: Columbia University Press. Pp. ix–xiv.

———. 1971. "The Statistical Approach: The Input-Output System," in George Rogers Taylor and Lucius F. Ellsworth (eds.), *Approaches to American Economic History.* Charlottesville: University Press of Virginia. Pp. 87–105.

Braithwaite, Richard B. 1953. *Scientific Explanation: A Study of the Function of Theory, Probability and Law in Science.* Cambridge, Eng.: Cambridge University Press.

Bridenbaugh, Carl. 1963. "The Great Mutation." *American Historical Review,* LXVIII (Jan.), 315–331.

Bridge, J. L. 1971. *Applied Econometrics.* Amsterdam: North-Holland.

Bridgeman, P. W. 1936. *The Nature of Physical Theory.* New York: Dover.

Brodbeck, May. 1962. "Explanation, Prediction and 'Imperfect' Knowledge," in Herbert Feigl and Grover Maxwell (eds.), *Scientific Explanation, Space and Time.* Minnesota Studies in the Philosophy of Science, vol. III. Minneapolis: University of Minnesota Press. Pp. 231–272.

Bronfenbrenner, Martin. 1966. "A Middlebrow Introduction to Economic Methodology," in Sherman R. Krupp (ed.), *The Structure of Economic Science.* Englewood Cliffs, N.J.: Prentice-Hall. Pp. 5–24.

———. 1970. "Radical Economics in America: A 1970 Survey." *Journal of Economic Literature,* VIII (Sept.), 747–766.

Brooke, John. 1964. "Namier and Namierism." *History and Theory,* III, No. 3, 331–347.

Brookings Institution. 1972. "Of Men and Models." *Bulletin,* IX (Summer), 5–9.

Brown, Murray. 1966. *On the Theory and Measurement of Technological Change.* Cambridge, Eng.: Cambridge University Press.

Bruchey, Stuart. 1968. "Econometrics and Southern History: Discussion." *Explorations in Entrepreneurial History,* 2d ser., VI (Fall), 59–65.

———. 1965. *The Roots of American Economic Growth, 1607–1861.* New York: Harper & Row.

Buchanan, James M. 1966. "Economics and Its Scientific Neighbors," in Sherman R. Krupp (ed.), *The Structure of Economic Science.* Englewood Cliffs, N.J.: Prentice-Hall. Pp. 166–183.

Budd, Edward C. 1960. "Factor Shares, 1850–1910," in National Bureau of Economic Research, *Trends in the American Economy in the Nineteenth Century.* Studies in Income and Wealth, vol. XXIV. Princeton, N.J.: Princeton University Press. Pp. 365–398.

Burks, Arthur W. 1951. "The Logic of Causal Propositions." *Mind,* LX (July), 363–382.

Burtt, Edwin Arthur. 1951. *The Metaphysical Foundations of Modern Physical Science.* New York: Humanities Press.

Cairnes, John E. 1888. *The Character and Logical Method of Political Economy.* London: Macmillan.

Callender, Guy S. 1913. "The Position of American Economic History." *American Historical Review*, XIX (Oct.), 80–97.

Cameron, Rondo E. 1965. "Has Economic History a Role in an Economist's Education?" *American Economic Review*, LV (May), 112–115.

Cannon, William T. 1972. "A Discussion of the Davis-North Model of Institutional Change with Particular Reference to its Application to the Early American Railroads." Unpublished paper, Department of Economics, Harvard University.

Carnap, Rudolf. 1956. "The Methodological Character of Theoretical Concepts," in Herbert Feigl and Michael Scriven (eds.), *The Foundations of Science and the Concepts of Psychology and Psychoanalysis*. Minnesota Studies in the Philosophy of Science, vol. I. Minneapolis: University of Minnesota Press. Pp. 38–76.

——. 1945. "On Inductive Logic." *Philosophy of Science*, XII (April), 72–97.

——. 1966. *Philosophical Foundations of Physics*. New York: Basic Books.

——. 1953. "The Two Concepts of Probability," in Herbert Feigl and May Brodbeck (eds.), *Readings in the Philosophy of Science*. New York: Appleton-Century-Crofts. Pp. 438–455.

Carr, Edward H. 1961. *What is History?* London: Macmillan.

Chamberlin, Edward H. 1933. *The Theory of Monopolistic Competition: A Reorientation of the Theory of Value*. Cambridge, Mass.: Harvard University Press.

Chandler, Alfred D., Jr. 1971. "Business History as Institutional History," in George Rogers Taylor and Lucius F. Ellsworth (eds.), *Approaches to American Economic History*. Charlottesville: University Press of Virginia. Pp. 17–24.

——. 1962. *Strategy and Structure: Chapters in the History of the Industrial Enterprise*. Cambridge, Mass.: M.I.T. Press.

Chisholm, Roderick M. 1946. "The Contrary-to-Fact Conditional." *Mind*, LV (Oct.), 289–307.

Christ, Carl F. 1955. "A Review of Input-Output Analysis," in National Bureau of Economic Research, *Input-Output Analysis: An Appraisal*. Studies in Income and Wealth, vol. XVIII. Princeton, N.J.: Princeton University Press. Pp. 137–169.

Clapham, J. H. 1957. *A Concise Economic History of Britain*. Cambridge, Eng.: Cambridge University Press.

——. 1922b. "The Economic Boxes: A Rejoinder." *Economic Journal*, XXXII (Dec.), 560–563.

——. 1931. "Economic History as a Discipline," in Edwin R. A. Seligman and Alvin Johnson (eds.), *Encyclopedia of the Social Sciences*, vol. V. New York: Macmillan. Pp. 327–330.

——. 1926. *Economic History of Modern Britain*. Cambridge, Eng.: Cambridge University Press.

——. 1922a. "Of Empty Economic Boxes." *Economic Journal*, XXXII (Sept.), 305–314.

Clark, G. Kitson. 1967. *The Critical Historian*. London: Heinemann.

Clarkson, Geoffrey P. E. 1963. "Interactions of Economic Theory and Operations Research," in Alfred R. Oxenfeldt (ed.), *Models of Markets*. New York: Columbia University Press. Pp. 339–361.

Cochran, Thomas C. 1960. "Cultural Factors in Economic Growth." *Journal of Economic History*, XX (Dec.), 515–530.

——. 1969. "Economic History, Old and New." *American Historical Review*, LXXIV (June), 1561–1572.

——. 1945. "The Economics in a Business History." *Journal of Economic History*, Supplement, V (Dec.), 54–65.

——. 1965. "The Entrepreneur in Economic Change." *Explorations in Entrepreneurial History*, 2d ser., III (Fall), 25–38.

——. 1964. *The Inner Revolution*. New York: Harper & Row.

——. 1947. "Research in American Economic History: A Thirty-Year Review." *Mid-America*, XXIX (Jan.), 3–23.

——. 1971. "Toward a Useful Model for Social Change," in George Rogers Taylor and Lucius F. Ellsworth (eds.), *Approaches to American Economic History*. Charlottesville: University Press of Virginia. Pp. 50–62.

Cohen, Morris R., and Ernest Nagel. 1934. *An Introduction to Logic and Scientific Method*. New York: Harcourt, Brace.

Cole, Arthur H. 1945. "Business History and Economic History." *Journal of Economic History*, Supplement, V (Dec.), 45–53.

——. 1968a. "Economic History in the United States: Formative Years of a Discipline." *Journal of Economic History*, XXVIII (Dec.), 556–589.

——. 1968b. "Meso-Economics: A Contribution from Entrepreneurial History." *Explorations in Entrepreneurial History*, 2d ser., VI (Fall), 3–33.

——. 1944. "A Report on Research in Economic History." *Journal of Economic History*, IV (May), 49–72.

Coleman, D. C. 1969. "An Innovation and Its Diffusion: The 'New Draperies.'" *Economic History Review*, XXII (Dec.), 417–429.

——. 1971. "Rejoinder: G. R. Hawke on—What?" *Economic History Review*, XXIV (May), 260–261.

——. 1972. *What Has Happened to Economic History?* Cambridge, Eng.: Cambridge University Press.

Coleman, James S. 1968. "The Mathematical Study of Change," in Herbert and Ann Blalock (eds.), *Methodology in Social Research*. New York: McGraw-Hill. Pp. 428–478.

Collingwood, R. G. 1956. *The Idea of History*. New York: Oxford Press.

Comte, Auguste. 1853. *The Positive Philosophy of Auguste Comte*. Translated by Harriet Martineau. London: John Chapman.

Conrad, Alfred H. 1968. "Econometrics and Southern History." *Explorations in Entrepreneurial History*, 2d ser., VI (Fall), 34–53.

——, and John R. Meyer. 1958. "The Economics of Slavery in the Ante Bellum South." *Journal of Political Economy*, LXVI (April), 95–130.

——, and John R. Meyer. 1964. *The Economics of Slavery and Other Studies in Econometric History*. Chicago: Aldine.

Cooper, Gershon. 1948. "The Role of Econometric Models in Economic Research." *Journal of Farm Economics*, XXX (Feb.), 101–116.

Cournot, Augustin. 1897. *Researches into the Mathematical Principles of the Theory of Wealth*. Translated by Nathaniel L. Bacon. New York: Macmillan.

Cox, Reavis. 1963. "Some Things We Know and Some Things We Do Not Know About Markets and Models," in Alfred R. Oxenfeldt (ed.), *Models of Markets*. New York: Columbia University Press. Pp. 3–19.

Curti, Merle. 1968. *Human Nature in American Historical Thought*. Columbia: University of Missouri Press.

——, and Peter Karsten. 1968. "Man and Businessman: Changing Concepts of

Human Nature as Reflected in the Writing of American Business History." *Journal of the History of the Behavioral Sciences*, IV (Jan.), 3–17.

Cyert, Richard M., and E. Grunberg. 1963. "Assumption, Prediction and Explanation in Economics," in Richard M. Cyert and J. G. March (eds.), *A Behavioral Theory of the Firm*. Englewood Cliffs, N.J.: Prentice-Hall. Pp. 298–311.

——, and Charles L. Hedrick. 1972. "Theory of the Firm: Past, Present, and Future: An Interpretation." *Journal of Economic Literature*, X (June), 398–412.

——, and J. G. March. 1963. *A Behavioral Theory of the Firm*. Englewood Cliffs, N.J.: Prentice-Hall.

D'Abro, A. 1952. *The Rise of the New Physics*. New York: Dover.

Dacey, Raymond. 1971. "On the Counterfactual Method of Economic History." Unpublished paper, University of Iowa, College of Business Administration Working Papers, No. 71–72, September.

Daems, Herman, and Glenn Porter. 1972. "Beyond Profit Maximization: A Historical Model of Institutional Change in the American Industrial Firm." Unpublished paper, Harvard Business School.

Danto, Arthur. 1965. *Analytical Philosophy of History*. Cambridge, Eng.: Cambridge University Press.

——, and Sidney Morgenbesser (eds.). 1960. *Philosophy of Science*. New York: Meridian Books.

Dasgupta, P., A. Sen, and S. Marglin. 1972. *Guidelines for Project Evaluation*. New York: United Nations.

David, Paul A. 1971. "Econometric Studies of History: Comments," in Michael D. Intriligator (ed.), *Frontiers of Quantitative Economics*. Amsterdam: North-Holland. Pp. 459–467.

——. 1964. "Economic History through the Looking Glass." *Econometrica*, XXXII (Oct.), 694–696.

——. 1966. "The Mechanization of Reaping in the Ante-Bellum Midwest," in Henry Rosovsky (ed.), *Industrialization in Two Systems*. New York: Wiley. Pp. 3–39.

——, and Peter Temin. 1974. "Slavery: The Progressive Institution?" *Journal of Economic History*, XXIV (Sept.), 739–783.

Davidson, Donald. 1967. "Causal Relations." *Journal of Philosophy*, LXIV (Nov. 9), 691–703.

Davis, Lance E. 1968. "'And It Will Never Be Literature': The New Economic History: A Critique." *Explorations in Entrepreneurial History*, 2d ser., VI (Fall), 75–92.

——. 1960. "New England Textile Mills and the Capital Markets: A Study of Industrial Borrowing, 1840–1860." *Journal of Economic History*, XX (March), 1–30.

——. 1966. "Professor Fogel and the New Economic History." *Economic History Review*, XIX (Dec.), 657–663.

——. 1957. "The Sources of Industrial Finance: The American Textile Industry; A Case Study." *Explorations in Entrepreneurial History*, IX (April), 189–203.

——. 1971. "Specification, Quantification and Analysis in Economic History," in George Rogers Taylor and Lucius F. Ellsworth (eds.), *Approaches to American Economic History*. Charlottesville: University Press of Virginia. Pp. 106–120.

——, and J. R. T. Hughes. 1960. "A Dollar-Stirling Exchange, 1803–1895." *Economic History Review*, XIII (Aug.), 52–78.

——, J. R. T. Hughes, and Duncan M. McDougal. 1961. *American Economic History.* Homewood, Ill.: Richard D. Irwin.

——, J. R. T. Hughes, and Stanley Reiter. 1960. "Aspects of Quantitative Research in Economic History." *Journal of Economic History*, XX (Dec.), 539–547.

——, and Douglass C. North. 1971. *Institutional Change and American Economic Growth.* Cambridge, Eng.: Cambridge University Press.

——, and Douglass C. North. 1970. "Institutional Change and American Economic Growth: A First Step towards a Theory of Institutional Change." *Journal of Economic History*, XXX (March), 131–149.

——, et al. 1972. *American Economic Growth.* New York: Harper & Row.

de Finetti, Bruno. 1968. "Probability: Interpretations," in David L. Sills (ed.), *International Encyclopedia of the Social Sciences*, vol. XII. New York: Macmillan. Pp. 496–504.

Degler, Carl H. 1963. "Do Historians Use Covering Laws?" in Sidney Hood (ed.), *Philosophy and History.* New York: New York University Press. Pp. 205–211.

Demsetz, Harold. 1967. "Toward A Theory of Property Rights." *American Economic Review*, LVII (May), 347–359.

Denison, Edward F. 1962. *The Sources of Economic Growth in the United States and the Alternatives Before Us.* New York: Committee for Economic Development.

——. 1964. "A Survey of Some Theories of Income Distribution: Comment," in National Bureau of Economic Research, *The Behavior of Income Shares.* Studies in Income and Wealth, vol. XXVII. Princeton, N.J.: Princeton University Press. Pp. 35–39.

Depillis, Mario S. 1967. "Trends in American Social History and the Possibilities of Behavioral Approaches." *Journal of Social History*, I (Fall), 37–60.

Desai, Meghnad. 1968. "Some Issues in Econometric History." *Economic History Review*, XXI (April), 1–16.

Devereux, Edward C., Jr. 1961. "Parsons' Sociological Theory," in Max Black (ed.), *The Social Theories of Talcott Parsons.* Englewood Cliffs, N.J.: Prentice-Hall. Pp. 1–63.

Dietl, Paul J. 1968. "Deduction and Historical Explanation." *History and Theory*, VII, No. 2, 167–188.

Dietz, Stephen M. 1970. "A Remark on Hempel's Replies to His Critics." *Philosophy of Science*, XXXVII (Dec.), 614–617.

Dodd, Stuart Carter. 1939. "A System of Operationally Defined Concepts for Sociology." *American Sociological Review*, IV (Oct.), 619–634.

Dollar, Charles M., and Richard J. Jensen. 1971. *Historian's Guide to Statistics: Quantitative Analysis and Historical Research.* New York: Holt, Rinehart and Winston.

Domar, Evsey D. 1970. "The Causes of Slavery or Serfdom: A Hypothesis." *Journal of Economic History*, XXX (March), 18–32.

——. 1947. "Expansion and Employment." *American Economic Review*, XXXVII (March), 34–55.

Donagan, Alan. 1959. "Explanation in History," in Patrick Gardiner (ed.), *Theories of History.* New York: Free Press. Pp. 428–443.

——. 1964. "Historical Explanation: The Popper-Hempel Theory Reconsidered." *History and Theory*, IV, No. 1, 3–26.

Dorfman, Robert. 1954a. "A Catechism: Mathematics in Social Science." *Review of Economics and Statistics*, XXXVI (Nov.), 374–377.

——. 1954b. "The Nature and Significance of Input-Output." *Review of Economics and Statistics*, XXXVI (May), 121–133.

——. 1964. *The Price System*. Englewood Cliffs, N.J.: Prenctice-Hall.

Dowie, J. A. 1967. "As If or Not As If: The Economic Historian as Hamlet." *Australian Economic History Review*, VII (March), 69–85.

Dray, William H. 1959. "'Explaining What' in History," in Patrick Gardiner (ed.), *Theories of History*. New York: Free Press. Pp. 403–408.

——. 1963. "The Historical Explanation of Actions Reconsidered," in Sidney Hook (ed.), *Philosophy and History*. New York: New York University Press. Pp. 105–135.

——. 1970. *Laws and Explanation in History*. Oxford: Clarendon Press.

——. 1971. "On the Nature and Role of Narrative in Historiography." *History and Theory*, X, No. 2, 153–171.

—— (ed.). 1966. *Philosophical Analysis and History*. New York: Harper & Row.

——. 1964. *Philosophy of History*. Englewood Cliffs, N.J.: Prentice-Hall.

——. 1967. "Philosophy of History," in Paul Edwards (ed.), *Encyclopedia of Philosophy*, vol. VI. New York: Macmillan. Pp. 247–254.

Droysen, Johann Gustav. 1893. *Outline of the Principles of History*. Translated by E. Benjamin Andrews. Boston: Ginn & Company.

Ducasse, C. J. 1966. "Critique of Hume's Conception of Causality." *Journal of Philosophy*, LXIII (March 17), 141–148.

Duesenberry, James S. 1954. "The Methodological Basis of Economic Theory." *Review of Economics and Statistics*, XXXVI (Nov.), 361–363.

Easterlin, Richard A. 1966. "Gross National Product in the United States, 1834–1909: Comment," in National Bureau of Economic Research, *Output, Employment and Productivity in the United States After 1800*. Studies in Income and Wealth, vol. XXX. New York: Columbia University Press. Pp. 76–90.

Eckaus, Richard S. 1972. *Basic Economics*. Boston: Little, Brown.

Edwards, Everett E. 1938. *The Early Writings of Frederick Jackson Turner*. Madison: University of Wisconsin Press.

Edwards, Paul (ed.). 1967. *Encyclopedia of Philosophy*. New York: Macmillan.

Edwards, Ward. 1968. "Decision Making: Psychological Aspects," in David L. Sills (ed.), *International Encyclopedia of the Social Sciences*, vol. IV. New York: Macmillan. Pp. 34–41.

Ellis, Howard S. 1950. "The Economic Way of Thinking." *American Economic Review*, XL (March), 1–12.

Elton, G. R. 1970. "Explanation and Cause," in his *Political History: Principles and Practice*. New York: Basic Books. Pp. 112–155.

——. 1967. *The Practice of History*. London: Methuen.

Engerman, Stanley L. 1971. "Human Capital, Education, and Economic Growth," in Robert W. Fogel and Stanley L. Engerman (eds.), *The Reinterpretation of American Economic History*. New York: Harper & Row. Pp. 241–256.

Fain, Hask. 1970. "History as Science." *History and Theory*, IX, No. 2, 154–173.

Feigl, Herbert. 1953. "Notes on Causality," in Herbert Feigl and May Brodbeck (eds.), *Readings in the Philosophy of Science*. New York: Appleton-Century-Crofts. Pp. 408–418.

——. 1954. "Scientific Method Without Metaphysical Presuppositions." *Philosophical Studies*, V (Feb.), 17–29.

——. 1956. "Some Major Issues and Developments in the Philosophy of Science of Logical Empiricism," in Herbert Feigl and Michael Scriven (eds.), *The*

Foundations of Science and the Concepts of Psychology and Psychoanalysis. Minnesota Studies in the Philosophy of Science, vol. I. Minneapolis: University of Minnesota Press. Pp. 3–37.

——, and May Brodbeck (eds.). 1953. *Readings in the Philosophy of Science.* New York: Appleton-Century-Crofts.

——, and Grover Maxwell (eds.). 1962. *Scientific Explanation, Space and Time.* Minnesota Studies in the Philosophy of Science, vol. III. Minneapolis: University of Minnesota Press.

Fine, Terrence L. 1973. *Theories of Probability.* New York: Academic Press.

Fischer, David H. 1970. *Historians' Fallacies: Toward a Logic of Historical Thought.* New York: Harper & Row.

Fisher, Franklin M. 1971a. "Aggregate Production Functions and the Explanation of Wages: A Simulation Experiment." *Review of Economics and Statistics,* LIII (Nov.), 305–325.

——. 1969. "The Existence of Aggregate Production Functions." *Econometrica,* XXXVII (Oct.), 553–577.

——. 1971b. "The Existence of Aggregate Production Functions: Reply." *Econometrica,* XXXIX (March), 405.

——. 1960. "On the Analysis of History and the Interdependence of the Social Sciences." *Philosophy of Science,* XXVII (April), 147–158.

Fisher, Irving. 1892. "Mathematical Investigations in the Theory of Value and Prices." Connecticut Academy of Arts and Sciences, *Transactions,* IX (July), 1–124.

Fisher, Sydney George. 1902. *The True History of the American Revolution.* Philadelphia: J. B. Lippincott.

Fishlow, Albert. 1965. "Antebellum Trade Reconsidered: Postscript," in Ralph L. Andreano (ed.), *New Views on American Economic Development.* Cambridge, Mass.: Schenkman. Pp. 209–212.

——. 1962. "Trends in the American Economy in the Nineteenth Century: A Review Article." *Journal of Economic History,* XXII (March), 71–80.

——, and Robert W. Fogel. 1971. "Quantitative Economic History: An Interim Evaluation; Past Trends and Present Tendencies." *Journal of Economic History,* XXXI (March), 15–42.

Fogel, Robert W. 1970. "Historiography and Retrospective Econometrics." *History and Theory,* IX, No. 3, 245–264.

——. 1966. "The New Economic History: Its Findings and Methods." *Economic History Review,* XIX (Dec.), 642–656.

——. 1964a. *Railroads and American Economic Growth: Essays in Econometric History.* Baltimore: Johns Hopkins Press.

——. 1964b. "Reappraisals in American Economic History—Discussion." *American Economic Review,* LIV (May), 377–389.

——. 1965. "The Reunification of Economic History with Economic Theory." *American Economic Review,* LV (May), 92–98.

——. 1967. "The Specification Problem in Economic History." *Journal of Economic History,* XXVII (Sept.), 283–308.

——, and Stanley L. Engerman. 1971a. "The Economics of Slavery," in their *The Reinterpretation of American Economic History.* New York: Harper & Row. Pp. 311–314.

——, and Stanley L. Engerman. 1971b. "A Model for the Explanation of Industrial Expansion during the Nineteenth Century: With an Application to the

American Iron Industry," in their *The Reinterpretation of American Economic History*. New York: Harper & Row. Pp. 148–162.

——, and Stanley L. Engerman (eds.). 1971c. *The Reinterpretation of American Economic History*. New York: Harper & Row.

——, and Stanley L. Engerman. 1971d. "The Relative Efficiency of Slavery: A Comparison of Northern and Southern Agriculture in 1860." *Explorations in Economic History*, VIII (Spring), 353–367.

——, and Stanley L. Engerman. 1974a. *Time on the Cross: The Economics of American Negro Slavery*. Boston: Little, Brown.

——, and Stanley L. Engerman. 1974b. *Time on the Cross: Evidence and Methods—A Supplement*. Boston: Little, Brown.

Foley, Duncan K., Karl Shell, and Miguel Sidrauski. 1969. "Optimal Fiscal and Monetary Policy and Economic Growth." *Journal of Political Economy*, LXXVII (July/Aug.), 698–719.

Fores, M. J. 1969. "No More General Theories." *Economic Journal*, LXXIX (March), 11–22.

Foust, James D., and Dale E. Swan. 1970. "Productivity of Ante-Bellum Slave Labor: A Micro Approach." *Agricultural History*, XLIV (Jan.), 39–62.

Francis, Darryl R. 1973. "The Usefulness of Applied Econometrics to the Policymaker." Federal Reserve Bank of St. Louis, *Review*, LX (May), 7–10.

Frank, Philip. 1962. *Philosophy of Science*. Englewood Cliffs, N. J.: Prentice-Hall.

Frankel, Charles. 1959. "Explanation and Interpretation in History," in Patrick Gardiner (ed.), *Theories of History*. Glencoe, Ill.: Free Press. Pp. 408–427.

Frey, Bruno S., and Hermann Garbers. 1971. "'Politico-Econometrics'—on Estimation in Political Economy." *Political Studies*, XIX (Sept.), 316–320.

Friedman, Milton. 1953. *Essays in Positive Economics*. Chicago: University of Chicago Press.

——, 1963. "More on Archibald versus Chicago." *Review of Economic Studies*, XXX (Feb.), 65–67.

——. 1955. "A Review of Input-Output Analysis: Comment," in National Bureau of Economic Research, *Input-Output Analysis: An Appraisal*. Studies in Income and Wealth, vol. XVIII. Princeton, N. J.: Princeton University Press. Pp. 169–174.

Fromm, Gary, and Paul Taubman. 1968. *Policy Simulations with an Econometric Model*. Washington, D. C.: Brookings Institution.

Galambos, Louis. 1966. "Business History and the Theory of the Growth of the Firm." *Explorations in Entrepreneurial History*, 2d ser., IV (Fall), 3–16.

Galbraith, John Kenneth. 1973a. *Economics and the Public Purpose*. Boston: Houghton Mifflin.

——. 1973b. "Power and the Useful Economist." *American Economic Review*, LXIII (March), 1–11.

Gallie, W. B. 1959. "Explanations in History and the Genetic Sciences," in Patrick Gardiner (ed.), *Theories of History*. New York: Free Press. Pp. 386–402.

——. 1963. "The Historical Understanding." *History and Theory*, III, No. 2, 149–202.

——. 1964. *Philosophy and the Historical Understanding*. London: Chatto & Windus.

Gallman, Robert E. 1960. "Commodity Output, 1839–1899," in National Bureau of Economic Research, *Trends in the American Economy in the Nineteenth*

Century. Studies in Income and Wealth, vol. XXIV. Princeton, N.J.: Princeton University Press. Pp. 13–67.

———. 1966. "Gross National Product in the United States, 1834–1909," in National Bureau of Economic Research, *Output, Employment, and Productivity in the United States After 1800.* Studies in Income and Wealth, vol. XXX. New York: Columbia University Press. Pp. 3–90.

———. 1972. "The Pace and Pattern of American Economic Growth," in Lance Davis *et al., American Economic Growth.* New York: Harper & Row. Pp. 15–60.

———. 1965. "The Role of Economic History in the Education of the Economist." *American Economic Review,* LV (May), 109–111.

———. 1971. "The Statistical Approach: Fundamental Concepts as Applied to History," in George Rogers Taylor and Lucius F. Ellsworth (eds.), *Approaches to American Economic History.* Charlottesville: University Press of Virginia. Pp. 63–86.

Garb, Gerald. 1964. "The Problem of Causality in Economics." *Kyklos,* XVII, Fasc. 4, 594–611.

———. 1965. "Professor Samuelson on Theory and Realism: Comment." *American Economic Review,* LV (Dec.), 1151–1153.

Gardiner, Patrick. 1952. *The Nature of Historical Explanation.* London: Oxford University Press.

——— (ed.). 1959. *Theories of History.* New York: Free Press.

Gay, Edwin F. 1941. "The Tasks of Economic History." *Journal of Economic History,* I, Supplement (Dec.), 9–16.

Gellner, E. A. 1964. "Model," in Julius Gould and William L. Kolb (eds.), *A Dictionary of the Social Sciences.* New York: Free Press of Glencoe. P. 435.

Georgescu-Roegen, Nicholas. 1966. *Analytical Economics: Issues and Problems.* Cambridge, Mass.: Harvard University Press.

———. 1952. "Toward Partial Redirection of Econometrics: Comment." *Review of Economics and Statistics,* XXXIV (Aug.), 206–211.

Gerschenkron, Alexander. 1967. "The Discipline and I." *Journal of Economic History,* XXVII (Dec.), 443–459.

———. 1971. "Mercator Gloriosus." *Economic History Review,* XXIV (Nov.), 653–666.

———. 1968. "Methodology," in his *Continuity in History and Other Essays.* Cambridge, Mass.: Belknap. Pp. 11–73.

Gershoy, Leo. 1963. "Some Problems of a Working Historian," in Sidney Hook (ed.), *Philosophy and History.* New York: New York University Press. Pp. 59–75.

Gifford, J. K. 1968. "Correlationism: A Virulent Disease in Economic Science." *Journal of Political Economy,* LXXVI (Sept.), 1091–1095.

Goldsmith, Raymond W. 1955. "Introduction," in National Bureau of Economic Research, *Input-Output Analysis: An Appraisal.* Studies in Income and Wealth, vol. XVIII. Princeton, N.J.: Princeton University Press. Pp. 3–8.

Goldstein, Leon J. 1970. "Collingwood's Theory of Historical Knowing." *History and Theory,* IX, No. 1, 3–36.

Goodman, Nelson. 1947. "The Problem of Counterfactual Conditionals." *Journal of Philosophy,* XLIV (Feb. 27), 113–128.

Goodrich, Carter. 1960. "Economic History: One Field or Two?" *Journal of Economic History,* XX (Dec.), 531–538.

Gordon, Donald F. 1955. "Professor Samuelson on Operationalism in Economic Theory." *Quarterly Journal of Economics*, LXIX (May), 305–310.

Gordon, R. A. 1965. "The New National Econometric Model: Discussion." *American Economic Review*, LV (May), 372–374.

Gordon, Robert J. 1970. "The Brookings Model in Action: A Review Article." *Journal of Political Economy*, LXXVIII (May/June), 489–525.

Gould, J. D. 1972. *Economic Growth in History*. London: Methuen.

——. 1969. "Hypothetical History." *Economic History Review*, XXII (Aug.), 195–207.

Gould, Julius, and William L. Kolb. 1964. *A Dictionary of the Social Sciences*. New York: Free Press of Glencoe.

Grabowski, Henry, and Dennis Mueller. 1970. "Industrial Organization: The Role and Contribution of Econometrics." *American Economic Review*, LX (May), 100–104.

Gras, N. S. B. 1931. "Economic History in the United States," in Edwin R. A. Seligman and Alvin Johnson (eds.), *Encyclopedia of the Social Sciences*, vol. V. New York: Macmillan. Pp. 325–327.

——. 1927. "The Rise and Development of Economic History." *Economic History Review*, I (Jan.), 12–34.

Gray, Lewis C. 1958. *History of Agriculture of the Southern United States to 1860*. Gloucester, Mass.: Peter Smith.

Green, George. 1968. "Comment on 'Potentialities and Pitfalls in Economic History.'" *Explorations in Entrepreneurial History*, 2d. ser., V (Fall), 109–115.

Grene, David (ed.). 1959. *The Complete Greek Tragedies*. Chicago: University of Chicago Press.

Gruchy, Allan G. 1968. "Economic Thought: The Institutional School," in David L. Sills (ed.), *International Encyclopedia of the Social Sciences*, vol. IV. New York: Macmillan. Pp. 462–467.

Grunberg, Emile. 1966. "The Meaning of Scope and External Boundaries in Economics," in Sherman R. Krupp (ed.), *The Structure of Economic Science*. Englewood Cliffs, N.J.: Prentice-Hall. Pp. 148–165.

——. 1957. "Notes on the Verifiability of Economic Laws." *Philosophy of Science*, XXIV (Oct.), 337–348.

——, and Franco Modigliani. 1954. "The Predictability of Social Events." *Journal of Political Economy*, LXII (Dec.), 465–478.

Gunnell, John G. 1968. "Social Science and Political Reality: The Problem of Explanation." *Social Research*, XXXV (Spring), 159–201.

Gurley, John G. 1971. "The State of Political Economics." *American Economic Review*, LXI (May), 53–62.

Haavelmo, Trygve. 1944. "The Probability Approach in Econometrics." *Econometrica*, XII (July), Supplement, 1–115.

——. 1958. "The Role of the Econometrician in the Advancement of Economic Theory." *Econometrica*, XXVI (July), 351–357.

Habakkuk, John. 1971. "Economic History and Economic Theory." *Daedalus*, C (Spring), 305–322.

Hacker, Louis M. 1966. "The New Revolution in Economic History: A Review Article Based on *Railroads and Economic Growth: Essays in Econometric History* by Robert William Fogel." *Explorations in Entrepreneurial History*, 2d ser., III (Spring), 159–175.

Hahn, F. H. 1970. "Some Adjustment Problems." *Econometrica*, XXXVIII (Jan.), 1–17.
——, and R. C. O. Matthews. 1964. "The Theory of Economic Growth: A Survey." *Economic Journal*, LXXIV (Dec.), 779–902.
Hall, Robert. 1959. "Reflections on the Practical Application of Economics." *Economic Journal*, LXIX (Dec.), 639–652.
Hampshire, Stuart. 1948. "Subjunctive Conditionals." *Analysis*, IX (Oct.), 9–14.
Hanson, Norwood R. 1959. "On the Symmetry between Explanation and Prediction." *Philosophical Review*, LXVIII (July), 349–358.
Harré, Romano. 1964. *Matter and Method*. London: Macmillan.
Harris, John R. 1970. "Some Problems in Identifying the Role of Entrepreneurship in Economic Development: The Nigerian Case." *Explorations in Economic History*, VII (Spring), 347–369.
Harrod, Roy. 1939. "An Essay in Dynamic Theory." *Economic Journal*, XLIX (March), 14–33.
——. 1968. "What Is a Model?" in J. N. Wolfe (ed.), *Value, Capital and Growth*. Chicago: Aldine. Pp. 173–191.
Hartwell, R. M. 1965. "The Causes of the Industrial Revolution: An Essay in Methodology." *Economic History Review*, XVIII (Aug.), 164–182.
——. 1969. "Economic Growth in England Before the Industrial Revolution: Some Methodological Issues." *Journal of Economic History*, XXIX (March), 13–31.
Hawke, G. R. 1971. "D. C. Coleman on the Counterfactual History of the New Draperies." *Economic History Review*, XXIV (May), 258–259.
Heaton, Herbert. 1942. "Recent Developments in Economic History." *American Historical Review*, XLVII (July), 727–746.
——. 1965. "Twenty-five Years of the Economic History Association: A Reflective Evaluation." *Journal of Economic History*, XXV (Dec.), 465–479.
Heckscher, Eli F. 1929. "A Plea for Theory in Economic History." *Economic History* (*A Supplement to the Economic Journal*), I (Jan.), 525–534.
——. 1939. "Quantitative Measurement in Economic History." *Quarterly Journal of Economics*, LII (Feb.), 167–193.
Hempel, Carl G. 1965a. "Aspects of Scientific Explanation," in his *Aspects of Scientific Explanation and Other Essays*. New York: Free Press. Pp. 331–496.
——. 1962. "Deductive-Nomological vs. Statistical Explanation," in Herbert Feigl and Grover Maxwell (eds.), *Scientific Explanation, Space and Time*. Minnesota Studies in the Philosophy of Science, vol. III. Minneapolis: University of Minnesota Press. Pp. 98–169.
——. 1964. "Explanation in Science and in History," in Robert G. Colodny (ed.), *Frontiers of Science and Philosophy*. London: George Allen and Unwin. Pp. 7–33.
——. 1942. "The Function of General Laws in History." *Journal of Philosophy*, XXXIX (Jan. 15), 35–48.
——. 1968. "Maximal Specificity and Lawlikeness in Probabilistic Explanations." *Philosophy of Science*, XXXV (June), 116–133.
——. 1966. *Philosophy of Natural Science*. Englewood Cliffs, N.J.: Prentice-Hall.
——. 1963. "Reasons and Covering Laws in Historical Explanation," in Sidney Hook (ed.), *Philosophy and History*. New York: New York University Press. Pp. 143–163.

——. 1958. "The Theoretician's Dilemma: A Study in the Logic of Theory Construction," in Herbert Feigl, Michael Scriven, and Grover Maxwell (eds.), *Concepts, Theories and the Mind-Body Problem*. Minnesota Studies in the Philosophy of Science, vol. II. Minneapolis: University of Minnesota Press. Pp. 37–98.

——. 1965b. "Typological Methods in the Natural and in the Social Sciences," in his *Aspects of Scientific Explanation and Other Essays*. New York: Free Press. Pp. 155–171.

——, and Paul Oppenheim. 1948. "Studies in the Logic of Explanation." *Philosophy of Science*, XV (April), 135–175.

Hexter, J. H. 1971. *Doing History*. Bloomington, Ind.: Indiana University Press.

——. 1968. "HISTORIOGRAPHY: The Rhetoric of History," in David L. Sills (ed.), *International Encyclopedia of the Social Sciences*, vol. VI. New York: Macmillan. Pp. 368–394.

——. 1966. "Some American Observations," in Walter Laquer and George L. Mosse (eds.), *The New History*. New York: Harper & Row. Pp. 5–23.

Hicks, John R. 1969. *A Theory of Economic History*. London: Oxford University Press.

Hidy, Ralph W. 1968. "HISTORY: Business History," in David L. Sills (ed.), *International Encyclopedia of the Social Sciences*, vol. VI. New York: Macmillan. Pp. 474–480.

——. 1972. "The Road We Are Traveling." *Journal of Economic History*, XXXII (March), 3–14.

Higgs, Robert. 1971. "Regional Specialization and the Supply of Wheat in the United States, 1867–1914: A Comment." *Review of Economics and Statistics*, LIII (Feb.), 101–102.

Higham, John. 1966. "The Schism in American Scholarship." *American Historical Review*, LXXII (Oct.), 1–21.

——. 1970. *Writing American History*. Bloomington, Ind.: Indiana University Press.

Hill, George B. (ed.). 1887. *Boswell's Life of Johnson*. Oxford: Clarendon Press.

Hobson, E. W. 1923. *The Domain of Natural Science*. New York: Macmillan.

Hodges, H. A. 1952. *The Philosophy of Wilhelm Dilthey*. London: Routledge & Kegan Paul.

Hofstadter, Richard. 1956. "History and the Social Sciences," in Fritz Stern (ed.), *Varieties of History*. New York: Meridian Books. Pp. 359–370.

Homans, George C. 1967. *The Nature of Social Science*. New York: Harcourt, Brace & World.

Hook, Sidney (ed.). 1963. *Philosophy and History: A Symposium*. New York: New York University Press.

Hoselitz, Bert F. 1957. "Noneconomic Factors in Economic Development." *American Economic Review*, XLVII (May), 28–41.

Houthakker, H. S. 1960. "Additive Preferences." *Econometrica*, XXVIII (April), 244–257.

——. 1965. "New Evidence on Demand Elasticities." *Econometrica*, XXXIII (April), 277–288.

Howe, Mark De Wolfe (ed.). 1961. *Holmes-Pollock Letters*. Cambridge, Mass.: Harvard University Press.

Hughes, H. Stuart. 1960. "The Historian and the Social Scientist." *American Historical Review*, LXVI (Oct.), 20–46.

Hughes, J. R. T. 1966. "Fact and Theory in Economic History." *Explorations in Entrepreneurial History*, 2d ser., III (Winter), 75–100.

———. 1965. "A Note in Defense of Clio." *Explorations in Entrepreneurial History*, 2d ser., II (Winter), 154.

Hume, David. 1894. *An Enquiry Concerning the Human Understanding*. Oxford: Clarendon Press.

———. 1956. *A Treatise of Human Nature*. London: J. M. Dent.

Humphreys, William C. 1968. "Discussion: Statistical Ambiguity and Maximal Specificity." *Philosophy of Science*, XXXV (June), 112–115.

Hunt, Edward H. 1968. "The New Economic History: Professor Fogel's Study of American Railways." *History*, LIII (Feb.), 3–18.

Hurwicz, Leonid. 1963. "Mathematics in Economics: Language and Instrument," in James C. Charlesworth (ed.), *Mathematics and the Social Sciences. A Symposium Sponsored by the American Academy of Political and Social Science*. Philadelphia: American Academy of Political and Social Science. Pp. 1–11.

Hutchison, T. W. 1960. "Methodological Prescriptions in Economics: A Reply." *Economica*, XXVII (May), 158–160.

———. 1956. "Professor Machlup on Verification in Economics." *Southern Economic Journal*, XXII (April), 476–483.

———. 1941. "The Significance and Basic Postulates of Economic Theory: A Reply to Professor Knight." *Journal of Political Economy*, XLIX (Oct.), 732–750.

Intriligator, Michael (ed.). 1971. *Frontiers of Quantitative Economics*. Amsterdam: North-Holland.

Isard, Walter. 1960. "Notes on the Use of Regional Science Methods in Economic History." *Journal of Economic History*, XX (Dec.), 597–600.

Jeffrey, Richard C. 1956. "Discussion: Valuation and Acceptance of Scientific Hypotheses." *Philosophy of Science*, XXIII (July), 237–246.

Jeffreys, Harold. 1955. "The Present Position in Probability Theory." *British Journal for the Philosophy of Science*, V (Feb.), 275–289.

Jenks, Leland H. 1949. "Role Structure of Entrepreneurial Personality," in Harvard University Research Center in Entrepreneurial History, *Change and the Entrepreneur*. Cambridge, Mass.: Harvard University Press. Pp. 108–152.

Jensen, Richard, and Charles M. Dollar. 1970. *Quantitative Historical Research*. New York: Holt, Rinehart and Winston.

Jewkes, John, David Sawers, and Richard Stillerman. 1958. *The Sources of Invention*. London: Macmillan.

Johnson, Arthur M. 1971. "Agenda for the 1970's: The Firm and the Industry." *Journal of Economic History*, XXXI (March), 106–117.

———. 1962. "Where Does Business History Go from Here?" *Business History Review*, XXXVI (Spring), 11–20.

Johnson, E. A. J. 1941. "New Tools for the Economic Historian." *Journal of Economic History*, Supplement, I (Dec.), 30–38.

Johnson, Harry G. 1961. "The General Theory after Twenty-Five Years." *American Economic Review*, LI (May), 1–17.

Johnston, J. 1963. *Econometric Methods*. New York: McGraw-Hill.

———. 1967. "Econometrics: Achievements and Prospects." *Three Banks Review*, LXXIII (March), 3–22.

Jorgenson, Dale W. 1971. "Econometric Studies of Investment Behavior: A Survey." *Journal of Economic Literature*, IX (Dec.), 1111–1147.

——. 1970. "Econometrics," in Nancy D. Ruggles (ed.), *Economics*. Englewood Cliffs, N.J.: Prentice-Hall. Pp. 55–62.

——. 1972. "Investment Behavior and the Production Function." *Bell Journal of Economics and Management Science*, III (Spring), 220–251.

——, and Zvi Griliches. 1967. "The Explanation of Productivity Change." *Review of Economic Studies*, XXXIV (July), 249–283.

——, Jerald Hunter, and M. Ishaq Nadiri. 1970. "A Comparison of Alternative Econometric Models of Quarterly Investment Behavior." *Econometrica*, XXXVIII (March), 187–212.

——, and C. D. Siebert. 1968. "A Comparison of Alternative Theories of Corporate Investment Behavior." *American Economic Review*, LVIII (Sept.), 681–712.

Joynt, C. B., and Nicholas Rescher. 1959. "On Explanation in History." *Mind*, LXVIII (July), 383–388.

——, and Nicholas Rescher. 1961. "The Problem of Uniqueness in History." *History and Theory*, I, No. 2, 150–162.

Kane, Edward J. 1968. *Economic Statistics and Econometrics: An Introduction to Quantitative Economics*. New York: Harper & Row.

Kantor, J. R. 1953. *The Logic of Modern Science*. Bloomington, Ind.: Principia Press.

Kaplan, Abraham. 1965. "Noncausal Explanation," in D. Lerner (ed.), *Cause and Effect*. New York: Free Press. Pp. 145–156.

Katona, George. 1968. "Consumer Behavior: Theory and Findings on Expectations and Aspirations." *American Economic Review*, LVIII (May), 19–30.

Kaufmann, Felix. 1944. *Methodology of the Social Sciences*. New York: Oxford University Press.

Kaysen, Carl. 1965. "Another View of Corporate Capitalism." *Quarterly Journal of Economics*, LXXIX (Feb.), 41–51.

Kennedy, C., and A. P. Thirlwall. 1972. "Technical Progress: A Survey." *Economic Journal*, LXXXII (March), 11–72.

Key, V. O., Jr. 1954. *A Primer of Statistics for Political Scientists*. New York: Thomas Y. Crowell.

Keynes, John Neville. 1891. *The Scope and Method of Political Economy*. London: Macmillan.

Kim, Jaegwon. 1967. "Explanation in Science," in Paul Edwards (ed.), *The Encyclopedia of Philosophy*, vol. III. New York: Macmillan. Pp. 159–163.

Klappholz, Kurt. 1964. "Value Judgements and Economics." *British Journal for the Philosophy of Science*, XV (Aug.), 97–114.

——, and J. Agassi. 1959. "Methodological Prescriptions in Economics." *Economica*, XXVI (Feb.), 60–74.

——, and J. Agassi. 1960. "Methodological Prescriptions in Economics: A Rejoinder." *Economica*, XXVII (May), 160–161.

Klein, L. R. 1954. "The Contributions of Mathematics in Economics." *Review of Economics and Statistics*, XXXVI (Nov.), 359–361.

——. 1971. "Forecasting and Policy Evaluation Using Large Scale Econometric Models: The State of the Art," in Michael Intriligator (ed.), *Frontiers of Quantitative Economics*. Amsterdam: North-Holland. Pp. 133–164.

Kneale, William. 1951. "Probability and Induction." *Mind*, LX (July), 310–317.

——. 1961. "Universality and Necessity." *British Journal for the Philosophy of Science*, XII (Aug.), 89–102.

Knight, Frank H. 1951. *The Ethics of Competition and Other Essays.* London: George Allen & Unwin.

——. 1952. "Institutionalism and Empiricism in Economics." *American Economic Review,* XLII (May), 45–55.

——. 1961. "Methodology in Economics." *Southern Economic Journal,* XXVII (Jan.), pt. I, 185–193; (April), pt. II, 273–282.

——. 1956. *On the History and Method of Economics.* Chicago: University of Chicago Press.

——. 1941. "The Significance and Basic Postulates of Economic Theory: A Rejoinder." *Journal of Political Economy,* XLIX (Oct.), 750–753.

——. 1940. "'What is Truth' in Economics?" *Journal of Political Economy,* XLVIII (Feb.), 1–32.

Komarovsky, Mirra (ed.). 1957. *Common Frontiers of the Social Sciences.* Glencoe, Ill.: Free Press.

Koopmans, Tjalling C. 1949a. "Identification Problems in Economic Model Construction." *Econometrica,* XVII (April), 125–144.

——. 1949b. "Koopmans on the Choice of Variables to be Studied: A Reply." *Review of Economics and Statistics,* XXXI (May), 86–91.

——. 1947. "Measurement without Theory." *Review of Economics and Statistics,* XXIX (Aug.), 161–172.

——. 1945. "Statistical Estimation of Simultaneous Economic Relations." *Journal of the American Statistical Association,* LX (Dec.), 448–466.

——. 1957. *Three Essays on the State of Economic Science.* New York: McGraw-Hill.

——. 1952. "Toward Partial Redirection of Econometrics: Comment." *Review of Economics and Statistics,* XXXIV (Aug.), 200–205.

Kracaver, Siegfried. 1969. *History: The Last Things before The Last.* New York: Oxford University Press.

Krieger, Leonard. 1963. "Comments on Historical Explanation," in Sidney Hook (ed.), *Philosophy and History.* New York: New York University Press. Pp. 136–142.

Krooss, Herman E. 1958. "Economic History and the New Business History." *Journal of Economic History,* XVIII (Dec.), 467–480.

Krupp, Sherman. 1963. "Analytic Economics and the Logic of External Effects." *American Economic Review,* LIII (May), 220–226.

——. (ed.). 1966a. *The Structure of Economic Science: Essays on Methodology.* Englewood Cliffs, N. J.: Prentice-Hall.

——. 1966b. "Types of Controversy in Economics," in his *The Structure of Economic Science.* Englewood Cliffs, N. J.: Prentice-Hall. Pp. 39–52.

Kuh, Edwin. 1965. "Econometric Models: Is a New Age Dawning?" *American Economic Review,* LV (May), 362–369.

Kuhn, Alfred. 1963. *The Study of Society: A Unified Approach.* Homewood, Ill.: Richard D. Irwin.

Kuhn, Thomas S. 1961. "The Function of Measurement in Modern Physical Sciences," in Harry Woolf (ed.), *Quantification: A History of the Meaning of Measurement in the Natural and Social Sciences.* Indianapolis: Bobbs-Merrill. Pp. 31–63.

——. 1962. *The Structure of Scientific Revolutions.* Chicago: University of Chicago Press.

Kuznets, Simon. 1971. *Economic Growth of Nations: Total Output and Production Structure.* Cambridge, Mass.: Belknap.

——. 1957. "The Integration of Economic Theory and Economic History—Summary of Discussion and Postscript." *Journal of Economic History*, XVII (Dec.), 545–553.

——. 1966. *Modern Economic Growth; Rate, Structure and Spread.* New Haven: Yale University Press.

——. 1959. "Notes on the Study of Economic Growth." Social Science Research Council, *Items*, XIII (June), 13–17.

——. 1965. "Notes on the Take-off," in W. W. Rostow (ed.), *The Economics of Take-off into Sustained Growth.* New York: St. Martin's. Pp. 22–43.

——. 1941. "Statistics and Economic History." *Journal of Economic History*, I (May), 26–41.

Lampard, Eric E. 1960. "The Price System and Economic Change: A Commentary on Theory and History." *Journal of Economic History*, XX (Dec.), 617–637.

Lancaster, Kelvin. 1966. "Economic Aggregation and Additivity," in Sherman Krupp (ed.), *The Structure of Economic Science.* Englewood Cliffs, N.J.: Prentice-Hall. Pp. 201–218.

Lane, Frederic C. 1948. "The Social Sciences and the Humanities." American Philosophical Society, *Proceedings*, XCII (Nov.), 356–362.

Lange, Edith. 1971. "Effects of Net Interregional Migration on Agricultural Income: The United States, 1850–1860." Unpublished Ph.D. dissertation, University of Rochester.

Lange, Oskar. 1945/46. "The Scope and Method of Economics." *Review of Economic Studies*, XIII, 19–32.

Laqueur, Walter, and George L. Mosse (eds.). 1966. *The New History: Trends in Historical Research and Writing Since World War II.* New York: Harper & Row.

Lazarsfeld, Paul F. 1961. "Notes on the History of Quantification in Sociology—Trends, Sources and Problems." *Isis*, LII (June), 277–333.

——. 1962. "Philosophy of Science and Empirical Social Research," in Ernest Nagel, Patrick Suppes, and Alfred Tarski (eds.), *Logic, Methodology and Philosophy of Science.* Stanford: Stanford University Press. Pp. 463–473.

Leach, James. 1966. "Discussion: Dray on Rational Explanation." *Philosophy of Science*, XXXIII (March–June), 61–69.

Lebergott, Stanley. 1964. "Factor Shares in the Long Term: Some Theoretical and Statistical Aspects," in National Bureau of Economic Research, *The Behavior of Income Shares.* Studies in Income and Wealth, vol. XXVII. Princeton, N.J.: Princeton University Press. Pp. 53–86.

——. 1966. "Labor Force and Employment, 1800–1960," in National Bureau of Economic Research, *Output, Employment and Productivity in the United States After 1800.* Studies in Income and Wealth, vol. XXX. New York: Columbia University Press. Pp. 117–204.

——. 1960. "Wage Trends, 1800–1900," in National Bureau of Economic Research, *Trends in the American Economy in the Nineteenth Century.* Studies in Income and Wealth, vol. XXIV. Princeton, N.J.: Princeton University Press. Pp. 449–498.

Leibenstein, Harvey. 1966a. "Allocative Efficiency vs. X-Efficiency." *American Economic Review*, LVI (June), 392–415.

——. 1968. "Entrepreneurship and Development." *American Economic Review*, LVII (May), 72–83.

——. 1966b. "Incremental Capital-Output Ratios and Growth Rates in the Short Run." *Review of Economics and Statistics*, XLVIII (Feb.), 20–27.

Lenz, John W. 1956. "Discussion: Carnap on Defining 'Degree of Confirmation.'" *Philosophy of Science*, XXIII (July), 230–236.

Leontief, Wassily. 1968. "The New Outlook in Economics." *Indian Economic Journal*, XVI (July–Sept.), 71–77.

——. 1936. "Quantitative Input and Output Relations in the Economic System of the United States." *Review of Economics and Statistics*, XVIII (Aug.), 105–125.

——. 1958. "The State of Economic Science." *Review of Economics and Statistics*, XL (May), 103–106.

——. 1941. *The Structure of the American Economy, 1919–1939.* Cambridge, Mass.: Harvard University Press.

——. 1971. "Theoretical Assumptions and Nonobserved Facts." *American Economic Review*, LXI (March), 1–7.

——. 1963. "When Should History Be Written Backwards?" *Economic History Review*, XVI (Aug.), 1–8.

Lerner, Abba P. 1965. "Professor Samuelson on Theory and Realism: Comment." *American Economic Review*, LV (Dec.), 1153–1155.

Lerner, Daniel (ed.), 1965a. *Cause and Effect.* New York: Free Press.

——. 1965b. "Introduction: On Cause and Effect," in his *Cause and Effect.* New York: Free Press. Pp. 1–10.

——, and Harold D. Lasswell (eds.). 1951. *The Policy Sciences.* Stanford: Stanford University Press.

Leslie, Thomas E. C. 1888. "On the Philosophical Method of Political Economy," in his *Essays in Political Economy*, 2d ed. Dublin: Hodges, Figgis. Pp. 163–190.

Lewis, William Arthur. 1955. *The Theory of Economic Growth.* Homewood, Ill.: Richard D. Irwin.

Liu, Ta-Chung. 1960. "Underidentification, Structural Estimation and Forecasting." *Econometrica*, XXVIII (Oct.), 855–865.

Lovell, Michael C. 1957. "The Role of the Bank of England as Lender of Last Resort in the Crises of the Eighteenth Century." *Explorations in Entrepreneurial History*, X (Oct.), 8–21.

Lucas, J. R. 1962. "Causation," in R. J. Butler (ed.), *Analytic Philosophy.* Oxford: Blackwell. Pp. 32–65.

Macaulay, Thomas B. 1880. "History," in *The Miscellaneous Writings, Speeches and Poems of Lord Macaulay*, vol. I. London: Longmans, Green. Pp. 55–107.

Machlup, Fritz. 1961. "Are the Social Sciences Really Inferior?" *Southern Economic Journal*, XXVII (Jan.), 173–184.

——. 1967. *Essays on Economic Semantics.* New York: Norton.

——. 1960. "Operational Concepts and Mental Constructs in Model and Theory Formation." *Giornale degli economisti*, XIX (Sept.–Oct.), 553–582.

——. 1966. "Operationalism and Pure Theory in Economics," in Sherman Krupp (ed.), *The Structure of Economic Science.* Englewood Cliffs, N.J.: Prentice-Hall. Pp. 53–67.

——. 1955. "The Problem of Verification in Economics." *Southern Economic Journal*, XXII (July), 1–21.

——. 1964. "Professor Samuelson on Theory and Realism." *American Economic Review*, LIV (Sept.), 733–736.

——. 1956. "Rejoinder to a Reluctant Ultra-Empiricist." *Southern Economic Journal*, XXII (April), 483–493.

——. 1967. "Theories of the Firm: Marginalist, Behavioral, Managerial." *American Economic Review*, LVII (March), 1–33.

——. 1936. "Why Bother with Methodology." *Economica*, III (Feb.), 39–45.

MacIntyre, Alasdair. 1967. "Ontology," in Paul Edwards (ed.), *Encyclopedia of Philosophy*, vol. V. New York: Macmillan. Pp. 542–543.

MacIver, R. M. 1942. *Social Causation*. New York: Ginn.

Mackie, J. L. 1962. "Counterfactuals and Causal Laws," in R. J. Butler (ed.), *Analytical Philosophy*. Oxford: Blackwell. Pp. 66–80.

Mandelbaum, Maurice. 1961. "Historical Explanation: The Problem of 'Covering Laws.'" *History and Theory*, I, No. 3, 229–242.

Manuel, Frank E. 1963. *Isaac Newton, Historian*. Cambridge, Mass.: Harvard University Press.

Marczewski, Jean. 1968. "Quantitative History." *Journal of Contemporary History*, III (April), 179–191.

Margenau, Henry. 1950. *The Nature of Physical Reality*. New York: McGraw-Hill.

——. 1967. "Quantum Mechanics, Free Will and Determinism." *Journal of Philosophy*, LXIV (Nov. 9), 714–725.

——. 1966. "What Is a Theory?" in Sherman Krupp (ed.), *The Structure of Economic Science*. Englewood Cliffs, N.J.: Prentice-Hall. Pp. 25–38.

Margolis, Joseph. 1970. "Puzzles Regarding Explanation by Reasons and Explanation by Causes." *Journal of Philosophy*, LXVII (April 9), 187–195.

Marhenke, Paul. 1950. "The Criterion of Significance." American Philosophical Association, *Proceedings and Addresses*, XXIII (Sept.), 1–21.

Marris, Robin. 1972. "Why Economics Needs a Theory of the Firm," *Economic Journal*, LXXXII (March), Supplement, 321–352.

Marschak, Jacob. 1950. "Statistical Inference in Economics: An Introduction," in Tjalling C. Koopmans (ed.), *Statistical Inference in Dynamic Economic Models*. New York: Wiley. Pp. 1–52.

Marshall, Alfred. 1925a. "The Old Generation of Economists and the New," in A. C. Pigou (ed.), *Memorials of Alfred Marshall*. London: Macmillan. Pp. 295–311.

——. 1925b. "The Present Position of Economics," in A. C. Pigou (ed.), *Memorials of Alfred Marshall*. London: Macmillan. Pp. 152–174.

——. 1952. *Principles of Economics*. 8th ed. London: Macmillan.

Martin, Anne. 1964. "Empirical and A Priori in Economics." *British Journal for the Philosophy of Science*, XV (Aug.), 123–136.

——. 1957. "How Economic Theory May Mislead." *British Journal for the Philosophy of Science*, VIII (Nov.), 225–236.

Marwick, Arthur. 1970. *The Nature of History*. London: Macmillan.

Massey, G. J. 1965. "Professor Samuelson on Theory and Realism: Comment." *American Economic Review*, LV (Dec.), 1155–1164.

McClelland, Peter D. 1969a. "The Cost to America of British Imperial Policy." *American Economic Review*, LIX (May), 370–381.

——. 1972a. "Discussion of Doctoral Theses," *Journal of Economic History*, XXXII (March), 423–427.

——. 1970. "Joseph Reid on the Navigation Acts: Reply." *American Economic Review*, LX (Dec.), 956–958.

——. 1969b. "New Perspectives on the Disposal of Western Lands in Nineteenth Century America." *Business History Review*, XLIII (Spring), 77–83.

——. 1968. "Railroads, American Growth, and the New Economic History: A Critique." *Journal of Economic History*, XXVIII (March), 102–123.

——. 1972b. "Social Rates of Return on American Railroads in the Nineteenth Century." *Economic History Review*, XXV (Aug.), 471–488.

McCloskey, Donald N. 1970. "Did Victorian Britain Fail?" *Economic History Review*, XXIII (Dec.), 446–459.

——. 1968. "Productivity Change in British Pig Iron, 1870–1939." *Quarterly Journal of Economics*, LXXXII (May), 281–296.

Meehl, Paul E. 1967. "Theory-Testing in Psychology and Physics: A Methodological Paradox." *Philosophy of Science*, XXXIV (June), 103–115.

——. 1958. "When Shall We Use Our Heads instead of the Formula?" in Herbert Feigl, Michael Scriven, and Grover Maxwell (eds.), *Concepts, Theories and the Mind-Body Problem*. Minnesota Studies in the Philosophy of Science, vol. II. Minneapolis: University of Minnesota Press. Pp. 498–506.

Meek, Ronald L. 1964. "Value-Judgements in Economics." *British Journal for the Philosophy of Science*, XV (Aug.), 89–96.

Melitz, Jack. 1965. "Friedman and Machlup on the Significance of Testing Economic Assumptions." *Journal of Political Economy*, LXXIII (Feb.), 37–60.

Mellor, D. W. 1967. "Imprecision and Explanation." *Philosophy of Science*, XXXIV (March), 1–9.

——. 1966. "Inexactness and Explanation." *Philosophy of Science*, XXXIII (Dec.), 345–359.

Meyer, John R. 1955. "An Input-Output Approach to Evaluating the Influence of Exports on British Industrial Production in the Late Nineteenth Century." *Explorations in Entrepreneurial History*, VIII (Oct.), 12–34.

——. and Alfred N. Conrad. 1957. "Economic Theory, Statistical Inference and Economic History." *Journal of Economic History*, XVII (Dec.), 524–544.

Meyerhoff, Hans (ed.). 1959. *The Philosophy of History in Our Time*. Garden City, N.Y.: Doubleday.

Mill, John Stuart. 1874. *Essays on Some Unsettled Questions in Political Economy*. London: Longmans, Green.

——. 1851. *A System of Logic*. London: J. W. Parker.

Miller, David W. 1963. "The Relevance of Game Theory," in Alfred R. Oxenfeldt (ed.), *Models of Markets*. New York: Columbia University Press. Pp. 265–306.

Mink, Louis O. 1968a. *Mind, History and Dialectic: The Philosophy of R. G. Collingwood*. Bloomington, Ind.: Indiana University Press.

——. 1968b. "Philosophical Analysis and Historical Understanding." *Review of Metaphysics*, XXI (June), 667–698.

Mischel, Theodore. 1966. "Pragmatic Aspects of Explanation." *Philosophy of Science*, XXXIII (March–June), 40–60.

Mommsen, Theodor. 1956. "On the Training of Historians," translated in Fritz Stern (ed.), *The Varieties of History*. New York: Meridian. Pp. 192–196.

Morgan, Theodore. 1969. "Investment versus Economic Growth." *Economic Development and Cultural Change*, XVII (April), 392–414.

Morgenstern, Oskar. 1937. *The Limits of Economics*. Translated by Vera Smith. London: William Hodge.

——. 1963a. "Limits to the Use of Mathematics in Economics," in James C. Charlesworth (ed.), *Mathematics and the Social Sciences*. Philadelphia: American Academy of Political and Social Science. Pp. 12–29.

——. 1963b. *On the Accuracy of Economic Observations*. Princeton, N.J.: Princeton University Press.

——. 1972. "Thirteen Critical Points in Contemporary Economic Theory: An Interpretation." *Journal of Economic Literature*, X (Dec.), 1163–1189.

Murphy, George G. S. 1969. "On Counterfactual Propositions." *History and Theory*, Beiheft 9, 14–38.

——. 1965. "The 'New' History." *Explorations in Entrepreneurial History*, 2d ser., II (Winter), 132–146.

——. and M. G. Mueller. 1967. "On Making Historical Techniques More Specific: 'Real Types' Constructed with a Computer." *History and Theory*, VI, No. 1, 14–32.

Myrdal, Gunnar. 1958. *Value in Social Theory: A Selection of Essays on Methodology*. London: Routledge & Kegan Paul.

Nabers, Lawrence. 1966. "The Positive and Genetic Approaches," in Sherman Krupp (ed.), *The Structure of Economic Science*. Englewood Cliffs, N.J.: Prentice-Hall. Pp. 68–82.

Nadiri, M. Ishaq. 1970. "Some Approaches to the Measurement of Total Factor Productivity: A Survey." *Journal of Economic Literature*, VIII (Dec.), 1137–1177.

Nagel, Ernest. 1963a. "Assumptions in Economic Theory." *American Economic Review*, LIII (May), 211–219.

——. 1953a. "The Causal Character of Modern Physical Theory," in Herbert Feigl and May Brodbeck (eds.), *Readings in the Philosophy of Science*. New York: Appleton-Century-Crofts. Pp. 419–437.

——. 1963b. "Relativism and Some Problems of Working Historians," in Sidney Hook (ed.), *Philosophy and History*. New York: New York University Press. Pp. 76–91.

——. 1959. "Some Issues in the Logic of Historical Analysis," in Patrick Gardiner (ed.), *Theories of History*. New York: Free Press. Pp. 373–385.

——. 1961. *The Structure of Science*. New York: Harcourt, Brace & World.

——. 1953b. "Teleological Explanation and Teleological Systems," in Herbert Feigl and May Brodbeck (eds.), *Readings in the Philosophy of Science*. New York: Appleton-Century-Crofts. Pp. 537–558.

——. 1965. "Types of Causal Explanation in Science," in Daniel Lerner (ed.), *Cause and Effect*. New York: Free Press. Pp. 11–32.

——. Patrick Suppes, and Alfred Tarski (eds.). 1962. *Logic, Methodology and Philosophy of Science*. Stanford: Stanford University Press.

Nef, John U. 1941. "The Responsibility of Economic Historians." *Journal of Economic History*, I (Dec.), Supplement, 1–8.

——. 1944. "What Is Economic History?" *Journal of Economic History*, IV (Dec.), Supplement, 1–19.

Nelson, Richard R. 1959. "The Economics of Invention: A Survey of the Literature." *Journal of Business* (University of Chicago), XXXII (April), 101–127.

——. (ed.). 1962. *The Rate and Direction of Inventive Activity*. Princeton, N.J.: Princeton University Press.

Nerlove, Marc. 1965. "The New National Econometric Model: Discussion." *American Economic Review*, LV (May), 370–372.

Newton, Isaac. 1819. *The Mathematical Principles of Natural Philosophy*. London: Sherwood, Neely, Jones.

Noether, Gottfried E. 1968. "Probability: Formal Probability," in David L. Sills (ed.), *International Encyclopedia of the Social Sciences*, vol. XII. New York: Macmillan. Pp. 487–496.

Nordhaus, William D. 1969a. *Invention, Growth and Welfare: A Theoretical Treatment of Technical Change*. Cambridge, Mass.: M.I.T. Press.

——. 1969b. "Theory of Innovation: An Economic Theory of Technical Change." *American Economic Review*, LIX (May), 18–28.

North, Douglass C. 1966. *Growth and Welfare in the American Past*. Englewood Cliffs, N.J.: Prentice-Hall.

——. 1968a. "HISTORY: Economic History," in David L. Sills (ed.), *International Encyclopedia of the Social Sciences*, vol. VI. New York: Macmillan. Pp. 468–474.

——. 1971. "Institutional Change and Economic Growth." *Journal of Economic History*, XXXI (March), 118–134.

——. 1958. "Ocean Freight Rates and Economic Development, 1750–1913." *Journal of Economic History*, XVIII (Dec.), 537–555.

——. 1963. "Quantitative Research in American Economic History." *American Economic Review*, LIII (March), 128–130.

——. 1968b. "Sources of Productivity Change in Ocean Shipping, 1600–1850." *Journal of Political Economy*, LXXVI (Sept./Oct.), 953–970.

——. 1965. "The State of Economic History." *American Economic Review*, LV (May), 86–91.

——, and Robert Paul Thomas. 1970. "An Economic Theory of the Growth of the Western World." *Economic History Review*, XXIII (April), 1–17.

——, and Robert Paul Thomas. 1971. "The Rise and Fall of the Manorial System: A Theoretical Model." *Journal of Economic History*, XXXI (Dec.), 777–803.

——, and Robert Paul Thomas. 1973. *The Rise of the Western World: A New Economic History*. Cambridge, Eng.: Cambridge University Press.

Oakeshott, Michael. 1966. *Experience and Its Modes*. Cambridge, Eng.: Cambridge University Press.

Ohlin, Goran. 1966. "No Safety in Numbers: Some Pitfalls of Historical Statistics," in Henry Rosovsky (ed.), *Industrialization in Two Systems*. New York: Wiley. Pp. 68–90.

Omer, I. A. 1970. "On the D-N Model of Scientific Explanation." *Philosophy of Science*, XXXVII (Sept.), 417–433.

Orcutt, Guy H. 1952a. "Actions, Consequences and Causal Relations." *Review of Economics and Statistics*, XXXIV (Nov.), 305–313.

——. 1970. "Simulation, Modeling and Data," in Nancy D. Ruggles (ed.), *Economics*. Englewood Cliffs, N.J.: Prentice-Hall. Pp. 63–72.

——. 1952b. "Toward Partial Redirection of Econometrics." *Review of Economics and Statistics*, XXXIV (Aug.), 195–200, 211–213.

Oxenfeldt, Alfred R. 1963a. "How Well Existing Market Models Meet the Needs of Businessmen," in his *Models of Markets*. New York: Columbia University Press. Pp. 61–92.

—— (ed.). 1963b. *Models of Markets*. New York: Columbia University Press.

Papandreou, Andreas G. 1963. "Theory Construction and Empirical Meaning in Economics." *American Economic Review*, LIII (May), 205–210.

Parker, William N. 1968. "American Economic Growth: Its Historiography in the Twentieth Century." *Ventures: The Magazine of the Yale Graduate School*, VIII (Fall), 71–82.

——. 1972a. "Economic History: Two Papers on the Development and State of the Art." Unpublished paper, University of Chicago Workshop in Economic History, March 3.

——. 1971. "From Old to New to Old in Economic History." *Journal of Economic History*, XXXI (March), 3–14.

——. 1972b. "Method and Methodology," in Lance E. Davis *et al.*, *American Economic Growth*. New York: Harper & Row. Pp. 7–9.

——. 1966. "Old Wine in New Bottles: A Review of *The Cambridge Economic History*, Volume VI." *Journal of Economic History*, XXVI (March), 99–106.

——. 1970. "Slavery and Southern Economic Development: A Hypothesis and Some Evidence." *Agricultural History*, XLIV (Jan.), 115–126.

Parks, Richard W. 1969. "Systems of Demand Equations: An Empirical Comparison of Alternative Functional Forms." *Econometrica*, XXXVII (Oct.), 629–650.

Passell, Peter, and Maria Schmundt. 1971. "Pre-Civil War Land Policy and the Growth of Manufacturing." *Explorations in Economic History*, IX (Fall), 35–48.

Passmore, John. 1962. "Explanation in Everyday Life, in Science, and in History." *History and Theory*, II, No. 2, 105–123.

——. 1958. "Review Article: Law and Explanation in History." *Australian Journal of Politics and History*, IV (Nov.), 269–275.

Peterson, Shorey. 1965. "Corporate Control and Capitalism." *Quarterly Journal of Economics*, LXXIX (Feb.), 1–24.

Phelps Brown, E. H. 1972. "The Underdevelopment of Economics." *Economic Journal*, LXXXII (March), 1–10.

Pigou, A. C. 1922. "Empty Economic Boxes: A Reply." *Economic Journal*, XXXII (Dec.), 458–465.

——. 1925. *Memorials of Alfred Marshall*. London: Macmillan.

Pikler, Andrew G. 1954/1955. "Utility Theories in Field Physics and Mathematical Economics." *British Journal for the Philosophy of Science*, V (May), 47–58; (Feb.), 303–318.

Pitt, Jack. 1959. "Generalizations in Historical Explanation." *Journal of Philosophy*, LVI (June 18), 578–586.

Plekhanov, Georgi. 1940. *The Role of the Individual in History*. New York: International Publishers.

Pollack, Norman. 1962. *The Populist Response to Industrial America*. Cambridge, Mass.: Harvard University Press.

Pope, Clayne, 1972. "The Impact of the Ante-Bellum Tariff on Income Distribution." *Explorations in Economic History*, IX (Summer), 375–422.

Popper, Karl. 1965. *Conjectures and Refutations: The Growth of Scientific Knowledge*. New York: Basic Books.

——. 1963. "The Demarcation between Science and Metaphysics," in Paul A. Schilpp (ed.), *The Philosophy of Rudolf Carnap*. LaSalle, Ill.: Open Court. Pp. 183–226.

——. 1959. *The Logic of Scientific Discovery*. New York: Basic Books.

——. 1949. "A Note on Natural Laws and So-Called Contrary-To-Fact Conditionals." *Mind*, LVIII (Jan.), 62–66.

——. 1957. *The Poverty of Historicism*. London: Routledge & Kegan Paul.

Postan, M. M. 1962. "Function and Dialectic in Economic History." *Economic History Review*, XIV (April), 397–407.

Price, Jacob M. 1969. "Recent Quantitative Work in History: A Survey of the Main Trends." *History and Theory*, Beiheft 9, 1–13.

——. 1963. "Review of E. H. Carr's *What Is History?*" *History and Theory*, III, no. 1, 136–145.

Quine, W. V. 1969. "Natural Kinds," in N. Rescher *et al.*, *Essays in Honor of Carl G. Hempel*. Dordrecht: D. Reidel. Pp. 5–23.

——. 1966. "Necessary Truth," in his *The Ways of Paradox and Other Essays*. New York: Random House. Pp. 48–56.

——. 1973. *The Roots of Reference*. LaSalle, Ill.: Open Court.

——. 1957. "The Scope and Language of Science." *British Journal for the Philosophy of Science*, VIII (May), 1–17.

——. 1953. "Two Dogmas of Empiricism," in his *From a Logical Point of View*. Cambridge, Mass.: Harvard University Press. Pp. 20–46.

Rasche, Robert H. 1972. "Comments on a Monetarist Approach to Demand Management." Federal Reserve Bank of St. Louis, *Review*, LIV (Jan.), 26–32.

Rashevsky, Nicholas. 1968. *Looking at History through Mathematics*. Cambridge, Mass.: M.I.T. Press.

Redlich, Fritz. 1962. "Approaches to Business History." *Business History Review*, XXXVI (Spring), 61–70.

——. 1965. "'New' and Traditional Approaches to Economic History and Their Interdependence." *Journal of Economic History*, XXV (Dec.), 480–495.

——. 1968. "Potentialities and Pitfalls in Economic History." *Explorations in Entrepreneurial History*, 2d ser., VI (Fall), 93–108.

Reichenbach, Hans. 1953. "The Logical Foundations of the Concept of Probability," in Herbert Feigl and May Brodbeck (eds.), *Readings in the Philosophy of Science*. New York: Appleton-Century-Crofts. Pp. 456–474.

——. 1954. *Nomological Statements and Admissible Operations*. Amsterdam: North-Holland.

——. 1940. "On the Justification of Induction." *Journal of Philosophy*, XXXVII (Feb. 15), 97–103.

——. 1951a. "Probability Methods in Social Science," in Daniel Lerner and Harold D. Lasswell (eds.), *The Policy Sciences: Recent Developments in Scope and Method*. Stanford: Stanford University Press. Pp. 121–128.

——. 1951b. *The Rise of Scientific Philosophy*. Berkeley: University of California Press.

Reid, Joseph D., Jr. 1970. "On Navigating the Navigation Acts with Peter D. McClelland." *American Economic Review*, LX (Dec.), 949–955.

Rescher, Nicholas. 1961. "Belief-Contravening Suppositions." *Philosophical Review*, LXX (April), 176–196.

——. 1958. "On Prediction and Explanation." *British Journal for the Philosophy of Science*, VIII (Feb.), 281–290.

——, and C. B. Joynt. 1959. "Evidence in History and in the Law." *Journal of Philosophy*, LVI (June 18), 561–578.

Rickman, H. P. 1967. "Wilhelm Dilthey," in Paul Edwards (ed.), *Encyclopedia of Philosophy*, vol. II. New York: Macmillan. Pp. 403–407.

Robbins, Lionel. 1962. *An Essay on the Nature and Significance of Economic Science*. 2d ed. London: Macmillan.

Roberts, Marc Jeffrey. 1969. "Models and Theories in Economics: An Exploration of the Logical Status of Economic Theory, with an Application to Welfare Economics." Unpublished Ph.D. dissertation, Harvard University.

Robinson, Enders A. 1967. "Model Building for the Human Sciences," in Herman O. A. Wold (ed.), *Model Building in the Human Sciences*. Entretiens de Monaco en Sciences Humaines. Session 1964. Monaco: Union Européene d'Editions. Pp. 125–162.

Robinson, Joan. 1962. *Economic Philosophy.* Chicago: Aldine.

——. 1961. "Equilibrium Growth Models: A Review Article." *American Economic Review,* LI (June), 360–369.

——. 1972. "The Second Crisis of Economic Theory." *American Economic Review,* LXII (May), 1–9.

——, and John Eatwell. 1973. *An Introduction to Modern Economics.* London: McGraw-Hill.

Rogers, Carl R. 1963. "Toward a Science of the Person." *Journal of Humanistic Psychology,* II (Fall), 72–92.

Roll, Eric. 1968. "The Uses and Abuses of Economics." *Oxford Economic Papers,* N.S., XX (Nov.), 289–302.

Rose, Arnold M. 1954. *Theory and Method in the Social Sciences.* Minneapolis: University of Minnesota Press.

Rosenberg, Nathan. 1972. *Technology and American Economic Growth.* New York: Harper & Row.

Rosovsky, Henry. 1965. "The Take-Off into Sustained Controversy." *Journal of Economic History,* XXV (June), 271–275.

Rostow, W. W. (ed.). 1965. *The Economics of Take-Off into Sustained Growth.* New York: St. Martin's Press.

——. 1971. "General Equilibrium Models in Economic History: Discussion." *Journal of Economic History,* XXXI (March), 76–86.

——. 1957. "The Interrelation of Theory and Economic History." *Journal of Economic History,* XVII (Dec.), 509–523.

——. 1960. *The Stages of Economic Growth.* Cambridge, Eng.: Cambridge University Press.

Rothman, Milton A. 1963. *The Laws of Physics.* Greenwich, Conn.: Fawcett.

Rothstein, Morton. 1970. "The Cotton Frontier of the Antebellum United States: A Methodological Battleground." *Agricultural History,* XLIV (Jan.), 149–165.

Rotwein, Eugene. 1966. "Mathematical Economics: The Empirical View and an Appeal for Pluralism," in Sherman Krupp (ed.), *The Structure of Economic Science.* Englewood Cliffs, N.J.: Prentice-Hall. Pp. 102–113.

——. 1959. "On 'The Methodology of Positive Economics.'" *Quarterly Journal of Economics,* LXXIII (Nov.), 554–575.

——. 1962. "On 'The Methodology of Positive Economics': Reply." *Quarterly Journal of Economics,* LXXVI (Nov.), 666–668.

Rowney, Don Karl, and James Q. Graham, Jr. (eds.). 1960. *Quantitative History: Selected Readings in the Quantitative Analysis of Historical Data.* Homewood, Ill.: Dorsey Press.

Ruggles, Nancy D. (ed.). 1970. *Economics.* Englewood Cliffs, N.J.: Prentice-Hall.

Russell, Bertrand. 1945. *A History of Western Philosophy.* New York: Simon & Schuster.

——. 1948. *Human Knowledge: Its Scope and Limits.* New York: Simon and Schuster.

——. 1918. *Mysticism and Logic and Other Essays.* New York: Longmans and Green.

——. 1953. "On the Notion of Cause, with Applications to the Free-Will Problem," in Herbert Feigl and May Brodbeck (eds.), *Readings in the Philosophy of Science.* New York: Appleton-Century-Crofts. Pp. 387–407.

———. 1956. *Portraits from Memory and other Essays.* London: George Allen and Unwin.

Salmon, Wesley C. 1967. "Carnap's Inductive Logic." *Journal of Philosophy*, LXIV (Nov. 9), 725–739.

Salsbury, Stephen. 1971. "The Economic Interpretation of History: Marx and Beard," in George Rogers Taylor and Lucius F. Ellsworth (eds.), *Approaches to American Economic History.* Charlottesville: University Press of Virginia. Pp. 37–49.

Samuelson, Paul A. 1952. "Economic Theory and Mathematics—An Appraisal." *American Economic Review*, XLII (May), 56–66.

———. 1973. *Economics.* 9th ed. New York: McGraw-Hill.

———. 1972. "Maximum Principles in Analytical Economics." *American Economic Review*, LXII (June), 249–262.

———. 1955. "Operationalism in Economic Theory: Comment." *Quarterly Journal of Economics*, LXIX (May), 310–314.

———. 1963. "Problems of Methodology—Discussion." *American Economic Review*, LIII (May), 231–236.

———. 1965a. "Professor Samuelson on Theory and Realism: Reply." *American Economic Review*, LV (Dec.), 1164–1172.

———. 1965b. "Some Notions on Causality and Teleology in Economics," in Daniel Lerner (ed.), *Cause and Effect.* New York: Free Press. Pp. 99–143.

———. 1964. "Theory and Realism: A Reply." *American Economic Review*, LIV (Sept.), 736–739.

Saraydar, Edward. 1964. "A Note on the Profitability of Ante-Bellum Slavery." *Southern Economic Journal*, XXX (April), 325–353.

Saveth, Edward. 1960. "Scientific History in America: Eclipse of an Idea," in Donald Sheehan and Harold C. Syrett (eds.), *Essays in American Historiography.* New York: Columbia University Press. Pp. 1–19.

Sawyer, John E. 1958. "Entrepreneurial Studies: Perspectives and Directions, 1948–1958." *Business History Review*, XXXII (Winter), 434–443.

Schaefer, Donald, and Thomas Weiss. 1971. "The Use of Simulation Techniques in Historical Analysis: Railroads versus Canals." *Journal of Economic History*, XXXI (Dec.), 854–884.

Scheffler, Israel. 1957. "Explanation, Prediction and Abstraction." *British Journal for the Philosophy of Science*, VII (Feb.), 293–309.

Scheiber, Harry N. 1970. "At the Borderland of Law and Economic History: The Contributions of William Hurst." *American Historical Review*, LXXV (Feb.), 744–795.

———. 1967. "On the New Economic History—And Its Limitations: A Review Essay." *Agricultural History*, XLI (Oct.), 383–396.

Scherer, F. M. 1970. *Industrial Market Structure and Economic Performance.* Chicago: Rand McNally.

Schilpp, Paul Arthur (ed.). 1949. *Albert Einstein: Philosopher–Scientist.* Evanston, Ill.: Library of Living Philosophers.

Schlesinger, Arthur, Jr. 1962. "The Humanist Looks at Empirical Social Research." *American Sociological Review*, XXVII (Dec.), 768–771.

Schmookler, Jacob. 1962. "Economic Sources of Inventive Activity." *Journal of Economic History*, XXII (March), 1–20.

———. 1966. *Invention and Economic Growth.* Cambridge, Mass.: Harvard University Press.

Schrödinger, Erwin. 1956. *What Is Life? And Other Scientific Essays*. New York: Doubleday.

Schultz, Charles L. 1971. "The State of Economics: The Reviewers Reviewed." *American Economic Review*, LXI (May), 45–52.

Schumpeter, Joseph A. 1947. "The Creative Response in Economic History." *Journal of Economic History*, VII (Nov.), 149–159.

——. 1965. "Economic Theory and Entrepreneurial History," in Hugh G. J. Aitken (ed.), *Explorations in Enterprise*. Cambridge, Mass.: Harvard University Press. Pp. 45–64.

——. 1954. *History of Economic Analysis*. New York: Oxford University Press.

Scitovsky, Tibor. 1964. "A Survey of Some Theories of Income Distribution," in National Bureau of Economic Research, *The Behavior of Income Shares*. Studies in Income and Wealth, vol. XXVII. Princeton, N.J.: Princeton University Press. Pp. 15–31.

Scriven, Michael. 1966. "Causes, Connections and Conditions in History," in William Dray (ed.), *Philosophical Analysis and History*. New York: Harper & Row. Pp. 238–264.

——. 1958. "Definitions, Explanations and Theories," in Herbert Feigl, Michael Scriven, and Grover Maxwell (eds.), *Concepts, Theories and the Mind-Body Problem*. Minnesota Studies in the Philosophy of Science, vol. II. Minneapolis: University of Minnesota Press. Pp. 99–195.

——. 1959a. "Explanation and Prediction in Evolutionary Theory." *Science*, CXXX (Aug. 28), 477–482.

——. 1962. "Explanations, Predictions and Laws," in Herbert Feigl and Grover Maxwell (eds.), *Scientific Explanation, Space and Time*. Minnesota Studies in the Philosophy of Science, vol. III. Minneapolis: University of Minnesota Press. Pp. 170–230.

——. 1963. "New Issues in the Logic of Explanation," in Sidney Hook (ed.), *Philosophy and History*. New York: New York University Press. Pp. 339–361.

——. 1956. "A Possible Distinction between Traditional Scientific Disciplines and the Study of Human Behavior," in Herbert Feigl and Michael Scriven (eds.), *The Foundations of Science and the Concepts of Psychology and Psychoanalysis*. Minnesota Studies in the Philosophy of Science, vol. I. Minneapolis: University of Minnesota Press. Pp. 330–339.

——. 1964. "The Structure of Science." *Review of Metaphysics*, XVII (March), 403–424.

——. 1959b. "Truisms as the Grounds for Historical Explanation," in Patrick Gardiner (ed.), *Theories of History*. New York: Free Press. Pp. 443–475.

Seligman, Ben B. 1967. "On the Question of Operationalism: A Review Article." *American Economic Review*, LVII (March), 146–161.

Sellars, W. S. 1953a. "Inference and Meaning." *Mind*, LXII (July), 313–338.

——. 1953b. "Is There a Synthetic A Priori?" *Philosophy of Science*, XX (April), 121–138.

——. 1958. "Counterfactuals, Dispositions and the Causal Modalities," in Herbert Feigl, Michael Scriven, and Grover Maxwell (eds.), *Concepts, Theories and the Mind-Body Problem*. Minnesota Studies in the Philosophy of Science, vol. II. Minneapolis: University of Minnesota Press. Pp. 225–308.

Shackle, G. L. S. 1968. "Economic Theory Since the Victorians." *Indian Economic Journal*, XVI (July-Sept.), 81–84.

Shepherd, James F. 1970. "Commodity Exports from the British North American

Colonies to Overseas Areas, 1768–1772: Magnitudes and Patterns of Trade." *Explorations in Economic History*, VIII (Fall), 5–76.

———, and Gary M. Walton. 1969. "Estimates of 'Invisible' Earnings in the Balance of Payments of the British North American Colonies, 1768–1772." *Journal of Economic History*, XXIX (June), 230–263.

Shryock, Richard H. 1944. "What Is Economic History—Discussion." *Journal of Economic History*, IV (Dec.), Supplement, 20–24.

Shubik, Martin. 1970. "A Curmudgeon's Guide to Microeconomics." *Journal of Economic Literature*, VIII (June), 405–434.

———. 1963. "Simulation and Gaming: Their Value to the Study of Pricing and Other Market Variables," in Alfred R. Oxenfeldt (ed.), *Models of Markets*. New York: Columbia University Press. Pp. 307–338.

Silberston, Aubrey. 1970. "Surveys of Applied Economics: Price Behavior of Firms." *Economic Journal*, LXXX (Sept.), 511–582.

Simon, Herbert A. 1953. "Causal Ordering and Identifiability," in William C. Hood and T. C. Koopmans (eds.), *Studies in Economic Methods*. New York: Wiley. Pp. 49–74.

———. 1965. "The Logic of Rational Decision." *British Journal for the Philosophy of Science*, XVI (Nov.), 169–186.

———. 1957. *Models of Man*. New York: Wiley.

———. 1962. "New Developments in the Theory of the Firm." *American Economic Review*, LII (May), 1–15.

———. 1963. "Problems of Methodology—Discussion." *American Economic Review*, LIII (May), 229–231.

———. 1959. "Theories of Decision-Making in Economics and Behavioral Science." *American Economic Review*, XLIX (June), 253–283.

———, and Nicholas Rescher. 1966. "Cause and Counterfactual." *Philosophy of Science*, XXXIII (Dec.), 323–340.

Simon, Julian L. 1970. "The Concept of Causality in Economics." *Kyklos*, XXIII, Fasc. 2, 226–254.

Smolensky, Eugene. 1963. "Composition of Iron and Steel Products, 1869–1909: Discussion." *Journal of Economic History*, XXIII (Dec.), 472–476.

Solow, Robert M. 1960. "Investment and Technical Progress," in Kenneth J. Arrow, Samuel Karlin, and Patrick Suppes (eds.), *Mathematical Methods in the Social Sciences*. Stanford: Stanford University Press. Pp. 89–104.

———. 1970. "Microeconomic Theory," in Nancy D. Ruggles (ed.), *Economics*. Englewood Cliffs, N.J.: Prentice-Hall. Pp. 31–43.

———. 1958. "A Skeptical Note on the Constancy of Relative Income Shares." *American Economic Review*, XLVIII (Sept.), 618–631.

———. 1957. "Technical Change and the Aggregate Production Function." *Review of Economics and Statistics*, XXXIX (Aug.), 312–320.

Soltow, James H. 1971. "American Institutional Studies: Present Knowledge and Past Trends." *Journal of Economic History*, XXXI (March), 87–105.

———. 1968. "The Entrepreneur in Economic History." *American Economic Review*, LVIII (May), 84–92.

Sombart, Werner. 1929. "Economic Theory and Economic History." *Economic History Review*, II (Jan.), 1–19.

Sorokin, Pitirim A. 1956. *Fads and Foibles in Modern Sociology and Related Sciences*. Chicago: Henry Regnery.

———. 1943. *Sociocultural Causality, Space and Time*. Durham, N.C.: Duke University Press.

Spector, Marshall. 1965. "Models and Theories." *British Journal for the Philosophy of Science*, XVI (Aug.), 121–142.

Spengler, Joseph J. 1968. "Economics: Its History, Themes, Approaches." *Journal of Economic Issues*, II (March), 5–30.

——. 1961. "On the Progress of Quantification in Economics." *Isis*, LII (June), 258–276.

Stebbing, L. S. 1946. *A Modern Introduction to Logic*. London: Methuen.

Stekler, Herman O. 1968. "Forecasting with Econometric Models: An Evaluation." *Econometrica*, XXXVI (July–Oct.), 437–463.

Stern, Fritz (ed.). 1956. *The Varieties of History, From Voltaire to the Present*. New York: Meridian Books.

Stigler, George J. 1963. "Archibald versus Chicago." *Review of Economic Studies*, XXX (Feb.), 63–64.

——. 1950. "The Mathematical Method in Economics," in his *Five Lectures on Economic Problems*. New York: Macmillan. Pp. 37–45.

Stone, Richard. 1964. "The A Priori and the Empirical in Economics." *British Journal for the Philosophy of Science*, XV (Aug.), 115–122.

——. 1966. *Mathematics in the Social Sciences and Other Essays*. Cambridge, Mass.: M.I.T. Press.

Supple, Barry E. 1960. "Economic History and Economic Growth." *Journal of Economic History*, XX (Dec.), 548–556.

——. 1963. "Economic History, Economic Theory and Economic Growth," in his *The Experience of Economic Growth*. New York: Random House. Pp. 3–46.

Sutch, Richard. 1965. "The Profitability of Ante-Bellum Slavery Revisited." *Southern Economic Journal*, XXXI (April), 365–377.

Swanson, Joseph, and Jeffrey Williamson. 1971. "Explanations and Issues: A Prospectus for Quantitative Economic History." *Journal of Economic History*, XXXI (March), 43–57.

Swierenga, Robert P. 1970. *Quantification in American History: Theory and Research*. New York: Atheneum.

Tarski, Alfred. 1965. *Introduction to Logic and to the Methodology of Deductive Sciences*. New York: Oxford University Press.

Taylor, George Rogers. 1970. "Economic History in the *International Encyclopedia of the Social Sciences*: A Review Article." *Journal of Economic Literature*, VIII (March), 35–39.

——. 1971. "Stage Theories of Economic History," in George Rogers Taylor and Lucius F. Ellsworth (eds.), *Approaches to American Economic History*. Charlottesville: University Press of Virginia. Pp. 25–36.

Taylor, Richard. 1967. "Causation," in Paul Edwards (ed.), *Encyclopedia of Philosophy*, vol. II. New York: Macmillan. Pp. 56–66.

Teigen, Ronald L. 1972. "A Critical Look at Monetarist Economics." *Federal Reserve Bank of St. Louis, Review*, LIV (Jan.), 10–25.

Temin, Peter. 1967. "The Causes of Cotton-Price Fluctuations in the 1830's." *Review of Economics and Statistics*, XLIX (Nov.), 463–470.

——. 1963. "The Composition of Iron and Steel Products, 1869–1909," *Journal of Economic History*, XXIII (Dec.), 447–471.

——. 1971a. "General Equilibrium Models in Economic History." *Journal of Economic History*, XXXI (March), 58–75.

——. 1966a. "In Pursuit of the Exact." *Times Literary Supplement*, No. 3361 (July 28), 652–653.

——. 1964a. *Iron and Steel in Nineteenth-Century America: An Economic Inquiry.* Cambridge, Mass.: M.I.T. Press.

——. 1969. *The Jacksonian Economy.* New York: W. W. Norton.

——. 1966b. "Labor Scarcity and the Problem of American Industrial Efficiency in the 1850's." *Journal of Economic History,* XXVI (Sept.), 277–298.

——. 1971b. "Labor Scarcity in America." *Journal of Interdisciplinary History,* I (Winter), 251–264.

——. 1964b. "A New Look at Hunter's Hypothesis About the Ante-Bellum Iron Industry." *American Economic Review,* LIV (May), 344–351.

Theil, Henri. 1970. "Operations Research and Economics," in Nancy D. Ruggles (ed.), *Economics.* Englewood Cliffs, N. J.: Prentice-Hall. Pp. 84–88.

Thernstrom, S. 1967. "The Historian and the Computer," in Edmund A. Bowles (ed.), *Computers in Humanistic Research: Readings and Perspectives.* Englewood Cliffs, N.J.: Prentice-Hall. Pp. 73–81.

——. 1968. "Quantitative Methods in History: Some Notes," in S. M. Lipset and R. Hofstadter (eds.), *Sociology and History: Methods.* New York: Basic Books. Pp. 59–78.

Thurow, Lester C., and L. D. Taylor. 1966. "The Interaction between the Actual and the Potential Rates of Growth." *Review of Economics and Statistics,* XLVIII (Nov.), 351–360.

Tinbergen, Jan. 1952. "Toward Partial Redirection of Econometrics: Comment." *Review of Economics and Statistics,* XXXIV (Aug.), 205–206.

Tintner, Gerhard. 1953. "The Definition of Econometrics." *Econometrica,* XXI (Jan.), 31–40.

——. 1966. "Some Thoughts about the State of Econometrics," in Sherman Krupp (ed.), *The Structure of Economic Science.* Englewood Cliffs, N.J.: Prentice-Hall. Pp. 114–128.

Tobin, James. 1970. "Macroeconomics," in Nancy D. Ruggles (ed.), *Economics.* Englewood Cliffs, N.J.: Prentice-Hall. Pp. 44–54.

Tolstoy, Leo. 1931. War and Peace. Translated by Constance Garnett. New York: Random House.

Topolski, Jerzy. 1972. "The Model Method in Economic History." *Journal of European Economic History,* I (Winter), 713–726.

Toulmin, Stephen. 1960. *The Philosophy of Science: An Introduction.* New York: Harper Torchbooks.

Toynbee, Arnold. 1958. *Civilization on Trail.* New York: Meridian.

U.S. Bureau of the Census. 1960. *Historical Statistics of the United States, Colonial Times to 1957.* Washington, D.C.: U.S. Government Printing Office.

Usher, Abbott Payson. 1932. "The Application of the Quantitative Method to Economic History." *Journal of Political Economy,* XL (April), 186–209.

Veblen, Thorstein. 1919. "The Preconceptions of Economic Science," in his *The Place of Science in Modern Civilization and Other Essays.* New York: B. W. Huebsch. Pp. 82–179.

——. 1898. "Why Is Economics Not an Evolutionary Science?" *Quarterly Journal of Economics,* XII (July), 373–397.

Vendler, Zeno. 1967. "Causal Relations." *Journal of Philosophy,* LXIV (Nov. 9), 704–713.

Vining, Rutledge. 1949a. "Koopmans on the Choice of Variables To Be Studied and Methods of Measurement." *Review of Economics and Statistics,* XXXI (May), 77–86.

——. 1949b. "Koopmans on the Choice of Variables To Be Studied: A Rejoinder." *Review of Economics and Statistics*, XXXI (May), 91–94.

——. 1950. "Methodological Issues in Quantitative Economics: Variations upon a Theme by F. H. Knight." *American Economic Review*, XL (June), 267–284.

von Mises, Richard. 1939. *Probability, Statistics and Truth*. New York: Macmillan.

——. 1957. *Theory and History: An Interpretation of Social and Economic Evolution*. New Haven: Yale University Press.

von Neumann, John, and Oskar Morgenstern. 1944. *Theory of Games and Economic Behavior*. Princeton, N.J.: Princeton University Press.

von Tunzelmann, G. N. 1968. "The New Economic History: An Econometric Appraisal." *Explorations in Entrepreneurial History*, 2d ser., V (Winter), 175–200.

——. 1966. "An Essay on the New Economic History." Unpublished M.S. Thesis, University of Canterbury.

Walras, Leon. 1954. *Elements of Pure Economics*. Translated by William Jaffé. Homewood, Ill.: Richard D. Irwin.

Walsh, William. 1960. *Philosophy of History*. New York: Harper & Row.

Walters, R. S. 1967. "Contrary-to-fact Conditionals," in Paul Edwards (ed.), *Encyclopedia of Philosophy*, vol. II. New York: Macmillan. Pp. 212–216.

——. 1961. "The Problem of Counterfactuals." *Australasian Journal of Philosophy*, XXXIX (May), 30–46.

Walton, Clarence C. 1962. "Business History: Some Major Challenges." *Business History Review*, XXXVI (Spring), 21–35.

Walton, Gary M. 1967. "Sources of Productivity Change in American Colonial Shipping, 1675–1775." *Economic History Review*, XX (April), 67–78.

Ward, Benjamin. 1966. "Institutions and Economic Analysis," in Sherman Krupp (ed.), *The Structure of Economic Science*. Englewood Cliffs, N.J.: Prentice-Hall. Pp. 184–200.

——. 1972. *What's Wrong with Economics?* New York: Basic Books.

Warner, R. Stephen. 1970. "The Role of Religious Ideas and the Use of Models in Max Weber's Comparative Studies of Non-Capitalist Societies." *Journal of Economic History*, XXX (March), 74–99.

Weber, Max. 1965. "Bureaucracy," in H. H. Gerth and C. Wright Mills (eds.), *Max Weber: Essays in Sociology*. New York: Oxford University Press. Pp. 196–244.

——. 1949. *Max Weber on the Methodology of Social Sciences*. Translated and edited by Edward A. Shils and Henry A. Finch. Glencoe, Ill.: Free Press.

White, Morton. 1965. *Foundations of Historical Knowledge*. New York: Harper & Row.

——. 1959. "Historical Explanation," in Patrick Gardiner (ed.), *Theories of History*. New York: Free Press. Pp. 357–373.

——. 1963. "The Logic of Historical Narration," in Sidney Hook (ed.), *Philosophy and History*. New York: New York University Press. Pp. 3–31.

——. 1968. "On What Could Have Happened." *Philosophical Review*, LXXVII (Jan.), 73–89.

White, William H. 1967. "The Trustworthiness of 'Reliable' Econometric Evidence." *Zeitschrift für Nationalökonomie*, XXVII (April), 19–38.

Whitehead, Alfred North. 1938. *Modes of Thought*. New York: Macmillan.

Whitney, William G. 1968. "The Structure of the American Economy in the Late Nineteenth Century." Discussion Paper Number 80, Department of Economics, University of Pennsylvania.

Wicksteed, Philip H. 1933. "Political Economy and Psychology," in his *The Common Sense of Political Economy*, vol. II. London: Routledge & Kegan Paul. Pp. 766–771.

———. 1938. "The Scope and Method of Political Economy in the Light of the 'Marginal' Theory of Value and Distribution," in his *The Common Sense of Political Economy*, vol. II. London: Routledge & Kegan Paul. Pp. 772–796.

Williamson, Harold F. 1966. "Business History and Economic History." *Journal of Economic History*, XXVI (Dec.), 407–417.

———. 1944. "What Is Economic History—Discussion." *Journal of Economic History*, IV (Dec.), Supplement, 25–28.

Williamson, Jeffrey G. 1967. "Consumer Behavior in the Nineteenth Century: Carroll D. Wright's Massachusetts Workers in 1875." *Explorations in Entrepreneurial History*, 2d ser., IV (Winter), 98–135.

Wilson, Fred. 1969. "Explanation in Aristotle, Newton and Toulmin." *Philosophy of Science*, XXXVI (Sept.), 291–310; (Dec.), 400–428.

Winch, Peter. 1967. "Max Weber," in Paul Edwards (ed.), *Encyclopedia of Philosophy*, vol. VIII. New York: Macmillan. Pp. 282–283.

Wold, Herman O. A. 1967. "The Approach of Model Building: The Crossroads of Probability Theory, Statistics and Theory of Knowledge," in his *Model Building in the Human Sciences*. Entretiens de Monaco en Sciences Humaines. Session 1964. Monaco: Union Européene d'Editions. Pp. 1–38.

———. 1954. "Causality and Econometrics." *Econometrica*, XXII (April), 162–177.

———. 1969. "Econometrics as Pioneering in Non-Experimental Model Building." *Econometrica*, XXXVI (July), 170–173.

Wong, Stanley. 1973. "The 'F-Twist' and the Methodology of Paul Samuelson." *American Economic Review*, LXIII (June), 312–325.

Wonnacott, Ronald J., and Thomas H. 1970. *Econometrics*. New York: Wiley.

Woodman, Harold D. 1972. "Economic History and Economic Theory: The New Economic History in America." *Journal of Interdisciplinary History*, III (Autumn), 323–350.

Worswick, G. D. N. 1972. "Is Progress in Economic Science Possible?" *Economic Journal*, LXXXII (March), 73–86.

Wright, Chester W. 1938. "The Nature and Objectives of Economic History." *Journal of Political Economy*, XLVI (Oct.), 688–701.

Wright, Gavin. 1971a. "Econometric Studies of History," in Michael D. Intriligator (ed.), *Frontiers of Quantitative Economics*. Amsterdam: North-Holland. Pp. 412–459.

———. 1971b. "An Econometric Study of Cotton Production and Trade, 1830–1860." *Review of Economics and Statistics*, LIII (May), 111–120.

Yoshihara, Kunio. 1969. "Demand Functions: An Application to the Japanese Expenditure Pattern." *Econometrica*, XXXVII (April), 257–274.

Youngson, A. J. 1956. "Marshall on Economic Growth." *Scottish Journal for Political Economy*, III (Feb.), 1–18.

Zemsky, Robert M. 1969. "Numbers and History: The Dilemma of Measurement." *Computers and the Humanities*, IV (Sept.), 31–40.

Index

Abstraction, 75–77; and formulating generalizations, 72–73; indispensability of, in causal explanation, 24, 42
Aitken, Hugh G. J., 175
Allport, Gordon W., 79
A priori, 114
Aristotle, 31, 32
Arithmetic interpolation and extrapolation: assessing legitimacy of, 226–227; assumptions of, 179; in cliometrics, 179–180
Aron, Raymond, 80, 165
Ashley, W. J., 177
Assessing relative importance, *see* Causal factors, relative importance
Assumption, 27
Axiom, 27, 28
Axiomatic system, 28

Bailyn, Bernard, 65
Baughman, James P., 169n
Baumol, William J., 114n
Beer, Samuel H., 92
Behavioral theories of the firm, 122
Bellman, Richard, 60n
Berlin, Isaiah, 78, 80, 85, 88
Bloch, Marc, 65, 72, 77, 80, 83; probabilistic nature of historical explanation, 85, 157–158
Born, Max, 241
Boulding, Kenneth E., 144
Bridge, J. L., 237
Brookings Institution, 133
Brookings model, 132–134
Brown, Murray, 194–195, 233n

Cairnes, John E., 106
Callender, Guy S., 202
Cannon, William T., 209
Capital-Output ratio, marginal, 201–206, 217, 237–238; aggregate, evidence not constant in short run, 237; explanation of, 202–203; Rostow's use of, 203–205
Carnap, Rudolf, 25, 49, 58, 59, 95
Causal explanation: abstraction, indispensable in, 42; assessment of, 41; basic requirements for, 152; constant conjunction and, 22, 23, 35–40, 47; contrasting views of, 23, 35–41;

criteria for adequacy of, 26, 30–31; mechanism ideas implicit in, 22, 23; two fundamental ideas underlying, 32–33; uncertainties in, inescapable, 24, 42–48, 170–171; unity of method in, 21, 63, 242; unrealism of, inevitable, 242; *see also* Abstraction; *Ceteris paribus*; Cliometrics, causal explanations of; Degree of confirmation; Economics, causal explanation in, summarized; History, causal explanation in; Homogeneity of sets; Necessary conditions; Probability; *and* Sufficient conditions
Causal factors, relative importance of: assessment of, in terms of changing probabilities, 154–158; assessment of, in terms of necessary conditions, 159–160; assessment of, in terms of numerical contribution, 160–161; counterfactual speculation and establishment of, 153–161; economists' desire to establish, 153, 160; historians' desire to establish, 153; proliferation of detail, effect upon assessment of, 164–165
Causal generalizations, 22, 25, 33, 35, 41, 46–47, 53, 66; *ceteris paribus* and formulation of, 45; uncertainty of, inevitable in applied disciplines, 44–48; universal, 24, 44, 48, 63, 93, 101–102; usefulness of, 62, 241
Causal laws, *see* Causal generalizations
Causation, efficient, 32; central tenet of, 21, 65, 86, 97; Newton's contribution to idea of, 36; popularity of, 32
Cause: four principal meanings of, 32; techniques for identifying, 43
Ceteris paribus, 74–75, 86; in causal explanation, 45–46; defined, 45; in economics, 112; merits of using, dubious in causal explanation, 46
Chronicle, 75
Clapham, J. H., 169, 170n, 177
Clark, G. Kitson, 78, 82, 146, 154, 212
Clifford, W. K., 31
Cliometrics, 15, 211; causal explanations of, 145, 170; counterfactual speculation in, 145, 146, 170, 172, 183–184; goals of, 104, 145, 170; inception of, problems of dating, 176; inevitable imprecision in causal explanations and counterfactual speculations of, 172–173, 241–242; models of, 170, 172; models of,

Causal Explanation and Model
Building in History, Economics,
and the New Economic History

Designed by R. E. Rosenbaum.
Composed by Syntax International Pte. Ltd.
in 10 point Monophoto Times New Roman, 2 points leaded,
with display lines in Monophoto Helvetica.
Printed offset by Vail-Ballou Press, Inc.
on Chenango Antique Offset, 50 pound basis
Bound by Vail-Ballou Press, Inc.